Prigg v. Pennsylvania

LANDMARK LAW CASES

AMERICAN SOCIETY

Peter Charles Hoffer
N. E. H. Hull
Series Editors

H. ROBERT BAKER

Prigg v. Pennsylvania

Slavery, the Supreme Court, and

the Ambivalent Constitution

UNIVERSITY PRESS OF KANSAS

© 2012 by the University Press of Kansas
All rights reserved

Published by the University Press of Kansas (Lawrence, Kansas 66045), which was
organized by the Kansas Board of Regents and is operated and funded by Emporia
State University, Fort Hays State University, Kansas State University, Pittsburg State
University, the University of Kansas, and Wichita State University

Library of Congress Cataloging-in-Publication Data

Baker, H. Robert.
Prigg v. Pennsylvania : slavery, the Supreme Court, and the ambivalent constitution/
H. Robert Baker.
p. cm. — (Landmark law cases and American society)
Includes bibliographical references and index.
ISBN 978-0-7006-1864-4 (cloth : alk. paper)
ISBN 978-0-7006-1865-1 (pbk. : alk. paper)
1. Prigg, Edward — Trials, litigation, etc. 2. Pennsylvania — Trials, litigation, etc.
3. Fugitive slaves — Legal status, laws, etc. — United States. I. Title.
KF228.P745B35 2012
342.7308'7 — dc23
2012016529

British Library Cataloguing-in-Publication Data is available.

Printed in the United States of America

10 9 8 7 6 5 4 3 2 1

The paper used in this publication is recycled and contains 30 percent postconsumer
waste. It is acid free and meets the minimum requirements of the American National
Standard for Permanence of Paper for Printed Library Materials z39.48-1992.

For my parents,

Fred S. Baker and Virginia H. Baker,

who still love me despite my having been both

a teenager and a graduate student.

CONTENTS

Watching the Missouri statehood debates of 1820 virtually shut down the federal government and hearing southern congressmen promise that blood would flow if slavery were impeded by federal legislation, Thomas Jefferson warned "We have the wolf by the ear, and we can neither hold him, nor safely let him go. Justice is in one scale, and self-preservation in the other." Like Jefferson, some southern whites feared slave rebellion, but even more they feared that valuable slaves would decamp and seek their freedom. Leaders of a posse of slave catchers like Edward Prigg roamed the free states seeking these runaways.

Prigg and his employers believed they acted in accord with the rendition clause of the U.S. Constitution and the recaption laws of slave states. The Fugitive Slave Act of 1793 required that "the person to whom such labor or service may be due, his agent or attorney, is hereby empowered to seize or arrest such fugitive from labor, and to take him or her before any Judge of the Circuit or District Courts of the United States, residing or being within the State, or before any magistrate of a county, city, or town corporate, wherein such seizure or arrest shall be made, and upon proof to the satisfaction of such Judge or magistrate" carry the individual or individuals back to their alleged masters.

In fact, relatively few slaves abandoned family and friends to venture far from home. If they left their owners, they stayed nearby. A few owners allowed slaves liberty of movement without actually signing the slaves' freedom papers. Maryland, sharing a border with the free state of Pennsylvania, was one such "middle ground," where white masters and black slaves mixed freely and where many slaves were allowed a freedom that appalled South Carolina and Mississippi slave masters.

One such slave was Margaret Morgan, who left Maryland in 1832 to marry and to raise her children in Pennsylvania. In 1826, Pennsylvania had enacted an antikidnapping law that provided in part that "any person or persons shall, from and after the passing of this act, by force and violence, take and carry away, or cause to be taken or carried away . . . any negro or mulatto, from any part or parts of this commonwealth . . . with a design and intention of selling and disposing of, or of causing to be sold, or of keeping and detaining" the captive, the accused could be indicted for a felony. The statute was one of the first of the so-called personal liberty laws in the North, clearly aimed at protecting the civil rights of free persons. It was not the work of abolitionists — their part in the story came later — but the debates over slavery in 1820 had rung a fire bell in the night, and free state legislatures took notice.

In 1837, Morgan's master had died, and her master's family sought her return, in part, perhaps, because she had children with the free black she married in Pennsylvania. While her use or exchange value might not be high, her children's potential value was. They hired Prigg and his crew to find her (she was not hiding), and he took her and her children back to Maryland against their will. He and four of his accomplices were indicted in absentia in a Pennsylvania court, and the governor sought their extradition from Maryland. Maryland refused, and the stage was set for a remarkable test case of whether the Constitution of the United States was a proslavery document. Certainly the rendition clause and the Fugitive Slave Act seemed to point in that direction, though the rising abolitionist movement found that the absence of the word *slavery* from the document proved the reverse. The case taxed the hearts and minds of the justices of the U.S. Supreme Court, and their various opinions demonstrated how right Jefferson was.

H. Robert Baker's account of the events leading up to the case could not be more exciting, for there was human drama in these events, as well as closely argued constitutional theory. Baker provides a model of balance between the personal and the legal stories. For most modern readers, the villains and the heroes of the tale may seem obvious, but to antebellum jurists, even those with abolitionist sympathies, the issues were not so clear cut. And this is where Baker excels, for he understands that one cannot impose one's own strong moral principles upon a past time and place — at least not until the end of the retelling.

ACKNOWLEDGMENTS

I would like to thank Peter Charles Hoffer for suggesting I undertake this project back in November of 2009 and Michael Briggs at the University Press of Kansas for providing me the formal opportunity. I am deeply indebted to both and to the entire editorial team at the press for their editorial prowess. Daniel Hamilton and Earl Maltz provided invaluable peer review that helped to focus my thinking. Rebecca Scott has stimulated me with critiques of the manuscript, as well as with her exciting scholarship on slavery and law. Maeva Marcus has been a powerful resource, and her service to the field of constitutional history is legend. David Sehat read the entire manuscript and helped straighten out the narrative when it became too circuitous. Bryan Camp also read the entire manuscript and provided invaluable legal and historical critiques. Fred Blue, Kristen Foster, Jared Poley, Jake Selwood, and Michelle Brattain all read and commented upon chapters. I have benefitted much from discussions of the project with my graduate students at Georgia State University, particularly Joseph Bagley, Mark J. Fleszar, Jeff Marlin, Jeff Morrison, and Lauren MacIvor Thompson. All errors, however, are my fault.

This book was made possible by a generous research grant from the William Nelson Cromwell Foundation. It has been a pleasure discussing my research with the foundation's secretary, John D. Gordan III. Georgia State University has funded my research as well, both through a Research Initiative Grant awarded by the College of Arts and Sciences and a summer research grant from the Department of History. The Newberry Library awarded me a short-term fellowship in 2010. And I would be remiss if I did not thank Jan Baker, who provided me with time release from parental and domestic duties in order to write. The fact that she did so while maintaining an international performance schedule cannot be overlooked.

This book is dependent upon a body of scholarship that has been built over the past half century. The mammoth contributions of John Hope Franklin, Paul Finkelman, William Wiecek, Earl Maltz, Mark Graber, Don E. Fehrenbacher, Phillip S. Paludan, Ira Berlin, Thomas D. Morris, and a host of other scholars who wrote trailblazing research in slavery, constitution, and law informs all my thinking on this subject and humbles any claim I have to originality. "The ugly fact is that books are made out of books," said the brilliant if reclusive author Cormac McCarthy. Of course, he was talking of novels and not history books, and in the same interview he allowed that "if there is an occupational hazard to writing, it's drinking." But the fundamental truth of the former statement is undeniable (I make no comment upon the latter), and I apologize in advance if I have not given enough credit to those who have given us all insight into the lost world of slavery and the Constitution.

Prigg v. Pennsylvania

Introduction

The primary character in the drama that is *Prigg v. Pennsylvania* was not even a named party in the case. She was Margaret Morgan. She was born in Maryland to slaves of John Ashmore. Some time before Margaret's birth, Ashmore had allowed Margaret's parents to live as free persons, and he never laid claim to Margaret. When he died in 1824, he did not list Margaret Morgan or her parents amongst his possessions. But neither did he formally emancipate them. Sometime in the 1820s, Margaret married a free man named Jerry Morgan. They had children together. They moved in 1832 to Pennsylvania and had at least one more child there. Then, in 1837, John Ashmore's widow (Margaret Ashmore) claimed Margaret Morgan as her slave. Several men, Edward Prigg among them, traveled to Pennsylvania as Ashmore's agents, obtained a warrant for Margaret Morgan's arrest and seized her and her children. Then, without securing a certificate of removal (required by Pennsylvania law), they took Margaret and her children back to Maryland. The state of Pennsylvania charged the slavecatchers with kidnapping under the Pennsylvania Personal Liberty Law of 1826. A grand jury indicted the slavecatchers and in 1837 Pennsylvania requested their rendition for trial. The state of Maryland protested. The two states negotiated a solution, and the Pennsylvania legislature initiated a case designed to come before the Supreme Court of the United States in 1842, known to us now as *Prigg v. Pennsylvania.*

Prigg v. Pennsylvania promised to settle one of the most contentious issues of the day: what exactly did the fugitive slave clause of the Constitution mean? On its face, the wording of Article IV, Section 2, seemed straightforward enough: "No person held to service or labour in one state, under the laws thereof, escaping into another, shall, in consequence of any law or regulation therein, be discharged from such service or labour, but shall be delivered up on claim of the party to whom such service or labour may be due." Pennsylvania certainly could not declare a slave who fled to its jurisdiction free — that was crystal clear. But the clause was ambiguous where it mattered most: Could a slaveholder simply seize his runaway slave in a free state without an arrest warrant or other legal process? If not, who would "deliver up" the fugitive? What if the fugitive claimed that it was a case of mistaken identity or outright kidnapping? What evidence would suffice to prove whether the person claimed was actually a fugitive slave? What constituted "escaping"? If a slaveholder took a slave into a free state or consented to the slave's travel there, and then the slave ran, was this an escape? And even if we concede that Margaret Morgan was a fugitive slave, was the child that she bore in Pennsylvania the legal property of Margaret's owner? Complicating this problem was the question of authority. The federal government and the state of Pennsylvania had created different legal procedures for answering these questions. But it was not entirely certain which sovereign entity had the authority under the Constitution to do so.

These questions reached beyond the fate of Margaret Morgan and her children. In the 1830s, conflicts over slavery dominated politics. Southerners demanded not only that the fugitive slave clause be upheld but also that Congress protect slaveholders' property rights in the territories and refuse abolitionist petitions. Reacting to the massive circulation of abolitionist literature in 1835, southerners demanded that Congress prohibit abolitionists from sending pamphlets via the federal mail and that the free states suppress abolitionist societies. Diehards among them claimed that failure to meet these demands imperiled union. Abolitionists saw it differently. They rested their right to petition Congress and agitate against slavery upon the First Amendment and claimed for Congress plenary power to ban slavery in the territories and to prohibit the interstate slave trade. Some abolitionists admitted the constitutional right of slaveholders to fugitive slaves but demanded that the states provide adequate protections for free blacks caught up in the rendition process. Slaveholders argued that this was but a thinly disguised means of impeding slaveholders' property rights, thus defeating the purpose of the fugitive slave clause. At the heart of *Prigg v. Pennsylvania* was a conflict between these competing rights claims. Slaveholders claimed a constitutional right to the return of their property without delay, and abolitionists demanded that black people ensnared by the law had a right to have their liberty determined in a court of law.

This was a pressing matter by 1842. At issue was the reach of slave-holders' property rights into the free states. At issue were the rights of free blacks. Also at issue was the question of whether the federal or the state governments had the power to enforce the fugitive slave clause. The Constitution was ambiguous, and both states and Congress had legislated procedures for fugitive slave rendition. If the power to legislate on the subject was exclusive in either the states or the federal government, then the question could be settled quite easily. If it was concurrent, then the possibility of conflict arose. Even if one granted that the supremacy clause in Article VI made federal law supreme, states could still claim to be exercising their reserved police power under the Tenth Amendment. "Police" was a broad category of powers inherent in sovereignty to regulate the health, welfare, and morals of a society. Under this heading in antebellum America fell the right to define the status of state residents and to protect their liberty. Free states broadly claimed this power to protect free blacks kidnapped under fraudulent rendition claims. This had explosive political potential in Jacksonian America. By the 1840s, slaveholders were complaining that the laws of free states impeded their constitutional right to fugitive slaves, and abolitionists argued that lax fugitive slave laws imperiled the liberty of free blacks and offended free states' sovereignty in the process. In short, answering the questions posed by fugitive slave rendition promised to answer some of the great constitutional questions of the day.

In *Prigg v. Pennsylvania*, the Supreme Court issued a landmark decision that announced federal supremacy in regulating fugitive slave rendition and denied that the states could dictate the terms of that rendition. But the decision reached further. It cast into doubt the ability of free states to define freedom and to protect their populations from potential kidnapping. Abolitionists complained mightily, and in many cases defied the decision. The controversy stretched on, well past the new congressional Fugitive Slave Act of 1850, right up through the Civil War. And while the Supreme Court upheld *Prigg v. Pennsylvania* on several occasions, the Court faced serious extrajudicial challenges to its supremacy.

All this speaks to why *Prigg v. Pennsylvania* is a landmark case. Yet the modern reader may be excused if she asks why *Prigg v. Pennsylvania* is relevant today. It is about exposition of the fugitive slave clause, a paragraph of the Constitution rendered defunct by the Thirteenth Amendment. We do not today have fugitive slaves. In this way, *Prigg v. Pennsylvania* is different from other antebellum cases that are still taught today as good constitutional law. *Marbury v. Madison* (1803) carved out a space for judicial review of legislative enactments. *Gibbons v. Ogden* (1824) and *Cooley v. Board of Wardens* (1851) interpreted the commerce clause. *Luther v. Borden* (1849) articulated the political questions doctrine. By way of contrast, *Prigg v. Pennsylvania* gave us a definitive judicial interpretation of the fugitive slave clause. While worthy of our curiosity, we might imagine that it is not necessarily relevant to our current constitutional regime.

But it is relevant. *Prigg* spoke to a question that still needles us: what exactly are the boundaries of federalism? As this book goes to press, the Supreme Court will consider whether Alabama and Arizona can pass laws enforcing U.S. immigration policy and whether the state of California can define marriage so as to exclude homosexual unions. In these cases, rights and powers are at issue, as are the question of who has the authority to determine, in the final instance, what is the meaning of the Constitution. These are all issues present in *Prigg v. Pennsylvania*. And *Prigg* in some respects is still good law when it comes to understanding the boundaries of federalism, and it has been cited as such. So we ought to understand precisely why the decision read the way it did. And that requires going beyond its text and into the factors that determined it.

We learn in this process that constitutional history cannot be told simply by reading constitutional law cases. Seven justices issued opinions in *Prigg* that read the Constitution in several distinct, and incompatible, ways. Story's opinion of the Court made an explicit appeal to a definitive original meaning of the fugitive slave clause. He also read the judicial precedents as unequivocally supporting his position. Nonetheless, he could not bring all of the justices around to his reasoning. Several read the sources of law differently from Story. But not one of them could claim a definitive interpretation. The justices slighted the complexity of the judicial precedents, and they read the Constitution's history in light of their contemporary problems. An intellectually honest reading of these sources produces a very different picture of the Constitution's original meaning and of the judicial interpretation of the fugitive slave clause.

Being critical of judges' use of history is important, but we should also be wary of privileging judges themselves. Constitutional law is created by many institutions, and the courts are only one particular set of them. Congress was the first interpreter of the fugitive slave clause, and its interpretation was worked out in successive intervals both in Congress and in the state assemblies. Both abolitionists and slaveholders pressed for their rights from the beginning. But they focused their efforts on petitioning the legislatures, which in the early republic were the places people primarily went to secure rights. As such, any history of the interpretation of the fugitive slave clause must first explain how Congress and the state legislatures interpreted the clause, before turning to the courts. The courts themselves demonstrated a remarkable deference to legislative construction of the Constitution, at least until the 1830s. And the Supreme Court was late to the game. Fugitive slave rendition had been an issue for half a century before the Supreme Court was invited into the fray. To treat that history as unimportant is to deny the obvious — that constitutional interpretation frequently takes place outside the Supreme Court.

It is because of this fact, not in spite of it, that *Prigg v. Pennsylvania* is a landmark case. The opinion of the Court was delivered by Joseph Story, a New Englander, but it supported immediate southern interests. It did so by unsettling the established constitutional regime governing fugitive slave rendition — a regime that had been challenged in petitions, negotiated in legislative enactments, and developed in court cases for over five decades. But that regime appeared to be collapsing. The 1830s had brought several constitutional crises over slavery onto the national stage, and the old means of balancing the interests of Maryland slaveholders with Pennsylvania abolitionists was failing. Moreover, slaveholders had put forward a set of assertions about the Constitution's meaning that tried both to reserve state sovereignty and compel strong federal action to protect slavery. Justice Joseph Story was a committed nationalist, devoted to both Union and Constitution. His opinion in *Prigg* agreed that the federal government was obliged to protect slavery (in certain ways) and in the process denied broad claims to reserve state sovereignty. His opinion, in short, attempted to solve more problems than just fugitive slaves.

Though it may be an important landmark, *Prigg v. Pennsylvania* ought not to be reduced solely to a number of constitutional law questions. Such an approach risks diminishing the people touched by the Court's naked power, relegating them to mere relevant "facts" in the development of legal doctrine. As much as *Prigg v. Pennsylvania* is about constitutional law in antebellum America, it is also about Margaret Morgan. The law defined her. The law took her freedom from her. It did so to thousands of others whose status as free or slave depended upon where they were born or whether their owners signed the right documents to emancipate them. But if law doomed Margaret Morgan, it also constrained slaveholders. In many cases it left them with no recourse if, for instance, they willingly took their slaves to free states and faced freedom suits there. And if slaveholders were willing to deny northern states the power to protect their free black residents from fraudulent rendition proceedings, then this would have implications for slave states' power to prevent the entry of free black citizens from northern states. Article IV, Section 2, contained not only the fugitive slave clause, but also the privileges and immunities clause. The logic of *Prigg v. Pennsylvania* had applications beyond fugitive slaves.

Margaret Morgan's fate was bound up with these intricate questions of law, but she was also heir to and at the mercy of deep historical forces. Slavery had been planted in North America along with other forms of unfree labor in the seventeenth century. Even "free labor" in colonial times was not free by modern standards because early modern concepts of social hierarchy did not imagine them as such and because an acute labor shortage made it impractical. A harsh legal regime that bound laborers to masters and ferreted out runaways was the colonial world's legacy. But even in the midst of this, an antislavery movement sprang to life in Britain and North America in the late eighteenth century that helped win freedom for thousands of slaves. Partly in fear of this movement, certain slaveholders in Philadelphia in 1787 demanded protections for slave property that found their way into the Constitution. They won the fugitive slave clause in the final document, although not entirely on the terms they wanted.

But the Constitution's protection of slavery, embodied in the fugitive slave clause, was muddled with notions of liberty and equality inherent in the document. It produced an opaque enough concoction for abolitionists white and black to nourish their movement. In short, the Constitution's compromises with slavery did not check antislavery sentiment. This was the matrix within which slaveholders and abolitionists and all those claimed as fugitive slaves argued for their rights. Margaret Morgan was born into this matrix. Her freedom, as well as her eventual enslavement, was in a large part determined by it. The point of this book is to recover the deep context of Margaret Morgan's dilemma; to explain a world over which she had little control and how it impacted her choices, her movements, and her fate.

Each chapter of this book explores a particular source of law, and in each we see a fundamental problem with interpreting these sources. They are by nature complex, and recovering their "true" meaning sometimes conflicts with the meaning ascribed to them by historical actors. In truth, sources of law often carry multiple meanings, and this destabilizes them. In constitutional law, this occurs most often when the constitutional text is ambiguous enough to allow for multiple interpretations. It is precisely at this moment that judges are compelled to justify a particular interpretive strategy and are most tempted to bring their preferences into decisions. *Prigg* is an instance of this kind of constitutional ambiguity, and the justices' differing opinions are testimony to how the same sources can be read to produce different results. My goal is not to find the "right" constitutional answer to the fugitive slave question. Rather, it is to show how the sources could bear multiple interpretations. This should not surprise us, as a certain level of indeterminacy accompanies all hard cases. And *Prigg* was a hard case.

Prigg was also a landmark in a more literal sense. It was a highly visible case that served as a marker for rupture. It altered constitutional law permanently. It convinced many abolitionists that the Constitution was the problem, not the solution, to slavery. It propelled other abolitionists to insist upon even stronger antislavery interpretations of the Constitution. State courts were not certain how to treat the decision, and several ignored it. Importantly, the principles of *Prigg* guided Congress when it passed a new Fugitive Slave Act in 1850. The new law proved far more effective at meeting slaveholders' demands that fugitive slave rendition be quick and cheap, even if it also inspired massive and sometimes savage resistance. *Prigg v. Pennsylvania* was the wellspring for all this, save one thing — the fugitives themselves. They ran from slavery before *Prigg*, and they ran from it after *Prigg*. No Supreme Court case — no matter how much of a landmark — would distract fugitives from their path to freedom.

A Short History of Fugitives in America and an African Named James Somerset

Fugitives had long been a part of the American fabric. Before the Supreme Court visited the matter in *Prigg v. Pennsylvania*, before the Underground Railroad was even a thought, and before the Constitution was framed, men, women, and children ran from their masters. They did so to find better employment elsewhere and to escape the servile conditions forced upon them. And because labor was scarce in the colonies, fugitives had a reasonable chance at bettering themselves. This was one reason that both the written and unwritten colonial law bound laborers to their masters even more tightly than in the old world. The same labor scarcity that encouraged runaways also compelled masters to chase them down. Recaption—the pursuit and capture of fugitives from labor—was authorized by the common law, by custom, and by practice. This was all the more common for those unfree laborers (indentured servant and slave alike) who did not willingly toil in tobacco fields and rice swamps. When willing immigrants stopped coming to the new world in numbers large enough to sustain colonial enterprises, masters sought others to supply the want. They turned to kidnappers, spiriting orphans and drunkards out of the English ports. And increasingly they turned to slave traders. In time, slavery would become a permanent part of the foundation of British North America, supported by private power and public authority.

This legal regime, however, did not go unchallenged. By the last third of the eighteenth century, British peoples in both England and the colonies began to examine critically the institution of slavery, and they found it incompatible with a common law tradition that exalted the freedom to contract. Those who harbored these antislavery impulses were few in number, but they began to demand that legal principles be applied consistently. By the time of the American Revolution, they had made considerable headway. In England, abolitionists won a stunning victory with *Somerset v. Stewart* (1772), a case in which the celebrated Lord Mansfield, Chief Justice of King's Bench, declared that slavery was so odious that it would be tolerated only if a legislature sanctioned it. Mansfield's opinion did nothing to free the millions of black slaves toiling in the corners of the British Empire, as the jurisdiction of King's Bench did not extend beyond England's shores and colonial legislatures had adopted slave codes in any case. But the principle that Mansfield intoned resonated with a British and American antislavery movement that was just finding its voice.

Thus, the roots of *Prigg v. Pennsylvania* ran deep in the history of fugitives in America and its intersection with a budding antislavery movement. It was not a tidy story. One encounters in the history of liberty and slavery and fugitives in America many contradictory strands: a legal regime that circumscribed virtually every laborer's liberty; masters who regularly pursued and captured fugitives and who cooperated with one another to do so across the colonies; a common law tradition of free will in contract that eroded slaveholders' claims to dominion; and a growing antislavery movement that demanded liberty be applied to all. By the eve of the Constitutional Convention's meeting, slaveholders might still have been strong in North America, but their position had been challenged in ways that were unimaginable only a few decades before.

Labor had always been dear in the American colonies. The speculators, investors, and colonists who wished to make fortunes in North America found themselves in constant shortage of the people to do the work necessary to produce even enough income to sustain a given colony year to year. The response to this labor crisis was by no means uniform. The Virginia Company eventually turned to the use of headrights and long-term indentures to bring laborers to the colony, a practice which continued after the monarchy assumed control of Virginia in 1624. The Puritans of Massachusetts Bay found themselves perpetually forced to relax entry requirements in order to attract enough immigrants — sacrificing in the process their vision of a colony populated primarily by rigorous Calvinists. When Pennsylvania opened up to settlement after 1681, an open immigration policy coupled with the recruitment of indentured servants and purchase of slaves made it the largest colonial enterprise of its time. Europeans, thirsty for religious liberty in the face of persecution, hurried to Pennsylvania. Still, by 1690 nearly one third of Pennsylvania's labor force was unfree. This regional diversity makes it quite difficult to generalize about the colonial experience of work and life. The rhythms of tobacco production in the Chesapeake differed from that of rice in the Carolinian Lowlands, and the dispersed farms of Pennsylvania did not resemble the nucleated villages of New England. Diversity of experience was the norm, even if all the colonies were united in a want for labor.

Labor scarcity partially explains why colonial authorities bound their labor so tightly. Indentured servants were expected to complete their contracts, and those who did not faced punishment. The laws of Virginia added double-time penalties for indentured servants who absconded before their service was up. Before 1662, runaways in Virginia were branded or had their hair cropped. Pennsylvania's "Act for the Better Regulation of Servants" of 1700 also extended runaways' length of servitude by five days for every one day they were absent. In Massachusetts, runaway servants were turned over to the courts, where the most common penalty was whipping. Colonial masters pushed the regime still further. Virginia planters in the seventeenth century made a trade of indentures, effectively turning white indentured servants into commodities. This was of dubious legality at best, given that no record was made of servants' consent, a requirement of English law. Not that this should surprise us. The record abounds with instances of masters using their superior power to manipulate the rules of law in order to hold servants longer than their period of indenture. They squeezed every ounce of blood from the stone.

Indentured servitude existed alongside slavery in the early-seventeenth-century colonies, and both were unfree forms of labor that shared much in common. The bonded white and black laborers toiled in the same fields, often shoulder to shoulder, and many died in service or without ever experiencing freedom. They ate the same coarse food, wore the same clothing, and were disciplined by the same hands. But there were differences too. Servant petitions collected from Maryland indicate that bonded whites enjoyed at least some privileges that slaves did not. And white servants never faced the terror of perpetual bondage, for themselves and their children, as did Africans. But such distinctions likely meant little in the first few decades of a colony's settlement, when malaria, malnutrition, and perpetual war cut lives short and dampened all expectations.

So the transition to black slavery was neither predetermined nor simple, and we should not forget that in the mid-seventeenth century the correlation between "white" and "free," as well as that between "black" and "slave," was still not completely certain. Free and voluntary migration to British North America declined between 1640 and 1661 for a number of reasons, and in its place came bonded servants. Among them were the victims of "spirits" — the men who haunted the British port cities of Bristol, Gravesend, and London looking for orphans, drunkards, or anyone else they could "spirit" onto ships bound for the colonies. The first such "spirit" in the English record was Owen Evans. After forging a royal commission, Evans demanded that petty officers in Somerset press maidens into service as concubines for colonists in Virginia and Barbados. The rogue in this case was sniffed out. Evans found himself in 1618 before a Somerset justice of the peace, to whom he confessed his crime. Despite this instance of justice being done, few kidnappers were ever caught. Glimpses of their work pepper both the legal and literary record. By the 1640s, kidnapping appeared to be an organized criminal enterprise, taking advantage of lax inspection and registration laws in England's port cities. The situation was serious enough that the Privy Council appointed a committee in 1660 to review the problem, and it reported back that only an act of Parliament would thwart kidnapping. Such a bill arrived in the 1662 session but was never passed. Nonetheless, Bristol and London authorities took their own actions, creating servant registries and checking logs to ferret out potential kidnappers.

The history of fugitive laborers is suffused with the kidnapped. Both were hunted down and both compelled to labor against their wishes. But while the legal regime punished fugitives by binding them for longer periods of time, it provided some protections for the kidnapped. If one sees the law as primarily serving the interest of the ruling class, this would appear at least mildly contradictory. After all, interest alone did not compel a distinction between the fugitive and the kidnapped. But the logic of social relations did. Kidnappers were loathed on both sides of the Atlantic because they threatened the legitimacy of hierarchical labor relations. Kidnappers exposed the naked need for labor and profit that underpinned the social system, and to tolerate them would have implicated other, legal forms of exploitation. At their heart, official actions against kidnapping reinforced the unquestioned premise that everyone had a place in the social order. This was as much a religious and moral belief as it was a material one, and it manifested itself as such. Strangers were regarded with suspicion and regularly warned out of towns. Masterless men were not to be tolerated. Even Pennsylvania, renowned for its open immigration and religious toleration, required servants to carry passports attesting to their status or risk spending time in jail. The burden lay with the defendant to prove his or her freedom. Nor was Pennsylvania alone — such laws were commonplace in North America.

These harsh laws distinguished the colonies from England, where apprenticeship contracts were shorter, pass laws were virtually unknown, and the laws governing absenteeism and fugitives from service were much more lenient. But the distinction should not be overdrawn. The English common law of persons governed the day-to-day life of servants, and this customary law gave wide latitude to masters. By this law, masters retained the right to regain their fugitive servants' labor by a general right of recaption — the legal authority to seize the runaway wherever he or she was found and forcibly return him or her to service. This right flowed from personal authority rather than the state and was implicit in the rigidly hierarchical early modern world. It pervaded every relationship, not just master-servant. Husbands could exercise recaption over their wives, and fathers over their children. A 1695 Massachusetts law reaffirmed this connection when it adopted measures to prevent both "Men's Sons or Servants" from leaving their service early. We should take note of the conflation of children and servants, which proves just how much hierarchical thinking dominated labor relationships in New England. Importantly, such statutes did not create but only reinforced the master's rights. The hunting down of fugitives — wives, children, servants, and slaves — did not require the legal cover of the legislature.

Intercolonial cooperation reinforced this right of recaption. By the terms of the New England Confederation of 1643, fugitive servants were to be returned from one colony to another upon the production of a magistrate's certificate or "other due proofe." This was extended to the New Netherlands in 1650. Requests for assistance in the recovery of fugitive servants and slaves often came in formal letters from one governor to another, as when Governor William Berkeley of Virginia asked for assistance in Massachusetts in recovering a merchant's servants, "it being but an accustomed favour reciprocally shown upon all occasions." Although the record indicates substantial cooperation between the colonies, indifference and intransigence sometimes strained relations. Georgia, for instance, was forced in 1733 to appeal to the imperial Board of Trade when South Carolina neglected to help return fugitive servants.

If intercolonial *cooperation* was common, so too was imperial *competition*. The settlement of Charles Town in (South) Carolina in 1670 presented a serious threat to Spanish Florida and its small port colony of St. Augustine. Skirmishes followed. In 1686, a motley crew of Spanish, blacks, and Indians raided the plantation of the governor of South Carolina, taking away (among other things), thirteen slaves. The British demanded their return, as well as the return of those slaves "who run dayly into your towns." This last bit was likely an exaggeration, but it proved prescient. In 1687, 11 slaves from South Carolina arrived in St. Augustine seeking refuge. After baptizing them into the Catholic faith, the Spanish refused to surrender them to the British. More would follow, and eventually the Spanish established the free black town of Gracia Real de Santa Teresa de Mose. Word of Spanish promises of freedom reached South Carolina's slaves. In 1738, some seventy slaves fled South Carolina for Spanish Florida. In 1739, slaves broke into the store at the Stono Bridge. Their initial motives were unclear, but their ultimate goal became obvious. After taking supplies, they made south for St. Augustine, killing the whites who got in their way. They never made it. But they left the South Carolinians a legacy of fear and loathing.

That black slaves resisted their bondage, just as white bound servants did, testified to the harshness of the regime under which they suffered. Rebelling and running away were only two ways in which blacks might protest their enslavement. Slaves had other means, violent and otherwise, at their disposal. Colonial authorities responded by tightening the screws. They also imported more slaves. In the Chesapeake, bonded white labor had predominated in the seventeenth century but then declined. Planters imported slaves in great numbers in the early eighteenth century. The Lowcountry was fundamentally different. Caribbean planters founded the first settlement in Carolina in 1670, and blacks outnumbered whites by 1708. The cultivation of rice and indigo in the Carolina Lowcountry required backbreaking work and large labor forces, which planters filled on the Caribbean model. Just south of Carolina, the colony of Georgia followed a different model with the same result. The Trustees who founded Georgia initially argued for a colony without slaves, and Parliament forbade slavery there in 1735. Settlers thought otherwise, and by 1750 had convinced Parliament to end the ban. By the eve of the Revolution, slave ships had brought nearly 16,000 Africans in chains to Georgia. Planters across North America imported slave codes from Caribbean sugar islands to define slavery and to differentiate Africans from Europeans. Slave law became distinct from the common law of master and servant that still governed white labor, both indentured and free. The association of "black" with "slave" may have had roots in seventeenth-century real-life experience, but by the mid-eighteenth century, it was a matter of law.

Such was the complicated colonial world at the cusp of the American Revolution. African slavery had become a legal institution separate from that which bound white servants. Nonetheless, the authority of masters stemmed from multiple and sometimes conflicting sources: from slave codes, customary practices, and the common law of master and servant. This authority, as well as the conditions of slavery itself, differed from colony to colony. However fractured and multivalent this world was, it did have some discernibly universal features. Slavery was a perpetual status that passed from mother to child. Slaves' diminished status meant they enjoyed far fewer privileges than even bonded white servants. In many cases, slaves lived under different criminal codes. Slave labor made fortunes for New England and Middle Atlantic merchants, as well as the tobacco and rice planters further south. And this prosperity would, paradoxically, work to weaken slavery in the long run. Economic opportunity attracted new immigrants, fueled trade, and integrated the North American colonies into the Atlantic commerce. But as port cities became denser and trade quickened, opportunities for freedom-hungry slaves broadened too. Rebels, resisters, and runaways became bolder and more numerous as the eighteenth century progressed.

To talk in such broad terms can obscure the ways in which this labor system impacted individual people and the ways in which individuals in turn impacted the system. Consider the case of James Somerset, whose encounter with the thirst for labor in the British Atlantic would reverberate throughout history. Somerset traveled the full length of the Atlantic twice and resided in multiple North American colonies in the 1760s before departing in 1769 for England. Shortly after that, he would encounter Granville Sharp. We will return to James Somerset in a moment, for by the time he met Granville Sharp, Sharp's tale would be critical to this story. Granville Sharp was born in 1735 to a prominent family. His grandfather had been the Archbishop of York, and his father the Archdeacon of Northumberland. His older brothers were philanthropists and well known amongst the aristocracy. But Granville was the ninth son in the family (six survived infancy), and for all his family's wealth he found himself a London draper's apprentice at the age of 15. The experience brought him into contact with a Jew, dissenting Protestants, and a Catholic. The cosmopolitan experience stimulated him. He taught himself Hebrew and Greek in order to better understand biblical prophesy. He never, however, took to the draper's trade. His apprenticeship ended in 1757, and he thereafter took up a clerk's position in the Ordnance office.

Sharp's first shocking encounter with slavery came in 1765 when he came across the half-dead Jonathan Strong, a Barbados slave brought to London by his master, David Lisle. Lisle had pistol-whipped Strong so badly as to nearly blind him. Then he cast him out. Granville Sharp was visiting his brother, a physician, when he discovered Strong lying upon a bench, awaiting treatment. Strong would spend four months in the hospital convalescing before he could work again, at which point the Sharps helped him obtain a position as a messenger and servant for a family acquaintance. It was nearly two years later, in 1767, that David Lisle spotted Strong on the street and had him seized. His plan was to sell Strong to a West Indies planter, but Strong got word to Granville Sharp. Sharp in turn convinced the Lord Mayor of London to release Strong from Lisle's custody. Lisle was furious. He sued Sharp, and challenged him to a duel. Sharp declined the duel and the lawsuit would ultimately fail. But Sharp's curiosity had been engaged. He threw himself into the study of the law both to defend himself and to discover slavery's legal foundation.

Sharp approached the study of the law much the way he had biblical texts. Ever the puritan, he endeavored to get to the law's textual heart, to search for purity of meaning and expose corrupt interpretations. Slavery, he found, was an analogous legal problem. It was an innovation with no basis in settled principles of the common law. If blacks were human beings, then in England they were entitled to the same protection by the king as other human beings. Masters' rights could only be secured by contract, and no one could contract permanently out of their personal liberty. Simply put: slavery could not exist under English law. Sharp's position was sound in logic but not square with reality. Sharp could quote the words of a sixteenth-century judge that the air of England was "too pure an air for slaves to breathe in," but plenty of slaves breathed English air. They were traded in the port cities of Liverpool and London throughout the seventeenth century. As overseas British plantations swelled with slaves, so were slaves brought to England. Newspaper advertisements promised bounties for runaways. Most notoriously, the British government protected and encouraged the slave trade, transporting over three million kidnapped Africans across the Atlantic during the eighteenth century (one of them being James Somerset).

Sharp had to contend, moreover, with a formidable legal opinion issued by two of England's legal luminaries. The legal opinion was itself an indication of just how unsettled was the common law's relationship with slavery. A consortium of West Indian slaveholders had approached several prominent lawyers at Lincoln's Inn (a prestigious legal society/law school) with prickly questions. Were their slaves considered property in England? Did English law make them free? Did baptism release a slave from perpetual bondage? The lawyers agreed to produce an opinion, and it would bear the name of two of the most prominent amongst them — Attorney General Philip Yorke and Solicitor General Charles Talbot. The Yorke-Talbot opinion was short in length, broad in application, and confident in tone. Slaves, the opinion held, did not become free by traveling to England. In fact, English law did not determine or vary the master's property right in any way. Nor did baptism free a slave. Masters retained power over their slaves and could compel their slaves to leave England's shores, by force or otherwise. It was precisely the legal cover the West Indian slaveholders wanted. But the Yorke-Talbot opinion was just that: an opinion. It did not have legal authority and it could not bind judges.

It was nonetheless influential, if only because of the notoriety of its authors (Philip Yorke, for instance, would go on to be Lord Chancellor). The brief cited no judicial opinions.

In truth, the common law's relationship with slavery was ambiguous. In 1677, judges indicated that the writ of trover — an action used to recover moveable property — lay for slaves. The rationale was twofold: merchants treated slaves as property, and slaves were infidels. However, King's Bench overruled this point in *Chamberlain v. Harvey* (1697). Rather than trover, Chief Justice Sir John Holt declared, a master should seek a writ that treated the slave as a servant absent from service. This was a point of procedure. At common law, selection of the right writ was essential to a plaintiff's case. But, as legal historian William Wiecek has argued, it was not merely technical. It laid down the principle that the common law did not recognize chattel slavery. In several cases over the next decade, King's Bench reaffirmed this principle. But this does not immediately lead to the conclusion — tendentiously drawn by Granville Sharp — that Chief Justice Holt had abolished slavery in England. In *Smith v. Gould* (1705–1707), the justices of King's Bench suggested various procedural remedies for a master asserting title to a slave in England. Thus, although chattel slavery could not exist in England, some of its vestiges could nonetheless be fit into common law pleading.

Such was the law that Granville Sharp encountered when he first sat down to study the subject in 1767. Two years later, he published the fruits of his research in *A Representation of the Injustice and Dangerous Tendency of Tolerating Slavery; or of Admitting the Least Claim of Private Property in the Persons of Men, in England*. His legal argument against slavery was both conservative and radical. It was conservative in the sense that it celebrated traditional authority and abhorred innovation. In Sharp's analysis, slavery was bad because it had never been recognized at common law. He began with the famous chapter 39 of Magna Carta, which declared no freeman would be imprisoned or dispossessed except by the law of the land. He found that the Parliament of Edward III in 1346 extended Magna Carta's provisions to all men and guaranteed that none would be imprisoned, dispossessed, or killed except by "due process of law." The famous 1679 Habeas Corpus Act guaranteed that any person could sue out the writ of habeas corpus. If all this were true, argued Sharp, then slavery did not exist as a legal category. And if this were true, it followed that slavery was a destructive innovation, foreign to the common law, and injurious to the personal liberty that the English held so dear.

Sharp's appeal to the common-law principle of liberty was thus deeply conservative in its nature. If Africans were people then they had access to the writ of habeas corpus. It was as simple as that. But it was here where the argument took a potentially radical turn. Habeas corpus was a writ used to test detention for its legality. As such, it had been traditionally confined to a review of whether the procedures that accompanied detention were regular. If a slave sued out a writ of habeas corpus because his or her master forcibly detained him or her, then the issue that would be pleaded was whether the master could hold the slave. If slavery did not exist in England, as Sharp believed, then the detention could not be legal. By 1769, the year Sharp published *A Representation of the Injustice*, there were some 15,000 blacks in England, many of whom were claimed in some way by a slaveholder. Sharp aimed to tell them they were all free.

Also in 1769, James Somerset arrived in London. He was a slave owned by an ambitious Scots peddler of various commodities (including slaves) named Charles Stewart. But Somerset had not always been a slave. Born free in western Africa, possibly Senegambia, James Somerset was kidnapped by African slavehunters as a boy. In 1749, he was sold to European slave traders and eventually to Charles Stewart. Somerset became one of Stewart's favorites as a personal servant, and he was rewarded with fine clothes and cloth. But it was freedom that Somerset desired above all else, for in November of 1771, two years after he arrived in England, he walked out on Charles Stewart and vowed never to return. Stewart reckoned otherwise. His agents located James Somerset within two months, seized him, and locked him up in the *Ann and Mary*. The ship was destined for the slave market in Jamaica, and Somerset might then contemplate a short life toiling on a sugar plantation. But before the ship set sail, Somerset's godmother obtained for him a writ of habeas corpus from King's Bench. Somerset was brought before Lord Chief Justice Mansfield, who set a hearing date and released Somerset in the mean time.

Somerset sought out Granville Sharp, by now the most famous figure in the antislavery movement. Sharp seized the opportunity and helped assemble a talented legal team. Stewart's lawyers were likewise picked with the help of the West Indies interests, as it quickly became clear that the case would have more import than the freedom or servitude of one man. Somerset's lawyers made the case clearly. Somerset may have been Charles Stewart's slave by the laws of Virginia, but those laws did not apply in England where chattel slavery was unknown to either common law or statute law. If English law did not recognize slavery, then it followed simply that Somerset was not a slave in England and his master could not compel him to leave the island.

Stewart's lawyers countered by invoking the principle of comity. Simply put, comity was the respectful admission of foreign laws (meaning foreign to one's own jurisdiction) when they did not otherwise conflict with one's law. Comity was not bound by hard and fast rules, but rather by general principles. Foreign laws could be admitted if necessary, provided that they did not contravene local custom, statute, or other law. One of Stewart's lawyers, the able John Dunning, made the point forcefully. He asked the court to imagine the "inconvenience" of every foreigner arriving in the country with his servants being suddenly informed that they were all of equal station. The servant would decide which commands to obey, and the master would be powerless to enforce his will. The result? "Both go without their dinner." Stewart's lawyers also pointed out that this was not solely a matter of comity, as the jurisdiction in question was part of the British Empire, and the laws of Virginia had the sanction of the royal government. Furthermore, Parliament had passed laws that legitimated the slave trade and otherwise tacitly approved of the institution. Imperial interests upheld slavery, and slavery ought as such to be recognized in the English courts.

For his part, Lord Chief Justice Mansfield would have preferred not to render a decision. At stake was more than just the fate of one African, but of the thousands who were held by British planters throughout England. At stake was also the ability of British subjects to travel freely with their slaves within the empire. More than once Mansfield urged the two sides to come to some agreement. He clearly hoped that Charles Stewart would accept a payment for Somerset's services in return for a relinquishing of his property rights in him. Mansfield postponed the case deliberately hoping for such a payoff. He even resorted to a warning, saying that "if the parties will have judgement, *fiat justitia, ruat cœlum*" (Let justice be done though the heavens may fall). But no settlement came.

So on Monday, June 22, 1772, Lord Mansfield and the judges of King's Bench announced in court that they had reached their decision. After reciting the facts of the case, Mansfield got to the heart of the matter. The seizing and detaining of Somerset for the purpose of transporting him out of the Realm was an act of "high dominion" and could be tolerated only if allowed by *positive law*, i.e., a statute passed by the legislature. He explained further that slavery was of such a nature that it derived its existence from no other source of authority than legislative enactment. Neither custom nor international practice would suffice. But as strong as such statements might appear on their face, Mansfield likely intended them to be read quite narrowly. He had held that the common law would not suffer the removal of a person against his or her will out of the realm of England. As he made clear in later pronouncements (both public and private), Mansfield did not wish to settle the question of whether slaves who came to England were instantly free. There were still ways for slaveholders from the corners of empire to bind their slaves should they travel to England. And Mansfield had not spoken at all about slaves held throughout the empire. There was doubt that he could in any case, as the jurisdiction of King's Bench did not reach the colonies.

Whatever Mansfield's intentions, the report of his decision acquired a life of its own. Abolitionists read Mansfield's opinion as differentiating slave property from other kinds of property. It was "so odious" that nothing but a statute could support it. Mansfield had handed an important weapon to the nascent antislavery movement. By 1773 it was widely reported in the mainland colonial press where its ringing invocation of English liberty dovetailed with revolutionary themes. Colonial protest of British imperial policy had invoked the pregnant concepts of "tyranny" and "liberty," and the fear of reducing freeborn Englishmen to "slavery" over taxes on, among other things, lead, glass, and tea. Africans seemed absent the equation, at least until an exasperated Samuel Johnson pointed out that the "loudest yelps for liberty come from the drivers of negroes." Nonetheless, there were some colonists who had brought the plight of enslaved Africans to their fellows' attention. The most prolific among them was Anthony Benezet, a Protestant of French descent whose family had arrived in Philadelphia fleeing religious persecution in Europe. Benezet married a Quaker and spent his early adulthood as a school-teacher. He eventually became a schoolmaster. He instructed black children and became convinced that society's stamp of inferiority on people of color owed more to vulgar prejudices than innate abilities. Beginning in 1762, Benezet published pamphlets denouncing the slave trade and initiated a correspondence with like-minded people, urging them to petition their assemblies and speak out on their own. Benjamin Franklin even credited Anthony Benezet for the Virginia House of Burgesses' 1772 petition to the king calling for an end to further slave importation. Franklin exaggerated Benezet's influence, but not his energy. He was abreast of every movement and missed no opportunity to strike at slavery. His search for ties to antislavery England led to a correspondence with Granville Sharp that commenced just as Mansfield delivered his opinion in *Somerset*. For his part, Sharp was thrilled that Benezet's letters carried news of several independent movements, from Virginia to Massachusetts, to end the slave trade and, hopefully, slavery as well.

We must be careful not to exaggerate antislavery sentiment in the colonies. In 1772, every colony tolerated slavery. The arguments deployed by colonists against British tyranny had relied more heavily on the concept of the rights of freeborn *Englishmen* than on natural law. Moreover, most antislavery activity was at first private and religious. Quakers had first disentangled themselves from slavery before turning to the public act of petitioning to bring an end to the slave trade. Those who adopted Anthony Benezet's arguments did so when it suited immediate political interests. For example, it was the surplus of slaves in the Chesapeake rather than humanitarian empathy that convinced the House of Burgesses to authorize a petition to the king calling for an end to the slave trade. But to concede this is not to suggest that antislavery sentiment had no independent moral force. Individuals had become troubled by the presence of perpetual slavery in an age of enlightenment, and in the conceptual space created by a revolution for liberty, an antislavery movement found a toehold. Benezet helped found the first formal society devoted to the abolition of slavery, the Society for the Relief of Free Negroes Unlawfully Held in Bondage, in Philadelphia in 1775. The Revolutionary War interrupted

{ *Chapter 1* }

it, but it was revived in 1784 and became known as the Pennsylvania Abolition Society. In that same year, the New York Manumission Society was founded. By that time, New England states had largely done away with the slave trade, and Pennsylvania had become the first state in the world to plan for the formal end of slavery in the form of a gradual abolition act, passed in 1780.

Independently of such political action, the surging efforts of blacks themselves undermined slavery. Runaways multiplied. The outbreak of war eventually brought with it British promises of emancipation, and slaves fled to British lines. Even here, one finds evidence of Lord Mansfield's influence. The *Williamsburg Evening Gazette* reported in 1773 that a Virginia slave couple had intended to escape to Great Britain in order to secure their freedom. But escape was not the only option. The first public petitions to legislatures by blacks appeared in Massachusetts in 1773. By 1774 a mass petition asking for freedom cited the principle that the common law did not recognize slavery, another clear reference to the power of Mansfield's opinion in *Somerset*. These public petitions were supplemented by private petitions, often in the form of "freedom suits." In Massachusetts, slaves initiated more than a dozen of these suits between the Stamp Act crisis of 1765 and the conclusion of the Treaty of Paris in 1783.

One such slave who took seriously the rhetoric and reality of freedom was Quaco "Quok" Walker. A slave in rural Massachusetts, Quok prevailed upon his owner, James Caldwell, to free him when he reached adulthood. He extracted the promise, but Caldwell's death and his widow's remarriage to a slaveholder named Nathaniel Jennison complicated the matter. Jennison refused to honor the promise. No matter to Walker. In 1781, he walked out on Jennison and went to work for James Caldwell's younger brothers. Jennison was furious. He took two white farmhands to the Caldwell farm, beat Quok Walker roundly, dragged him back to his farm, and locked him in a barn. Quok escaped, hired the prominent Massachusetts lawyer Levi Lincoln, and sued Jennison for assault and battery. Jennison launched a countersuit against the Caldwell brothers for employing Quok and thus depriving Jennison of Quok's labor.

As if this situation were not confusing enough, both Quok and Jennison won their cases. One court said, in essence, that Quok Walker could not be restrained by Jennison; another said that Jennison had dominion over Quok Walker. Appeals took Quok Walker's case (also known as *Commonwealth v. Jennison*) to the Massachusetts Supreme Judicial Court in 1783. The appeal was decided by jury, but Chief Justice William Cushing's charge left little doubt about what it would decide. True, said Cushing to the jury, Quok Walker was born a slave. True, slavery had existed in all of the colonies for some time. However, slavery was not "expressly enacted or established" by Massachusetts statute. Furthermore, the Revolution had changed the hearts of men, and now people were "more favorable to the natural rights of mankind." Cushing ended by alluding to Massachusetts' Declaration of Rights, which preceded the state's landmark 1780 Constitution. "All men are born free and equal," quoted Cushing, and therefore "the idea of slavery is inconsistent with our own conduct and Constitution." It took the jury (which deliberated in the corner of the same room where they had heard the case and would deliver their verdict) a few minutes to find for Quok Walker.

Here were traces of Mansfield's influence in North America. Cushing, like Mansfield, had required slaveholders to plant their claims in express, positive law. Also like Mansfield, Cushing had required that slavery be construed strictly. And like Mansfield's opinion, Cushing's would be consistently misinterpreted. Contrary to popular belief (then and now), Cushing had merely charged a jury, not ended slavery by judicial fiat. The legislature easily could have overruled him (although it did not), and slaves would still have had to sue for their freedom should masters continue to exercise authority over them. And the case — a charge of assault and battery by a Massachusetts slave against a Massachusetts man — did not address a plethora of other situations that might arise. If a Virginian or New Yorker traveled to Massachusetts with his slave, would his slave instantly become free? If a slave fled from another state, would that slave be free?

Chief Justice Cushing addressed these questions in two subsequent cases. In *Exeter v. Hanchett*, Cushing considered whether Oliver Hanchett, a resident of Connecticut, had committed kidnapping when he sent agents to arrest a fugitive slave. The fugitive was a woman named Flora, who was married to a freeman in Massachusetts by the name of Exeter. Flora ran to Exeter in Massachusetts, and Hanchett sent agents to arrest her. Exeter brought suit, claiming that Flora's owner had kidnapped his wife and stolen some of their belongings in the process. Exeter won a jury verdict in the Court of Common Pleas in Hampshire County. Hanchett appealed, and Cushing reversed the verdict. He gave no rationale, but the ruling betrayed Cushing's understanding that slavery was not a dead letter in Massachusetts. In a second case, *Affa Hall*, Cushing hedged his ruling in Quok Walker's case further. *Affa Hall* was complicated. Some 35 South Carolinian slaves captured by British privateers during the Revolutionary War had come into the custody of the state of Massachusetts. After news was communicated to the government of South Carolina, 25 were claimed. Two slaveholders waited some four years to claim their slaves, who by then had integrated themselves into Boston's free black community. The South Carolinians employed a Boston lawyer who secured a writ of mittimus (used to hold criminals for trial) to jail their slaves. Cushing released them on writs of habeas corpus, prompting a furious diplomatic exchange. The slaveholders petitioned their legislature and governor, and South Carolina Governor Benjamin Guerard wrote a blustering letter demanding to know why his citizens' property had not been restored. The Massachusetts governor asked his chief justice for an explanation. Chief Justice Cushing demurred. The writ of mittimus could only hold criminals, and no crime had been alleged. The blacks were entitled to a writ of habeas corpus (all persons were), and the detention under the writ of mittimus was deficient. Therefore, the blacks were released. In short, it was a legal technicality that freed them, not judicial principle.

Cushing had erected two hedges around Quok Walker's case. In *Exeter* he intimated that although the Massachusetts Constitution did not permit slavery, it did not control a resident of Connecticut who came to Massachusetts to recover a fugitive slave. In *Affa Hall*, Cushing reaffirmed that purported slaves were to be treated as persons at law and were entitled to relief just as any other person. But Cushing denied that he had decided whether the blacks in question owed service. He denied that his court had in any way abrogated the South Carolinian slaveholders' legal rights. But in practice, he had. The South Carolinians proved unable to secure the return of their slaves, and the practical result of *Affa Hall* was that the former slaves were now free. Perhaps more importantly, virtually everyone at the time believed that the slaves in question had been freed by the principles laid down by Cushing in Quok Walker's case. It was not a ringing victory for North American abolitionists, but it would do.

Thus was the law of slavery and freedom unsettled at the end of the Revolutionary War. Americans had fought a war for English liberty yet had retained African slavery. They had embraced reform and experimented with grand new ideas, but they still clung to traditional concepts of authority, among which the persistence of slavery was only the most naked. Indentured white servitude, albeit quite rare, still existed in post-Revolutionary America. And even contractual labor was not yet fully free, as masters retained immense authority over their servants. Their authority was old in a land where labor was dear. Pass systems and long-term contracts operated on the assumption that everyone belonged to someone in some way. In this world, fugitives from labor were regularly advertised for, hunted down, and chained up. Slaves had the worst of it, and they contended with a social and political order that had long collaborated — internally and with other jurisdictions — to prevent fugitives from realizing the freedom they sought.

Somerset disrupted this system by giving abolitionists several potent new arguments to deploy, one of which was that slavery could now find no other sanction except express, positive law. After *Somerset*, lawyers defending slaves could demand that a specific statute be produced granting slaveholders their rights. But slaveholders were even more vulnerable than this. Given that slave property had been divorced conceptually in *Somerset* from other kinds of property, abolitionists might convince legislatures to curtail slaveholders' rights or end them altogether. In the newly independent United States of America, this possibility had big implications. South Carolina slaveholders had little to fear — they controlled their sovereign state's legislature, and abolitionists were not likely to make headway there. But any other state might abolish the practice and perhaps refuse to return fugitive slaves. The Articles of Confederation, formally adopted in 1781, supplied only vague provisions for securing interstate comity. Article IV contained a poorly worded privileges and immunities clause, granting "the free inhabitants" of one state "all privileges and immunities of free citizens in the several States." It contained a clause guaranteeing that fugitives from justice would be delivered back to the jurisdiction from whence they fled and provided that "full faith and credit shall be given" to the records, acts, and judicial proceedings of the various states. These were basic principles of comity for confederation, but they had left much power in the hands of the individual states.

This was why Massachusetts Chief Justice Cushing's rulings were of such import. In Quok Walker's case (1783), he signaled to Massachusetts slaveholders that the judiciary would not support their property claims in human beings under the 1780 constitution. While Cushing's ruling did not preclude the legislature from overturning the decision, either directly or by simply passing a statute giving explicit sanction to slavery, there was little chance that the legislature would do so. The writing was on the wall, and by the 1790 federal census, slavery had disappeared from Massachusetts. In *Exeter v. Hanchett* and *Affa Hall*, however, Cushing created conceptual space for the continuation of slavery, even if on attenuated terms. For instance, fugitive slaves from other states could not claim rights under the Massachusetts Constitution. Nonetheless, the practical inability of powerful South Carolinians, backed by the full power of their state, to secure the return of their slaves in 1783 – despite Cushing's smug assertion that he had not abrogated their property rights in any way – exposed the vulnerability of slaveholders in the new United States.

CHAPTER 2

The Original Meaning of the Fugitive Slave Clause

Just as abolitionists were organizing their first official societies devoted to the gradual end of slavery and preparing for concerted action, America's political elite considered fundamental revisions to their national charter of government. The Articles of Confederation had sufficed during wartime but proved ineffectual at curbing the individual interests of the states or promoting national unity in peacetime. Structural defects — especially the inability of Congress to raise its own revenues — left the central government prostrate at the feet of the individual states. At the same time, all the states suffered from a crippling recession, partly owing to the fact that American merchants were no longer being favored in British markets and partly because the nation could not enact a unified economic policy to manage debt and boost productivity. Tax revolts in 1785 and 1786 startled an elite leadership into realizing that the Revolution had unintended consequences for the nature of authority in general. After some cajoling and a few false starts, most of the states appointed delegates to meet in Philadelphia in the summer of 1787 to consider appropriate revisions to the Articles of Confederation.

For the millions of slaves who would live in the United States of the nineteenth century, 1787–1788 would prove a decisive moment, for it altered forever the power held by the federal government, the relations between the states, and the protections claimed by slaveholders. By any measure, the new Constitution strengthened slavery. Slaveholders had guaranteed their political power by securing representation for slaves on the three-fifths (or "federal") ratio. Slaveholders demanded that the slave trade be protected for a period of at least twenty years. The Constitution obliged the new federal government (if asked) to intervene in any state in the case of invasion or insurrection, a potential hedge against Spanish intrigue or slave uprisings in the Lowcountry. And, most importantly for fugitive slaves, an explicit clause in the Constitution guaranteed that the *Somerset* principle would not apply among the states. Article IV, Section 2, positively read: "No person held to service or labour in one state, under the laws thereof, escaping into another, shall, in consequence of any law or regulation therein, be discharged from such service or labour, but shall be delivered up on claim of the party to whom such service or labour may be due." No wonder South Carolina's delegates proved among the most trenchantly nationalist during the secret Convention and public ratification debates.

The U.S. Constitution would structure disputes over slavery for the next seven decades. Integral to this would be the Constitution's shift in the location of sovereignty. The Articles of Confederation had unambiguously placed sovereignty with the states, but the Constitution apportioned it between the federal and state governments. This was federalism: the idea that absolute power might be divided. The new federal government may have been greatly augmented by the Constitution, but its powers were limited to a specific number of subjects. In all the residual areas, the states were left supreme. But this simple proposition belied a nettlesome problem – how would disagreements over the correct division of power be resolved?

The Constitution itself did not provide an answer. No clause indicated who might be the final arbiter if the meaning of the Constitution was in dispute. Nor was it even entirely clear what rules would govern constitutional interpretation. Today, many give preference to *originalism*, the idea that the Constitution's meaning was fixed at the time of its adoption. There are several varieties of originalism, ranging from the vulgar to the sophisticated. Without entering a discussion on the relative merits of interpretive strategies, we can at least agree that the historical meaning of the Constitution is important, both for its own sake and because it provides a benchmark for subsequent interpretations. We must remember an important set of distinctions. We must distinguish between *intent* (what the Framers at the Constitutional Convention meant when they drafted the final document) and *understanding* (what the ratifiers believed the Constitution meant when they ratified it). And even once these distinctions are made, finding a coherent and stable meaning for any particular clause of the Constitution is problematic. The Founders found plenty of occasion to disagree with one another over the meaning of the Constitution's text, and their debates were often quite sharp. The particular meaning of the fugitive slave clause — and whether it empowered Congress or the states or both to enforce it — would become one of those disagreements in the antebellum era. To understand it properly, we must turn to the clause's drafting, adoption, and context.

On May 17, 1787, a passenger ship arrived in Philadelphia carrying Charles Pinckney, one of South Carolina's four delegates to the Convention charged with proposing amendments to the Articles of Confederation (a fifth, Henry Laurens, declined to serve due to flagging health). Pinckney was young — only twenty-nine — of smooth complexion, agile intelligence, and ample confidence. He was an able political thinker and not above preening. Resistance to British authority informed his first political memories, and the Revolutionary War forged his character. In all, experience proved a harsh teacher. The British captured Charles Pinckney when Charleston fell on May 12, 1780. Within months, virtually the entire state was in the hands of the British. President John Rutledge (South Carolina's executive was titled a president rather than a governor) fled to North Carolina. Charles's father capitulated and accepted British protection. Charles himself would spend months in captivity before a prisoner exchange sent him back to Philadelphia (he had been there in 1777–1778 as a member of the Continental Congress). Perhaps bitter over his father's fecklessness, he declined to return to South Carolina even after the state returned to patriot hands, instead making plans to tour Europe and continue his education there. Only his father's death and the need to settle his estate persuaded him to return to Charleston.

Circumstances returned Charles Pinckney to South Carolina, but his passion and talent for the public life took him back to service in the Continental Congress in 1784. He already harbored nationalist sentiments, having authored a pamphlet calling for an independent revenue for Congress. Pinckney's experience soon convinced him of the dire need for a stronger national government, for trouble with imperial powers lurked on the borders. The British had never evacuated their frontier forts, in violation of the Treaty of Paris. The Spanish refused to allow navigation of the Mississippi and threatened to ally with hostile tribes in the Southeast. Such dangers disquieted Pinckney, as any violence on the frontier would spill into South Carolina. Pinckney warned South Carolina's governor to prepare the militia, and he expressed the hope that his fellow delegates from South Carolina to the Continental Congress would stand united in support of solving these national problems.

But Pinckney's vision was grander. Following the lead of James Monroe, who had introduced resolutions seeking an augmentation of congressional power to regulate foreign trade, Pinckney advocated that the entire power of commercial regulation ought to be in the hands of Congress. He did so with full knowledge that the cost of encouraging native shipping could be retaliatory tariffs against the very products he and his fellow planters marketed. Pinckney took the long view, believing that a strong nation would in the end benefit planters more than hurt them. In fact, Pinckney became one of the first to make a public call for a new Convention; he did so while delivering an address to the New Jersey Assembly at Trenton on March 13, 1786. That occasion was fraught with tension. New Jersey's legislature had just passed a resolution refusing to comply with Congress's requisition of 1785. Pinckney was one of three congressional delegates to New Jersey charged with convincing the state to end its defiance.

Pinckney was not alone amongst the South Carolina delegates in his nationalist sentiments. The delegation's leader was the redoubtable John Rutledge, the state's wartime president. Rutledge was heir to a large estate and had studied law at Oxford. When he returned from Oxford in 1761 at the age of twenty-one, he discovered that his fortune had been decimated. He used his persuasive talents to secure more credit, to win a seat in the assembly, and to establish a successful law practice, all of which helped him rebuild his family's estate in a matter of years. This meant he had much to lose when South Carolinians debated separation from Great Britain. He proved a reluctant patriot, at first resigning his post due to misgivings about South Carolina's new constitution. Or so he said. More likely he was holding out for reconciliation with the British. He eventually came around, and proved himself a capable leader. He would serve in the Continental Congress during peacetime and there, like Charles Pinckney, became a committed nationalist. The third South Carolina delegate, Charles Cotesworth Pinckney (a cousin of fellow delegate Charles Pinckney's father), had been, along with Rutledge, a member of the congressional committee that recommended in 1786 that the states cede all control of foreign trade to the national Congress for a period of fifteen years. The fourth delegate was Pierce Butler. He carried a noble pedigree but, being the second son of an English lord, his pedigree did not come with property, so he pursued a career in the British army. He sailed to British America in 1765 and eventually landed a fortune when he married the South Carolina heiress Mary Middleton.

These were four delegates with much in common. They were all planters from leading families, whether by marriage or birth. Their wealth came from rice cultivation, a cash crop that reaped massive profits but required the brutal application of labor. The long growing season meant that during the hottest part of the year slaves worked in the marshy swamp. After the August harvest, slaves turned to processing, after which the fields, dykes, dams, and floodgates would be prepared for the next season. There was virtually no time off. Indigo, South Carolina's secondary cash crop, was not any easier to produce. In South Carolina, slaves toiled throughout the malarial season and died by the thousands. Well into the nineteenth century, the rice plantations would maintain the highest mortality rates anywhere in North America. For mid-eighteenth-century planters, the labor want could be met by the flourishing Atlantic slave trade. So long as profits flowed from rice cultivation, the killing cycle continued.

The intense labor and capital requirements for cultivation of rice and indigo in the Lowcountry had done much during the eighteenth century to concentrate wealth in the hands of a few. The result was a scattering of "first families" who cultivated a lifestyle fitting for a new gentry. Charles Town (Charleston) grew spectacularly, becoming one of North America's wealthiest and largest cities — 12,000 strong — by the time of the Revolution. These planters hired drivers to work their plantations and spent the malarial summer months in Charleston or in port towns further north. In this way, the planters of the Revolutionary era were far more insulated from the primal violence of slave labor than their fathers and grandfathers had been. The brutality with which planters dealt with their laborers on rice plantations had long shocked Christian missionaries, who periodically denounced their reliance on the lash — and worse — to discipline slaves. By absenting themselves from the plantation, even if only for certain periods of time, planters like Rutledge and the Pinckneys could cultivate their more genteel sides. They founded literary societies, promoted religion, and put a new emphasis on sophisticated metropolitan etiquette.

Yet even the wealthy Rutledges and Pinckneys were not men of leisure. They maintained their estates and kept side businesses. Rutledge may have boasted of never losing a case in twenty-six years of advocacy, but his boast revealed the need for a wealthy planter to maintain a law practice. Charles Cotesworth Pinckney also practiced law (and, incidentally, boasted that he had beaten Rutledge in court). Charles Pinckney's family suffered financially from his father's submission to the British, and Charles returned home to find his family in a desperate state. Importantly, the men of the South Carolina delegation were all men who had been confronted, at some point, with ruin. Pierce Butler's good birth was not good enough: the accident of being the second-born son cost him an inheritance and forced him to cast his lot with the army instead. Rutledge had stared down creditors and imminent bankruptcy and had gambled his way out of it with a bid for public office. Charles Pinckney had spent a month aboard a prison frigate before learning that his own father had surrendered to the British. These were men accustomed to bold stands, to bluffing, and to boasting. And they were familiar with desperation and the cruelty of fate.

If something did separate Charles Pinckney from the other delegates, it was his intellectual curiosity. He studied the art of politics and took to the subject. He arrived in Philadelphia prepared to present ideas that would facilitate union and alter the fundamental charter of government. His arrival on May 17 was technically late—the Convention had opened three days previous—but he was ahead of most other delegates. Only the Virginia and Pennsylvania delegations were represented, and they had quickly transformed the delay into an opportunity to conspire. Each day, after formally visiting the Pennsylvania State House, the Pennsylvanians and Virginians repaired to the Indian Queen tavern for refreshment and conversation. There they discussed the bold plan to dispense entirely with the Articles of Confederation and draft a new plan of government. These discussions had already begun when Charles Pinckney arrived. Did he participate? The written record does not say. But he took up his lodging at Mrs. Mary House's boardinghouse, where James Madison and Edmund

Randolph of the Virginia delegation were staying. He would have taken his breakfast there, and certainly some exchange of warm and allied sentiments with the like-minded Virginians would have occurred. But whether he knew of the plan to have Edmund Randolph introduce the series of resolutions fated to become known as the "Virginia Plan," or whether he shared details of his own draft of a new constitution, we do not know.

By Friday, May 25, enough delegates had arrived in Philadelphia to establish a quorum and begin business. For the next four months, the Convention would meet regularly on Monday through Saturday from ten or eleven in the morning until three thirty in the afternoon. Thereafter, the delegates were on their own. Delegates often repaired in groups of six to eight men to dine together, and evening tea was usually taken at eight or nine at night. Although the Convention's regular meetings would be broken by several vacations, and the delegates would wander in and out on their own schedules throughout the summer, after May 25 the Convention acquired a sense of stability. The first few days of business were spent deciding the ground rules. Voting in the Convention would be by state delegation, and the states would retain their equality of suffrage there. Voting was also to be informal, without the necessity of entering yeas and nays on the record. Members could also ask for reconsideration of any issue previously voted upon. This had the effect of relaxing the proceedings, with the clear hope that it would allow delegates to persuade and be persuaded, to change votes and manufacture consensus. One rule would have far-reaching consequences. At Pierce Butler's suggestion, the body adopted a vow of secrecy. Deliberations would be kept from the public, to such an extent that the windows and doors were kept shut while the Convention was in session during the long, hot Philadelphia summer.

On Tuesday, May 29, the Virginians, in concert with Pennsylvanians, made their play. Edmund Randolph stood to deliver a set of resolutions now known as the Virginia Plan. Authored primarily by James Madison, the Virginia Plan promoted a powerful national sovereignty with sweeping and undefined legislative powers and an explicit right to veto state laws. The Virginia and Pennsylvania conspirators succeeded in setting the agenda by putting aside the present articles and starting fresh. They also caused panic. Robert Yates of

New York complained of Randolph's "elaborate" speech that it promoted a consolidated union "in which the idea of states should be nearly annihilated." William Paterson of New Jersey understood the consequences in express terms. "Objn. – ," he scribbled in his notes, "sovereignty is an integral thing." Indeed it was, and the Virginia Plan could not be mistaken for anything other than the creation of a national sovereignty at the expense of the states.

Randolph's presentation was followed by Charles Pinckney, who presented his own plan of national government to the Convention. Precisely what he presented that day, or how he did so, remains in dispute. Madison scarcely mentioned it in his meticulous notes, which suggests he was piqued by Pinckney's attempt to steal the Virginia delegation's thunder. Not that Pinckney was above such antics. Sensing the fame that would follow participation in the Convention, Pinckney arranged in July to have his speech given at Trenton a year earlier printed, implicitly taking credit for being the first to advocate for a constitutional convention. Later in life he would take every opportunity to claim paternity for the final document and would boast of being the youngest of the delegates. He was not the youngest, and he knew it. But such was Charles Pinckney's ego.

Historians today generally – if reluctantly – accept that Pinckney contributed some important ideas to the final shape of the Constitution: the bicameral Congress and the use of the three-fifths clause for determining representation; the independent and energetic executive; the clause securing the writ of habeas corpus; and the clause securing that no religious test would be applied to officeholding. His plan also resembled the Virginia Plan in many respects. But no one could mistake the import of Pinckney's plan, least of all those committed to the sanctity of state sovereignty. And if they did, Pinckney relieved them of doubt. "The idea which has been so long and falsely entertained of each being a sovereign State, must be given up," he explained, "for it is absurd to suppose there can be more than one sovereignty within a Government." The states would retain "nothing more than mere local legislation." If Pinckney was to have his way, sovereignty – absolute, uncontrollable power – would reside with a new, national government.

But Pinckney was not to have his way. Despite repeatedly angling for broad national powers, including an absolute veto over all state laws, the nationalists could not support so clear a grab for power. Nor, however, could their opponents retain a system in which sovereignty remained squarely with the states. And many believed that sovereignty would have to rest absolutely in one or the other and could not rest in both. They had reached the limits of eighteenth-century political theory, which held that *imperium in imperio* (a state within a state) was a solecism. So the delegates turned to experience rather than theory. They had long been accustomed to a hybrid system in which disputes between colony and metropole were negotiated rather than authoritatively declared. Why not model a new federal system upon that principle? As Oliver Ellsworth pointedly asked during the ratification debates: why cannot sovereignties coexist? "It is not enough to say they cannot. I wish for some reason." As he went on to note, "They actually have done it."

We know this solution as *federalism*. It was neither simple nor complete in its formulation in 1787–1788, nor is it today. James Wilson provided the theoretical justification for this during the Pennsylvania ratification convention when he argued that sovereignty lay not with either the states or the national government, but with the people themselves. The powers exercised by either level of government, Wilson argued, were all of a limited nature derived from the sovereign people. This left open the question of precisely how the Constitution's text and structure balanced state and national authority. James Madison explained it in Federalist 39 as a kind of hodgepodge. The House of Representatives, wrote Madison, derived its power from the people of the United States and was thus a national body. The Senate derived its power and equality of suffrage from the states but gave senators independent votes (rather than voting by state delegation) and was thus a federal body. The Executive was a compound office, thanks to that most divinely grotesque of founding ideas, the electoral college. As to the extent of congressional power, Madison informed his readers that it was national in the sense that it could now act directly upon individuals regardless of their state allegiance. He then reassured his audience that congressional power was not general, but rather was specific and limited to enumerated subjects. As Madison summed up for his audience: "The proposed Constitution, therefore, is, in strictness, neither a national nor a federal Constitution, but a composition of both. In its foundation it is federal, not national; in the sources from which the ordinary powers of the government are drawn, it is partly federal and partly national; in the operation of these powers, it is national, not federal; in the extent of them, again, it is federal, not national." What could be clearer?

The boundaries were blurry because the Framers had intended them to be. The specific enumeration of the subjects of congressional power left the bulk of legislation in the hands of the states, including the regulation of status, individual rights, and personal relationships. This meant that the legal regulation of slavery was with the states, and this was well understood during both the convention and ratification debates. But once the objects of national power were defined and thus limited, the Framers made two additions. The first was the necessary and proper clause, which authorized Congress to pass any law necessary to carry out one of its enumerated goals. The second was the supremacy clause, which bound state judges by oath to treat federal law and treaties as the supreme law of the land, "any thing in the constitution or laws of any state to the contrary notwithstanding." Antifederalists seized upon these clauses during the ratification debates to argue that the national government would absorb and annihilate the states. Federalists worked hard to reassure Americans that the Constitution *limited* the national government while giving it the means necessary to carry out its essential functions. It would remain for practice and experience to bring the precise workings of federalism into focus.

If the boundaries between national and state authority were fuzzy at best, the same could not be said for the necessity of distributing power through representation. That problem was solved unambiguously. Representation was the first question addressed by the delegates, and it proved to be vexatious precisely because it came down to raw power. The small states were loath to relinquish their equal suffrage, partly for fear of being swallowed up by their larger neighbors and partly just because they did not want to diminish their power within the federal system. The forced compromise was the bicameral Congress, with one house — the Senate — composed upon the principle of equality of suffrage. The small states would have one body in which they could, if unified, resist the encroachments of the power of the larger states. The other body, with its proportional representation, would come closer to representing the people themselves as a national whole.

But how to count the people themselves? Who would be represented in the Congress? Should one count people? Only men? Only free men? Wealth? This was a most serious question, and one which roused the greatest passions. Remarkably, the Convention adopted, without any discussion, James Wilson's suggestion that all inhabitants (men, women, and children) ought to be counted, rather than just men. But this did not settle the question of whether slaves should be counted. The delegates settled this by reverting to an old formula — the counting of three slaves for every five. It was originally proposed in 1783 as a way of gauging wealth in order to determine quotas of contribution from each of the states under the Articles of Confederation. Charles Pinckney had included the three-fifths ratio in his plan for a new Constitution. On Monday, June 11, after John Rutledge had intimated that he would accept a strong national government only if slave wealth were represented, James Wilson moved that representation be apportioned to the "whole number of white and other free Citizens and inhabitants of every age sex and condition including those bound to servitude for a term of years and three fifths of all other persons not comprehended in the foregoing description, except Indians not paying taxes." Seconding the motion was Charles Pinckney.

Scholars have regarded this as an essential compromise for the adoption of a new national constitution. The fact that the Pennsylvanian James Wilson proposed it and Charles Pinckney seconded suggests that a deal had been worked out ahead of time. It would take another month for the Convention to come to something like a formal agreement, and even that would not stop South Carolina's delegates from threatening to revisit the issue if the Convention did not supply additional securities for slave property. In August, John Rutledge and Charles Pinckney did precisely that, demanding that the Constitution provide protections for the African slave trade. This startled several delegates. By 1787, abolitionist literature had brought public opinion around to the notion that the slave trade was a special kind of evil. Even if one accepted slavery as necessary, it was more difficult to defend the African slave trade as morally permissible. George Mason, a wealthy Virginia slaveholder himself, denounced the slave trade at the Convention. Nonetheless, northern delegates (as well as the more morally scrupulous of the southern delegates) caved. They prohibited Congress from banning the slave trade for a period of twenty years.

Yet that was not enough for the South Carolina delegates. On August 28, the Convention took up Article XIV, which read that "the Citizens of each State shall be entitled to all privileges and immunities of citizens in the several States." James Madison recorded that Charles Cotesworth Pinckney was dissatisfied and that "he seemed to wish some provision should be included in favor of property in slaves." His proposal, whatever it was, went nowhere, and South Carolina stood alone in opposing the article. Next up was the fugitives from justice clause. Charles Pinckney and Pierce Butler moved to add a provision "to require fugitive slaves and servants to be delivered up like criminals."

This was the fugitive slave clause's first introduction, three months into the Convention, with the major issues apparently settled and business winding down. Nonetheless, it drew objections from northern delegates. James Wilson of Pennsylvania pointed out that the clause would obligate the executive of the state to provide for the seizure of runaways, at the public expense. Roger Sherman of Connecticut — a man renowned for his honesty, oratory, and proud simplicity — put it in starker terms: seizing a fugitive slave was more like seizing a horse than a criminal. Would you oblige the state, at the public expense, to chase after runaway horses? Of course not.

The analogy may — and should — strike modern readers as perverse. To so blithely compare people with horses betrays the coarseness of both the speaker and the audience who received his words. For all our admiration of the Framers, these were men inured to the traffic in human flesh. Slavery had made the colonies wealthy, and not just the Rutledges and Pinckneys of South Carolina. New England merchants engaged in the slave trade and trafficked in the goods produced by the appropriated labor of slaves. One of the major reasons for a strong national government was precisely to favor New England shippers over foreigners. Charles Pinckney had explicitly stated this in advance of the Convention, and the South Carolinians came to the table ready to sacrifice some of their self-interest (say, a cheaper carrying trade thrown open to the Spanish, French, or British) in exchange for security. Roger Sherman's comparison of a refugee seeking freedom with a beast of burden draws our modern attention to the complicity of northerners in nurturing slavery in the nation's bosom.

But Sherman was not simply being callous. The Connecticut lawyer was drawing a distinction between public duties and private rights. Criminals offended the public peace. When they fled a state's jurisdiction, they in essence flouted public order. If their rendition was left to the principle of comity—to be complied with by the states as a matter of grace rather than by command—there was potential for an undermining of that public order. The liberty so cherished by the Framers depended upon order, and the fugitives from justice clause reflected this commitment. Property rights, by contrast, were private. When a horse fled its owner's field to another, it offended not the public order but the owner. It followed that the owner could assert his property right without obliging the government to do so for him. The analogy had its intended effect. Pierce Butler withdrew his motion. But the next day, Pinckney and Butler reintroduced it as a separate article: "If any Person bound to service or labor in any of the United States shall escape into another State, He or She shall not be discharged from such service or labor in consequence of any regulations subsisting in the State to which they escape; but shall be delivered up to the person justly claiming their service or labor." It passed unanimously. With only a few alterations in the weeks following, it would become the fugitive slave clause.

On September 8, the Convention appointed a Committee of Style to attend to what many delegates likely believed were cosmetic matters—cleaning up odd bits of language and arranging the articles in appropriate order. Serving on the committee were James Madison, Alexander Hamilton, Rufus King, and Gouveneur Morris. The committee entrusted Morris with writing the document, and his eloquence has become the stuff of legend. It was Morris who replaced "We the People of the States of New Hampshire, Massachusetts" and so forth with "We the People of the United States." It was a simple change, but one that immediately inspired questions. Was the document the sovereign expression of the people of the states or the people of the nation? If the former, did this mean that the people of the states could opt out the same way they opted in? Morris's change suggested not, and unionists would later cite this text against secessionists. Never has so simple a stylistic edit produced so much theoretical tumult. His continuation of the preamble "to establish justice, insure domestic tranquility, provide for the common defense, and secure the blessings of liberty to ourselves and posterity" infused the document with a purpose expressed in straightforward, elegant prose. He, and the Committee of Style with him, transformed the Constitution into a document that would be revered for its beauty as well as its substance.

This beauty was not just a matter of prose, but also of architecture. Hitherto, the delegates had voted on twenty-three separate articles. Article I, produced by the Committee of Detail, read: "The stile of this government shall be. 'The United States of America.'" Article II read, "The Government shall consist of supreme legislative, executive, and judicial powers." And so on. In place of this, the Committee of Style created seven articles. The first three organized each branch of government—Congress, the presidency, and the judiciary. Upon this edifice the remaining articles filled in important spaces. The fourth article dealt with interstate relations, admission of new members, and the territories. The fifth covered future alterations of the document. The sixth covered oaths of office, and the seventh ratification. To alter the metaphor a bit, it was a roadmap of sorts, taking its audience through the three grand departments of state and the means by which the union would be bound together. It was followed by an even more literal roadmap, as the delegates signed their names by state convention, from north to south—from Delaware to Georgia on left side, and New Hampshire to Pennsylvania on the right.

In important ways, the Constitution's aesthetics would shape its interpretation. Congress's enumerated powers fell into Article I, Section 8, and constitutional restrictions on Congress came immediately after in Section 9. Section 10 listed restrictions on the state legislatures. But the articulation of congressional power was not limited to Article I. Article II, for instance, gave Congress the authority to determine the day and time of national elections for president. Article III gave Congress the power to establish inferior courts and to declare the punishment for treason (within limits). Article IV contained four separate sections, three of which contained explicit grants of congressional power. In Article IV, section 1, Congress was granted the power to "prescribe the manner" in which full faith and credit would be given to the public acts, records, and judicial proceedings of one state by another. In section 3, Congress was given the power to admit new states and "to dispose of and make all needful Rules and Regulations respecting the Territory or other Property belonging to the United States." Section 4 charged the United States with guaranteeing a republican form of government to the states and to protecting them in times of invasion or rebellion. In fact, only Section 2 of Article IV omitted a congressional grant of power. Section 2 included the privileges and immunities clause, the fugitives from justice clause, and the fugitive slave clause.

One cannot help but to espy this architectural flaw in the Constitutional fabric. Was the fugitive slave clause primarily a restriction on the states? Then why was it not housed in Article I, Section 10? Was it the granting of a substantive property right enforceable by Congress? Then why not fit it into Article I, Section 8? One might argue that the committee hewed to the language, substance, and order in which the article came up before the Convention, which necessitated its being placed in a separate article. If so, then why not provide an enabling clause giving Congress the power to enforce it? This would have required some substantive revision by the Committee of Style, thus exceeding its instructions, but the committee was not above such behavior. At Rufus King's urging, for instance, the committee had added the contracts clause to Article I, Section 10 despite its having never been adopted by the Convention. The committee certainly could have provided an additional clause to clarify the document's intention regarding the responsibility for the rendition of fugitive slaves, but it did not. The result was ambiguity—the fugitive slave clause could be interpreted either as directing the states or the federal government to enforce it.

The Committee of Style submitted its report on Wednesday, September 12. The rest of the week was spent mopping up some details, rejecting a few late-suggested additions to the Constitution (from securing freedom of the press to granting Congress the power to regulate people's choice of clothing), and preparing to transmit the document to the states for ratification.

Ratification was not a given. A print war erupted between September 1787 and August 1788 that was far more ferocious than felicitous. Not only did the Constitution threaten to shift power structures—thus challenging the establishment—but it also played upon people's worst fears. Opponents of the Constitution did have legitimate concerns. The document had been produced in secret. It established a powerful new executive with a lengthy term of office and no limitation on how many terms he might serve. The states' power was significantly eroded by a federal government that now had an independent revenue stream and the ability to establish law enforcement apparatus. And congressional statutes — even if limited to an enumerated list of subjects — were to be the supreme law of the land, "any Thing in the Constitution or Laws of any State to the Contrary notwithstanding." Several of the Convention's own turned on the Constitution. The well-respected and well-heeled Edmund Randolph opposed it, and George Mason swore he would rather cut off his right hand than put his name to it. The towering Revolutionary figure Patrick Henry thundered against it. The tumult made James Madison nervous, and as early as December he expressed his fears that Patrick Henry was angling for a southern confederacy that would tank the union and the Constitution with it.

For their part, the South Carolinian delegates who had repeatedly threatened to walk out of the Convention if it did not meet their every demand now just as vigorously defended the finished product. They did so in the face of real opposition, reflected in the fact that the South Carolina legislature held a debate in January about the merits of the Constitution before calling a ratification convention. Against such opposition, the delegates themselves extolled the document's virtues. Charles Cotesworth Pinckney reminded the legislature that South Carolina could not go it alone and that the Declaration of Independence had established that "our freedom and independence arose from our union." One benefit of the new Constitution, he noted, was that "we have obtained a right to recover our slaves in whatever part of America they may take refuge, which is a right we had not before." The delegates and their Federalist allies proved effective, and South Carolina ratified the Constitution on May 23, 1788.

It is tempting to cite Charles Cotesworth Pinckney in support of the idea that the Constitution was granting slaveholders a new right, but one should not make too much of his comment. As we saw in the last chapter, fugitive slave recaption had always been a generally recognized right. Pinckney overdrew the distinction between the Articles of Confederation's silence on the subject and the Constitution's explicit inclusion of it to make the case to slaveholders for ratification. North Carolina's delegation did the same thing in its report to the legislature, and James Madison trumpeted the fugitive slave clause as an additional security for slaveholders. These were rhetorical ploys, and there is no evidence that they proved decisive in any of the conventions. It follows that we cannot read the statements of Pinckney or Madison as the definitive original understanding of the fugitive slave clause.

In ratifying conventions north of the Mason-Dixon Line, the fugitive slave clause occasioned little controversy. The return of fugitive slaves and servants, even across state and colonial lines, had been commonplace. Even Pennsylvania's landmark statute, of 1780, for the gradual abolition of slavery and the Northwest Ordinance of 1787 (which prohibited slavery in the Northwest Territories) contained fugitive slave clauses. One might reasonably conclude that northerners ignored the fugitive slave clause because recaption had been so common for so long. But in truth, northerners raised few objections about the Constitution's entanglement with slavery at all. A satirist writing in support of the Constitution put it best when he published a "recipe" for an antifederalist essay. The recipe listed 114 portions, including (among others) "nine parts well-born, eighteen parts Aristocracy, thirteen parts Liberty of the press, and nineteen parts Mr. Mason's hand in a cutting box." African slavery counted for only one part. It was a fitting reminder of how interest-driven was the debate and how much contemporary principles hewed to an eighteenth-century world that expressed more concern over the tyranny of the aristocrat than that of the slavemaster.

Some were not fooled. The abolitionist Quakers understood precisely what the fugitive slave clause meant, and in their correspondence they lamented that it could only be designed to destroy the "asylum of Massachusetts." The Quakers clearly believed that the holding in *Somerset* had been incorporated into Massachusetts law in Quok Walker's case (*Commonwealth v. Jennison*, 1783). That the South Carolina delegation insisted on the fugitive slave clause during the Convention reflected just how prevalent was this popular belief. Given that only a few years earlier South Carolina had been unable to retrieve several slaves from Boston and that the courts had stood in the way, their insistence was understandable. But such concern hardly came up in public debate in the North. The Quakers wrote privately to each other about their concerns; they wrote no missives to the public. The ratification debate itself — in every state — was marked by indifference to the fugitive slave clause and only slightly less indifference to slavery at all.

The adoption of the Constitution proved an important step in the long-term evolution of rights in the United States, but it was of no immediate help to refugees from slavery. For slaveholders, it created (or acknowledged) the property right in human beings who fled to jurisdictions that did not recognize the institution of slavery. But the Constitution was ambiguous on how this right would be enforced. The innovative reconciling of dual sovereignties into a federalist system depended upon a few clear boundaries and many blurry ones. On the one hand, Congress had enumerated powers listed in Article I, Section 8. And the states were prohibited certain powers in Article I, Section 10. Congress could claim other powers in Articles II, III, and IV. Was enforcing the fugitive slave clause amongst them? The historical reading of the clause suggests that it was. The initial proposal by Charles Pinckney and Pierce Butler was rebuffed because northerners did not want the burden to lie on the states to assist slaveholders in retrieving their property. This could suggest that the Constitution's framers and ratifiers understood the clause to create a national right that would require national enforcement. In short, the historical meaning of the fugitive slave clause — both its framing and its acceptance — suggests that it created a national property right that should have been protected by Congress.

Nonetheless, slavery was a domestic relation controlled by state law, and the Constitution left such matters solely to the states. Congress had not been given any warrant to interfere with state domestic relations, leaving one to believe that the fugitive slave clause's lack of an explicit granting of power to Congress left the matter with the states. Its placement in Article IV strengthened this interpretation, as the section containing the fugitive slave clause was the only section to lack an enabling clause specifically granting power to Congress. Especially after ratification of the Tenth Amendment in 1791, a strict reading of the Constitution required that all powers not granted to the federal government were reserved to the states. If one accepts this interpretive theory, the affirmative power of enforcing the fugitive slave clause could lie only in the states. In short, the strict textual and structural interpretation in this case defies the historical one: whereas the language of the fugitive slave clause had been revised specifically to take the burden off the states, the final language did not place the burden on the federal government. The consequence is a solecism.

There was a third option. The power might be concurrent, something which either Congress or the states (or both) might legislate upon. And there was a fourth option. The clause might not require legislation at all. A private right created by the Constitution could still be enforced by state and federal officers, all of whom took an oath to uphold the U.S. Constitution. If anything, this ambiguity speaks to the very real problem of indeterminacy in constitutional law. Simply put, there was no definitive way to interpret the fugitive slave clause.

Confusing or not, the fugitive slave clause was also now part of the supreme law of the land. But at least one man thought it a nullity. Granville Sharp, the man who had done so much to help free James Somerset in 1772 and set the jurisprudential course of the antislavery movement, wrote Benjamin Franklin in 1788 to complain that he was "sincerely grieved" to see the fugitive slave clause in the Constitution because it was in opposition to the express command of Deuteronomy 23:15 to "not deliver up to his Master the Servant which is escaped from his master unto thee." The fugitive slave clause, Sharp continued, was "*null and void*. . . . It would be even *a crime* to regard [it] as Law." To Sharp, the Constitution was not — could not — be the highest source of law. Others would agree.

CHAPTER 3

The Fugitive Slave Act, Kidnapping, and the Powers of Dual Sovereigns

It is a problem of classification. While a plain reading of the Constitution demanded that fugitive slaves be returned to their masters, what of the kidnapper who stole a free black? In both cases, human beings were being carried against their will across state lines and their condition reduced from freedom to slavery. But in the first instance, a slaveholder was exercising a constitutional right. In the second, a criminal was committing the crime of kidnapping. At first blush, the difference might seem obvious. But what if a slaveholder traveled with his slave to a free jurisdiction and the slave then fled? Or what if a slaveholder claimed a fugitive slave and her child, but her child had been born in the free state to which she had fled? Could the slaveholder carry these people back across state lines legally? The devil, it might be said, was in the details.

Complicating this matter was the prickly problem of citizenship in the republic. Before the Fourteenth Amendment created a birthright national citizenship in 1868, it was the individual states that defined someone's rights, duties, and place in society. More important than political notions of citizenship was the legal notion of status. One's status depended on a welter of conditions. Was one black or white? Man or woman? Was a woman married or single? Was one free or bound to service of some kind? The answers to these questions often determined precisely what kind of law governed someone. Slavery was nothing more than a legal status that enabled a master to exploit another's body. Complicating this matter greatly was that each state defined status for itself. The rights of a free black, for instance, varied from one state to another. So too did the legal incidents of slavery. The fugitive slave clause admonished the free states not to extirpate the slave status from refugees who crossed their borders, but the real question left unanswered by the clause was who was to decide the status of an *alleged* fugitive slave.

Congress provided the first answer when it passed the Fugitive Slave Act of 1793. In so doing, it provided the first interpretation of the fugitive slave clause's meaning, an interpretation that would dominate both the understanding and practice of fugitive slave rendition for the next half century. The statute made fugitive slave rendition a matter of private law and authorized both federal and state judges and petty magistrates to issue "certificates of removal" authorizing the transport of someone across state lines. But this federal law governed only slaveholders' claims; it did not penalize kidnappers for making fraudulent claims or for failing to follow proper legal process. The states, however, did. Several states set forth punishment for kidnapping before passage of the Constitution, and virtually all would come to, including many slave states.

Because rendition and kidnapping described the same naked act—taking a person against their will across state lines—but clothed it with different meaning, conflict between slaveholders and fugitives was bound to occur. The first body of fugitive slave jurisprudence necessarily dealt with sorting out the competing claims of slaveholders and abolitionists. But we should understand these early court cases as more about *power* than about *rights*. At issue was the power of the states to inquire into the status of people within its jurisdiction. At issue was the extent of congressional power to enforce Article IV, Section 2. As the judges of the early republic made clear over and over again, they were not interested in adjudicating the rights of slaveholders or free blacks. They wished only to carry out the instructions of the legislators under the dictates of the Constitution.

John Davis of Pennsylvania was black, and in the eyes of Pennsylvania law at the time of the Constitution's ratification debates in 1788 he was free. He was born a slave and lived in a region of western Virginia, along its border with Pennsylvania. The precise location of the border was disputed, and in 1779 the legislatures of the two sovereign states had appointed commissioners to survey the border and set an agreed-upon boundary. In 1780, Pennsylvania passed its Act for the Gradual Abolition of Slavery. Under this law, all slaves had to be registered so the state could make good on its promise to free all slaves born after passage of the act after 28 years of service. Failure to register slaves immediately freed them. This put slaveholders in the disputed border region (the western Pennsylvania counties of Washington and Westmoreland) in a pickle. Should they register their slaves with Pennsylvania before the border was determined? If they registered and turned out to be living in Virginia, then they would have conceded Pennsylvania's jurisdiction and lost a future interest in their property. If they did not register them and turned out to be living in Pennsylvania, they would lose their slaves altogether. Pennsylvania's legislature was not blind to the problem. They extended registration deadlines in those counties until January 1, 1783. But with the border not yet precisely determined (the legislatures would not come to a formal agreement until April 1, 1784), several slaveholders – once Virginians but now Pennsylvanians – neglected to register their slaves. John Davis, a resident of Washington County, Pennsylvania, was one of those slaves. He became free by the law of Pennsylvania, where he and his former master resided.

But whether ignorant of the law or simply indifferent to it, Davis's former owner rented him out to a Virginia farmer named Miller in 1788. Abolitionists in western Pennsylvania caught wind of this, found John Davis, and returned him to Pennsylvania. Miller hired three men to bring John Davis back. The three crossed into Pennsylvania, seized John Davis, and forcibly took him to Virginia. In November of 1788, these three Virginians were indicted in Pennsylvania for kidnapping. The indictments did not lead to trials as the three Virginians neglected to appear before the court. In 1791, the Pennsylvania Abolition Society petitioned Governor Thomas Mifflin to request his help. Mifflin wrote his counterpart, Virginia Governor Beverly Randolph, requesting the rendition of the three fugitives under Article IV, Section 2 of the Constitution. Governor Randolph in turn asked for the opinion of James Innes, his attorney general, on the rendition request.

James Innes had succeeded the prominent Edmund Randolph as Virginia's attorney general. He was known as an able orator as well as lawyer and had defended the Constitution in Virginia's ratification convention several years earlier. His answer to Pennsylvania's extradition request was a sophist's masterpiece. He began by admitting that the request came under Article IV, Section 2, in so far as the indictments supplied by Governor Mifflin demonstrated that the alleged fugitives from justice were "charged with Treason, Felony, or other Crime." But then his opinion took a bizarre turn. The crime, said Innes, would be judged according to Virginia law. Since the offense of kidnapping listed in the indictment amounted only to a minor breach of the peace in Virginia, no extradition was required. The plaintiffs could appoint attorneys to represent them, and the trial could proceed. If they were acquitted, then no extradition was necessary. If they were found guilty, then Pennsylvania could again request extradition.

Innes's claim that extradition requests had to be tethered to the law of the state to which the criminal fled was patently absurd. It also made a mockery of Virginia law. A Virginia statute of 1788 punished the kidnapping of a free negro with one to ten years of imprisonment—hardly just a breach of the peace. But Innes's opinion did not rest solely on this argument. He also pointed out that the extradition request contained no evidence that the fugitives were even in Virginia. Here he was on more solid ground, as the state executive could not be obliged to hunt for the men (and expend state resources in the process) without some proof that they were actually there. Innes also argued that Virginia's governor had no authority to arrest the fugitives, as neither Virginia nor U.S. law provided a mode of arrest and delivery. Therefore, any arrest for extradition would be backed only by naked force rather than due process. Although arguable, this was a strong point.

The frustrated Pennsylvania governor submitted the matter to President Washington, who was conveniently in Philadelphia where the U.S. government had made a temporary home. Washington in turn sought the opinion of his attorney general, Edmund Randolph, the former Virginia attorney general. Randolph dismissed the "untenable reasoning" in Innes's position. But he nonetheless agreed that formal rendition required more evidence than had been provided by the Pennsylvania governor—namely, proof of escape (there must be *flight* to make a *fugitive*) and some evidence that the fugitives were actually in the state, before the executive was obliged to expend public money to seek them out. Randolph also cautioned against President Washington's intervention. This was a matter of interstate relations, and it was up to the states to work it out. Of course, Pennsylvania's governor "appears to be anxious that the matter should be laid before Congress," Randolph noted. "Perhaps, such a step might content all scruples." Aware that every act of the Washington administration would set a precedent, Randolph signaled that the appropriate venue for settling interstate disputes over constitutional meaning would be Congress.

Washington agreed, laying the matter before Congress in October 1791. A Senate committee reported a bill on December 20, 1792. The bill covered both fugitives from justice and fugitive slaves, obliging state officers in both cases to assist with recovery. Senators balked. They recommitted the bill to the committee, now enlarged to include John Taylor of Virginia and Roger Sherman of Connecticut, the very same Sherman who had argued during the Constitutional Convention that fugitive slave rendition ought to be a private affair. This committee reported a bill back on January 3, 1793. The new bill made reclamation the slaveholder's duty, although it largely preserved the legal procedure of the first bill and modified the legal requirements for fugitive slave reclamation. It contained a new provision as well, protecting free blacks claimed as fugitives. After debate and further amendments, the Senate passed the bill and sent it to the House, which returned it with amendments of its own—most notably the deletion of the clause protecting free blacks. This final version would become law.

We know the law now as the "Fugitive Slave Act," but the original title of the bill was "an Act respecting fugitives from justice, and persons escaping from the service of their masters." The more detailed portion of the bill dealt with the extradition of suspected criminals, which was defined as a public responsibility. The bill went on to specify the duties of state officers if an extradition request was made. By contrast, fugitive slave rendition was defined as a matter of private law. A slaveholder could seize a fugitive slave wherever the slave was found. If the slaveholder could then convince either a court—a state or federal judge or magistrate—that the person seized was in fact his or her slave, then the statute authorized the court to issue a certificate of removal (to "remove" the slave across state lines). The Fugitive Slave Act's last section gave slaveholders additional security for their property right. If anyone prevented the slaveholder from removing her slave, the slaveholder could sue for up to $500. President Washington signed it into law on February 12, 1793.

This law was, therefore, the first authoritative interpretation of the fugitive slave clause. Several of those in Congress who debated, drafted, and amended the law had been active in the Constitutional Convention and the ratification debates, yet this did not smooth over disagreement about how the clause distributed powers between the federal and state governments. Various permutations of the bill had given more explicit commands to state officers, provided protections for free blacks, and required different levels of proof to obtain certificates of removal. The final form likely owed its composition to a combination of political and constitutional factors, not the least of which was the limit of federal authority to command state officers.

Following passage of the Fugitive Slave Act, Congress took up the subject of kidnapping. On April 18, 1796, a memorial from the Delaware legislature was laid before Congress, complaining of the kidnapping of free blacks in the coastal trade. Just as the "spirits" of Liverpool and London a century and a half before had reduced orphans and mendicants to bondage in the colonies, so now did kidnappers haunt the port cities of the United States, stealing free blacks for sale in the rice swamps of South Carolina or the sugar islands of the West Indies. The petition before Congress asked for federal legislation since the kidnapping was clearly committed in the stream of interstate commerce. Congress committed the petition to the Committee of Commerce and Manufactures, indicating that Congress would derive its power to prevent kidnapping from the commerce clause. The committee reported a bill that would require ship captains to carry certificates attesting to the status of any person of African descent on board. The bill met with serious objections in the House, largely on states' rights grounds. Representatives from Connecticut and New York argued that kidnapping was a crime that the Constitution left to the states to punish. Any law passed by Congress would therefore be a usurpation of state authority and might be construed — as William Smith of South Carolina put it — as an "entering wedge" for the enlargement of national power at the expense of the states.

The report of the debate indicates that it was measured and thoughtful. Representatives north and south had rested on the proposition embodied in the Tenth Amendment that the states were sovereign in all areas not delegated to the federal government. The fact that northerners joined southerners in protest was a strong indication that the defense of slavery was not the only political context for opposition. The 1790s had witnessed the spectacular rise of Alexander Hamilton and his program as Secretary of the Treasury to expand federal power. Hamilton exploited the Constitution's broad and hazy clauses to gain approval for the assumption of state debt, to pay off speculators who had accumulated depreciated paper, and to found a national bank. So when the House considered a bill that would broadly interpret the commerce clause to grant a new criminal jurisdiction to the federal government, representatives indifferent to slavery understandably balked because they feared that it could inadvertently strengthen Hamilton's program by sapping state sovereignty. It fell to John Swanwick of Pennsylvania to argue in favor of the bill. He focused on the commission of the crime *during* interstate commerce. True, Swanwick conceded, the states have passed laws against kidnapping, but those laws were being broken with impunity. Congress, he said, was duty-bound to act.

The strict interpretation of federal power under the commerce clause won out. The House recommitted the bill to the committee, which reported in January 1797 its recommendation that Congress ought not to legislate. Key in this decision were unarticulated assumptions about political and social membership that are foreign to our contemporary notions of universal citizenship. The states did not regard all their residents equally. Black slavery was only the most obvious manifestation of this. A welter of laws limited voting largely to propertied white men, restricted married women's access to courts, and stripped the indigent of their liberty. Someone's status — man or woman; married or single; black or white; free or slave; mulatto or other mixed blood — was a matter of state law. The Constitution had only designated that a citizen of one state might, if traveling to another, be entitled to the same "privileges and immunities" of a citizen of that state. There was no substantive federal citizenship created by the United States Constitution. True, the federal government represented its citizens on the high seas, including issuing certificates to free black sailors attesting to their status as citizens of the United States in order to protect them from impressment. But international relations were an area where the states were explicitly prohibited from acting, and as such Congress obtained the right and duty to act to protect its citizens in that arena. But outside this area, many worried that the danger of national supremacy was too great for the federal government to be involved in what they considered a state matter.

For their part, the states provided antikidnapping protections for their free black residents. Connecticut passed such laws in 1784 and 1788, and Pennsylvania and Massachusetts passed antikidnapping laws in 1785. In 1787, the kidnapping of free blacks was punishable by, in Virginia, one to ten years' imprisonment and by fine in Delaware. Delaware strengthened its law in 1793, giving convicted kidnappers (including those who stood mute and chose to "not directly answer to the indictment") thirty-nine lashes and an hour in the pillory (disfigurement followed, as both ears were nailed to the pillory and then the soft part cut off). In 1796, Maryland punished kidnapping with an $800 fine or service on the roads for up to five years.

From a theoretical perspective, one could argue that fugitive slave rendition was a federal matter and the prevention of kidnapping a state matter. But two problems undercut this neat analysis. First, fugitive slave rendition might itself become cover for kidnapping. A 1799 memorial to Congress complained of just this problem in Philadelphia. In short, fugitive slave rendition hearings in federal courts would necessarily intersect with the states' sovereign duty to protect their residents' liberty. Second, the Fugitive Slave Act of 1793 had conferred jurisdiction directly on state officers to conduct rendition proceedings. This raised the constitutional question of whether Congress could direct state officers. James Madison was one of several Framers who voiced his opinion to the contrary. Nonetheless, the early congresses repeatedly did direct state officers. In 1789, Congress directed how state officers would take their Article VI oaths to support the Constitution. The Seamen's Act of 1790 conferred jurisdiction on state justices of the peace to hear cases of desertion, fix penalties, and mediate between crew and captain on questions of vessels' seaworthiness. In 1792, Congress directed governors to deliver lists of certified candidates for the presidency to the electors. Each of these bills drew constitutional objections on the floor of the House of Representatives, but not enough to interfere with their passage. Whether intentionally or not, Congress had laid down the interpretive principle that if the Constitution spoke to an issue, Congress could legislate on it. Congress had also acted practically, acknowledging in both the Seamen's Act of 1790 and the Fugitive Slave Act of 1793 that the weak federal infrastructure could not enforce federal law. State help was needed, and Congress prescribed it.

If Congress had laid down the principle that it could direct state officers when necessary, the states also asserted their will. In the first two decades of the nineteenth century, Ohio, New York, and Indiana passed laws governing procedure in fugitive slave cases. These laws clearly intended to be fair to slaveholders but also made clear that if status was in doubt, it would be determined in that state's jurisdiction. These statutes worked within the guidelines established by the Fugitive Slave Act, although there were some notable departures. Indiana's law, for instance, allowed either party to insist upon a jury trial, which conflicted with the federal law's requirement of a summary hearing. But for the most part, fugitive slave acts passed by the states conformed to federal law.

Most of the clashes over fugitive slave rendition occurred because abolition societies had resolved to protect fugitives from slavery with the same zeal with which they protected free blacks from kidnapping. The Pennsylvania Abolition Society assigned all such legal work to its acting committee, which itself reported a steady increase in the number of cases from the 1790s through the 1810s. Perversely, the increase in the legal work of protecting free blacks from kidnapping came from one of the abolition movement's great successes—the closing of the African slave trade by Congress in 1808. Thereafter, the demand for slaves in the southern interior outstripped the natural supply, and a robust internal slave trade developed. Abolitionists deplored this interstate slave trade, but their efforts to have it banned by Congress came to naught. Between the official closing of the trade and the onset of the Civil War, slave traders carried one million men, women, and children across the Appalachians in chains to meet the labor demand. It was a dark moment in American history. But it was lucrative, and few who conducted such a trade spared a scruple for the kidnapped free blacks who ended up amongst the slaves, marching in coffles to their misery.

Northerners moved to combat kidnapping. The Pennsylvania Assembly appointed a committee in 1804 to address the "cruel and infamous practice" of kidnapping free blacks from Philadelphia. Before Congress, Joseph Stanton of Rhode Island rose to point out that "the high price offered for negroes by the Southern people" had enticed unscrupulous Rhode Islanders to kidnap free blacks. The American Convention for Promoting the Abolition of Slavery reported in 1812 that "the diabolical practice of kidnapping is still continued," and went further to note that clandestine conduct had given way to "open claims under the fugitive [slave] act." Newspapers reported the rise independently of abolitionists, and southerners themselves decried the practice. Abolitionists committed themselves to protecting kidnapped free blacks, but they did so on humanist grounds. As such, they made no distinction between the slaveholder who claimed a fugitive and the kidnapper who attempted to steal a free black.

It should surprise no one that the major early conflicts occurred in Pennsylvania. The active abolition society there and the proximity of a large free black population from which kidnappers poached led to heightened activity and tensions over slavery. Few felt it more acutely than the state's chief justice, William Tilghman. Tilghman had himself been a slaveholder at one time before emancipating his slaves, although his tarrying in this regard has led some historians to wonder just how genuine were his antislavery principles. Nonetheless, he displayed an evenhandedness regarding fugitive slave rendition despite private lobbying from slaveholders on the one hand and public pressure exerted by abolitionists on the other.

Tilghman first encountered fugitive slaves in *Commonwealth v. Holloway* (1816), a case concerned with the status of the children of fugitives. Mary, the slave of a Marylander named James Corse, fled to Philadelphia where she lived for two years before giving birth to a daughter, Eliza. Corse captured Mary and her daughter and had them both committed to the Philadelphia jail. Lawyers retained by the Pennsylvania Abolition Society obtained a writ of habeas corpus to the Pennsylvania Supreme Court. The judges there confronted a problem in the conflict of laws. Pennsylvania law held that all slaves born there after passage of the gradual abolition act would be free, subject only to a limited period of servitude. The fugitive slave clause was silent about the children of fugitives, but did make clear that the status of the fugitive slave would not be altered by the laws of the state into which he or she fled. Lawyers for the slaveholder Corse argued that Eliza's status followed that of her mother, as her mother was still governed by Maryland law. Ergo she was a slave. The Pennsylvania

Supreme Court rejected this reasoning. Tilghman was not suggesting that Pennsylvania law trumped the U.S. Constitution. "If there be a repugnancy," he explained, "there is no doubt but the act of [Pennsylvania's] assembly must give way." But the Constitution was silent on the subject of the children of fugitives, and in the face of such silence Tilghman proved unwilling to extend slaveholders' rights by judicial fiat. Eliza was free by Pennsylvania law and the U.S. Constitution. A U.S. district court judge had reached a similar conclusion a year earlier in *Kitty's Case*, reading the fugitive slave clause and the Fugitive Slave Act of 1793 narrowly and refusing to extend slaveholders' property rights to the children of their fugitives.

Tilghman's cautious reading of the law worked against refugees from slavery as often as it did against slaveholders. In *Wright v. Deacon* (1819), abolitionists asked the Pennsylvania Supreme Court to intervene in a fugitive slave rendition currently under way and order a jury trial for the alleged fugitive. How this request came before the court is instructive. Slaveholders had, in conformity with the Fugitive Slave Act, been granted a hearing before a state judge to obtain a certificate of removal. Lawyers for the Pennsylvania Abolition Society, however, brought the fugitive before a different judge on a writ of habeas corpus. (This was, it should be noted, the exact same procedure that resulted in Eliza's freedom in *Commonwealth v. Holloway*.) Unfortunately for the abolitionists, the habeas corpus proceeding did not go as planned. Instead of taking the opportunity to free the fugitive, the judge instead issued a certificate of removal so that the slaveholder could remove his slave to Maryland.

Abolitionists asked the Pennsylvania Supreme Court to intervene by issuing a writ *de homine replegiando*. This was an old common law writ long since fallen into disuse, in England as well as in America. It literally "replevied" someone's body from custody. Unlike the writ of habeas corpus, which was conducted in a summary manner before a judge, *de homine replegiando* required a jury to decide the issue. Lawyers for the slaveholders complained that the certificate of removal had already been issued and that the writ interfered with their client's constitutionally secured right to his fugitive's labor. Tilghman agreed. "Whatever may be our private opinions on the subject of slavery," he answered, "it is well known that our southern brethren would not have consented to become parties to a constitution under which the *United*

States have enjoyed so much prosperity, unless their property in slaves had been secured." It was his duty, he went on to say, to give to the laws a fair and candid construction. The Fugitive Slave Act had prescribed a summary hearing for fugitives in order to obtain a certificate of removal, and the demand for a jury trial was thus in conflict with federal law and the Constitution. The writ was quashed and the fugitive was sent to Maryland.

Taken together, these two cases give a fair glimpse of the principles that governed fugitive slave rendition in Pennsylvania. In both cases, the Pennsylvania Supreme Court regarded habeas corpus hearings as being in conformity with the Fugitive Slave Act. They were, after all, summary proceedings that determined status and had — in the case of *Commonwealth v. Holloway* — resulted in the issuance of certificates of removal. The fugitive slave clause had been read narrowly as protecting only the right of the slaveholder to his fugitive slave's labor. He had no claim under Pennsylvania law to the body of a fugitive's child born on Pennsylvania soil. When conflict of federal and state law did occur, Tilghman indicated that the Pennsylvania law must recede.

These cases did not occur in a vacuum. Slavery had reentered national politics with a vengeance following the War of 1812. The protest against the admission of Missouri as a slave state in 1819 brought the issue to a head. On February 13, 1819, in the House of Representatives, James Tallmadge from New York introduced an amendment to the Missouri admission bill prohibiting the further introduction of slavery into the state and providing that all children born of slaves shall be free after twenty-five years of service. Rufus King in the Senate (one of the only Framers still alive), supported the Tallmadge Amendment by arguing that Congress was well within its power to lay a restriction on admission through the territories and admissions clauses. John Jay (the one-time chief justice of the Supreme Court and one of the *Federalist* Papers authors) wrote a public letter in support of the amendment. Slaveholders recoiled, arguing that Congress was but a trustee of territory that was common property in a union where all the states ought to have equal access to the territories. The final resolution of the Missouri crisis was to admit both a slave state and a free state and to divide the remaining U.S. territory into predetermined slave and free portions. But it took two years to complete this shaky transaction, and not all parties received it well.

In such a climate, judges were painfully aware of the import of their decisions regarding the disposition of this or that alleged fugitive slave. Chief Justice William Tilghman decided *Wright v. Deacon* in 1819, after the Missouri Question had exploded upon the national consciousness but before anyone was quite sure what would be its aftermath. Thomas Jefferson himself wrote that he had heard the knell of the Union while talk of secession and the formation of regional confederacies permeated the public press. This partly explains Tilghman's labored explanation that various securities for slaveholders were necessary for national union and that returning fugitives—however disagreeable to one's individual conscience—was a constitutional duty. Such a statement had nothing to do with the case before him. It spoke instead to abolitionists' increasingly pointed demand that northern judges bend the law to favor refugees from slavery over slaveholders. As Tilghman's opinion in *Wright v. Deacon* indicates, judges were not disposed to do so.

Nor were judges inclined to assume a power that abolitionists increasingly urged upon them: to declare the Fugitive Slave Act unconstitutional. The first such case to register a written opinion on that subject was *In re Susan* (1818), before the federal circuit court of Indiana. The case was classic conflict-of-laws. In 1816 Indiana had passed a law requiring slaveholders who were making fugitive slave claims to obtain a certificate of removal from a state judge who could, at his discretion, order a jury trial. A Kentucky slaveholder had sought a certificate of removal from a state judge before turning to the federal district court. Abolitionist lawyers moved for dismissal of the federal case and argued that the Constitution conferred on Congress no power to pass fugitive slave laws. It was a plausible argument. Article IV, Section 2, had no enabling clause explicitly conferring authority on Congress. The other sections in Article IV—containing the full faith and credit clause; admission of new states; territories clause; guarantee clause—all did. Following the common law rule of *expressio unius est exclusio alterius* (express mention of one thing excludes all others not on the list), then the omission was intentional and should be read as such. Given that the Tenth Amendment reserved to the states all powers not expressly granted to the federal government, it followed that only the states could legislate fugitive slave laws. In short, the "strict constructionist" reading of the Constitution (a position championed by Virginians Thomas Jefferson, Spencer Roane, and John Taylor of Caroline County) concluded that the Constitution conferred no authority on Congress to legislate in this area.

The federal district judge refused this argument, although he never specifically refuted it. He ruled that congressional power to pass fugitive slave laws was "in conformity to the constitutional provision." He noted the Fugitive Slave Act's long operation and its recognition "before the judges and courts of this country." He saw no reason to deviate from that authority. Abolitionist lawyers were not through, however. In a second argument, they averred the Fugitive Slave Act's constitutionality but argued that state law took precedence. The judge rejected this argument as well, arguing from the supremacy clause. Once Congress had legislated, the new law immediately superseded any state law on the subject. To admit concurrent legislation that proscribed different modes of fugitive slave rendition as well as different penalties for noncompliance was "pregnant with the greatest mischief, and the source of perpetual collisions between the states and the general government."

The state of Indiana thought otherwise. After the slaveholder in question returned to Kentucky, Indiana's governor sought his rendition for kidnapping, which was rejected by resolutions from the Kentucky legislature. The governor referred the matter to his legislature, which produced a report that asserted the rights of the state of Indiana. The Fugitive Slave Act of 1793, the report noted, could not bind state officers who were pledged to protect the constitutional liberties of Indiana's residents. A federal judge may have declared Indiana's antikidnapping law "useless," and the Kentucky legislature may have complained it was unconstitutional, but the report doggedly claimed the "right and duty of our state" to pass it. The legislature fulfilled this duty in 1824 when it passed a new personal liberty law that provided a summary mode for fugitive slave rendition. The law also provided protections for free blacks caught up in the process by giving them opportunities to prove their freedom. It was a compromise on Indiana's part, putting it in conformity with federal law but maintaining its right to hear and determine rendition claims.

Conflict with state law was not the only concern of federal judges. Supreme Court Justice Bushrod Washington complained mightily in *Worthington v. Preston* (1824), a case he decided while riding circuit in

Pennsylvania, that the Fugitive Slave Act did not authorize federal judges to issue arrest warrants. He hoped Congress would remedy the ill. He also admitted in his opinion that he had always felt free to hold alleged fugitives in order to give them time to get witnesses together to disprove the claims of a slavecatcher, despite the lack of a specific statutory authority to do so. Even Supreme Court judges bent the rules when necessary to do justice.

Above all else, northern judges proved willing and able to make the distinction between fugitive slave rendition and potential kidnapping, as demonstrated by the case of *Commonwealth v. Griffith* (1823). The case originated in 1822 when a slavecatcher named Camillus Griffith seized a fugitive named Randolph in the town of New Bedford, Massachusetts. Randolph had fled five years earlier, settled in New Bedford, and ultimately acquired property there. Griffith had gone to the federal district judge to procure a warrant, but the judge refused to issue it because the Fugitive Slave Act did not explicitly authorize it. So, without a warrant, Griffith and a deputy sheriff seized Randolph and imprisoned him, intending to take him before the same federal judge in order to procure a certificate of removal. For his pains, Griffith found himself under indictment by a Massachusetts grand jury for assault and battery and for false imprisonment. The trial ended in his conviction, even though it was proved in court that Randolph was indeed a slave by Virginia law and thus a fugitive from labor under the U.S. Constitution. An appeal removed the case to the Massachusetts Supreme Court in 1823 as *Commonwealth v. Griffith*.

Massachusetts' attorney general and his assistants argued that state protections of liberty applied to *alleged* fugitives because it was within the state's power to hear and determine status. This meant that the Fugitive Slave Act was invalid because it violated the Fourth Amendment's protection against unreasonable searches and seizures. Lawyers for the commonwealth recalled the furor in pre-Revolutionary days over the "writs of assistance," search warrants that were general in nature rather than specifically listing what an authority was looking for. The Fugitive Slave Act, they argued, was much worse. The alleged fugitive, Randolph, had been domiciled in Massachusetts and was to be considered at law a freeman until proven otherwise. There was no excuse for violating his rights on the *presumption* that he was a slave. This might lead to a freeman being seized without a warrant, in clear violation of the Massachusetts Constitution. The state pushed this argument further. If the fugitive were found in a Massachusetts citizen's barn or home, by the terms of the Fugitive Slave Act the slaveholder might enter and remove him without any warrant whatsoever. What plainer violation of a Massachusetts citizen's property rights could there be?

At this point, Chief Justice Isaac Parker intervened and admonished counsel that the argument had been carried too far. A case had come before him in Middlesex where a constable had, without a warrant, gone into a citizen's house after a slave and Parker had held this to be a trespass. The *Griffith* case, Parker was reminding counsel, would be decided on the basis of what rights a fugitive slave had. And so the attorney general staked his claim: in Massachusetts, one could not presume that a person was a slave. Before any rights were surrendered, the person's status had to be proven in a court of law. It followed that seizure without a warrant was illegal and therefore the Fugitive Slave Act was void.

In response, Camillus Griffith's lawyer denied that a fugitive slave could claim any rights under the Constitution. "We the People," he argued, did not include slaves. As such, they could claim no protection under the Bill of Rights. To do so courted absurdity. Given that it was protection under the U.S. Constitution that the fugitive Randolph was now claiming, it must apply equally throughout the United States. If Randolph could not be seized without a warrant in Massachusetts, the same must be true in Virginia. The better analogy, Griffith's lawyer contended, was to the state laws that governed the master's right to seize an apprentice, or a parent's right to seize a child, "in which cases no warrant is necessary."

The Massachusetts Supreme Court agreed with Griffith's attorney and discharged the defendant. Slaves were not parties to the Constitution, Chief Justice Isaac Parker related, and as such could claim none of its protections. And because the Constitution governed the status of fugitives, Massachusetts could not demand that the seizure of fugitives be in conformity with its laws. This by itself settled the issue, and was sufficient rationale to discharge the defendant. Nonetheless, Chief Justice Parker added a final thought. Noting the objection that a freeman might be seized in this summary manner as a fugitive — thus potentially violating both federal and state guarantees of individual liberty—he explained that "mischievous consequences" awaited anyone who made such a seizure, and habeas corpus would lie ready to obtain liberty for the wronged freeman. Federal process, it would seem, did not always trump state process.

A tacit constitutional settlement governed the division of power regarding fugitive slave rendition in the early republic. Congress had claimed the power to define fugitive slave rendition procedure, but it had declined to distinguish kidnapping from fugitive slave rendition. Congressional reticence to legislate the distinction had a political dimension, to be sure, but it also fit within the framework of federalism in the early republic. Because the individual states determined status, they held the power to define and punish kidnapping. This was an artificial division, as both fugitive slave rendition and antikidnapping legislation required a status determination. But the Fugitive Slave Act's dependence upon state judges and magistrates for its execution masked the artificiality of this division. It enabled Pennsylvania judges to hear evidence in habeas corpus proceedings and then end them by issuing certificates of removal or by freeing the alleged fugitive. It enabled a federal judge in Indiana to declare that federal law prescribed the mode for fugitive rendition hearings, without striking down state law. And in Massachusetts, it allowed the Supreme Court to declare that a fugitive slave had no rights while a freeman had every right afforded by the Massachusetts Declaration of Rights. The distinction was artificial, but it worked.

The cases from Pennsylvania and Massachusetts also revealed the judge's proper role in the early republic. The judges in these cases did not uphold the supremacy of federal law over state law. True, the courts had refused arguments to strike down the Fugitive Slave Act as unconstitutional, but they had also kept their decisions narrow to avoid setting aside state law that assisted in fugitive slave reclamation or protected free blacks from kidnapping. Although judges frequently complained of the mischiefs of collision, their cautious course reconciled conflicting statutes and procedures rather than declaring them void. Even in *In re Susan*, the federal judge in Indiana declined to strike down state law even as he declared that federal law trumped it. If one thing held constant in these cases, it was judges' deference to the will of the legislatures and their desire to avoid rule by judicial fiat.

What the courts did do was settle some of the particulars of the law governing fugitive slave rendition in the early republic. Fugitive slave rendition was conducted privately, and slaveholders could seize their fugitives wherever they found them. State laws preventing warrantless searches and seizures could not touch slaveholders or their agents when they lawfully seized a fugitive. The certificate of removal necessary to transport a fugitive across state lines was to be granted in a proceeding more akin to a hearing than a trial (i.e., no jury was necessary), although nothing prevented judges from admitting evidence on behalf of the alleged fugitive that might prove his or her freedom. Federal law had extended jurisdiction to state judges and magistrates to conduct these hearings. There were some rumblings that Congress might not have the authority to direct state officers, but Congress had long done so, and no judge was willing to overturn the law on those grounds. Instead, judges had interpreted the loose procedure outlined in the Fugitive Slave Act as conforming to a variety of judicial functions. Writs of habeas corpus issued by state judges, for instance, could interrupt state or federal process to determine the status of an alleged fugitive. And in Pennsylvania, at least, the Fugitive Slave Act was read narrowly to apply only to the fugitive. Her children, if born on free soil, would not be governed by slave law.

It was in this way that the same bare act — the moving of a person across state lines against his will and reducing him to slavery — was clothed as either legitimate fugitive slave rendition or kidnapping.

The Rights of Slaveholders and Those of Free Blacks in Pennsylvania's Personal Liberty Law of 1826

From virtually the moment of the Constitution's ratification, both slaveholders and free blacks sought rights. Free blacks demanded that the vision of equality and autonomy embodied in the Declaration of Independence and the Constitution be taken seriously. They contended with a society still moored in eighteenth-century social and legal conventions, which subjugated wives to husbands, women to men, and servants and slaves to their masters. Abolitionists white and black proved to be in the vanguard of a movement that developed a rights consciousness by attacking the hierarchy enshrined in American law. But slaveholders claimed rights, too. They repeatedly demanded that their property rights be respected, especially those rights protected by the Constitution. Against the aspirational vision of equality put forward by abolitionists, slaveholders insisted that their rights were founded in nature and law as well. They pointed to the sanctity of property in the American constitutional order, and they demanded that the letter of the law be enforced. Slaveholders claimed rights, albeit upon a different foundation than abolitionists.

The struggle between abolitionists and slaveholders over fugitive slaves was a rights struggle in the most fundamental sense. On the one hand, slaveholders claimed a property right backed by the full force of state and federal law and guaranteed by the Constitution itself. Slaveholders repeatedly complained that northerners disrespected their property rights by employing fugitive slaves, harboring them, or manipulating the law to impede slaveholders' rights. For their part, abolitionists called attention to the unfair laws under which people of African descent lived. They published reports of kidnapping, and they demanded stronger legislation protecting the rights of free blacks and fugitive slaves alike.

In the early republic and antebellum era, rights were sought primarily through political action. Slaveholders and abolitionists alike drafted and circulated petitions, published pamphlets, and sought to influence the passage of legislation. Both sides won recognition and suffered defeats regarding fugitive slave rendition, but the victories did not always track the way we would expect them. Both slaveholders and abolitionists petitioned and lobbied Congress for federal legislation friendly to their cause, but neither succeeded. Nonetheless, this conflict inspired a national discussion about the proper role of the federal government in securing rights, a discussion that would endure for the next six decades. Slaveholders and abolitionists also petitioned the state legislatures. In Pennsylvania, at least, both parties were successful. Abolitionists scored a huge victory with Pennsylvania's tough antikidnapping law of 1820. But protest from Maryland slaveholders ultimately won the day, and the compromise Maryland and Pennsylvania reached resulted in Pennsylvania's Personal Liberty Law of 1826 — the very law that would be at issue in *Prigg v. Pennsylvania*.

Abolitionists began their national campaign against slavery immediately following the adoption of the Constitution. Quakers presented a memorial to Congress in 1790 asking that body to take steps to end the slave trade. The ferocity of the reply by representatives from Georgia and South Carolina was stunning. Slaveholders summoned every available argument to defeat the Quakers, many without any constitutional tether. William Smith of South Carolina, for instance, argued that the Constitution prevented Congress from even discussing the slave trade until 1808. An incredulous James Madison replied that the very constitutional clause that Smith quoted allowed Congress to impose a $10-per-head tax on slave imports. How was Congress to tax the slave trade if, as Smith would have it, members of Congress could not even discuss it? Madison took his argument further, noting that the commerce clause allowed for other kinds of regulations of the slave trade. For instance, Congress might prohibit American vessels from transporting slaves from Africa to the West Indies. Georgia's representative protested that any such prohibition threatened slavery itself. These proslavery arguments were patently absurd, and slaveholders were bested in virtually every constitutional argument. But they won the political fight, as none of the abolitionists' petitions came to anything.

The Pennsylvania Abolition Society never quit petitioning as a form of political action, despite its failure in 1790. Petitioning was an ancient right, a bulwark of freedom. No matter how indignant slaveholders were with abolitionist petitions, abolitionists had no intention of abandoning them. They did, however, moderate them. Abolitionists came to the realization that petitions could not simply call for the federal government to pursue justice and right. Besides being politically inexpedient, broad federal action was constitutionally impermissible. The new federal government may have had significant grants of power, but control over the domestic institutions of the states was not among them. The federal government could no more free slaves than it could extend the vote to women. Its power was limited to certain enumerated subjects, and the subjects of petitions needed to carefully hew to that course. Most obviously, Congress could act against the slave trade, indirectly before 1808 and directly after 1808. By implication, Congress could also abolish slavery in the "Ten Miles Square" of the federal capitol, and through Article IV, Section 3, it could prohibit slavery in the territories and prevent new slave states from entering the republic. Over time, petitions from abolitionist societies would embrace all these issues, politely begging for relief in ways that reflected the limited power of the federal government.

More immediately, the Pennsylvania Abolition Society sought to influence its state legislature, lobbying for laws to ameliorate the condition of the free black population or to defeat laws subjecting its black population to legal hardship. Such lobbying would pay dividends, especially in an era when stratified legal status might impinge the rights of whole groups of people. To be black in America in the early republic was not to be a free citizen, but rather to be presumed a freed slave. The upper south followed North Carolina's lead in requiring free blacks to wear patches signaling their status as free. Without such proof, a free black in a slave state was always subject to the possibility of being whipped into jail and sold into slavery. Ohio's infamous Black Law of 1804 required all black or mulatto immigrants to the state to register and provide proof of their freedom. In 1807, the Ohio legislature further prohibited blacks from testifying in cases involving whites.

In such ways even the "free states" throttled blacks' liberty, restricting their movement, access to education, and other privileges and immunities. The federal government also reinforced the whiteness of the republic. In 1810, Congress prohibited blacks from carrying the mail, and it repeatedly passed municipal codes for the District of Columbia that greatly restricted the movement and rights of its black residents. It was precisely these kinds of laws that the Pennsylvania Abolition Society sought to prevent, albeit without much success.

Others took a different path. In 1813, the brilliant black abolitionist James Forten of Philadelphia published a stirring attack on the racial prejudice enshrined in law. There were few better equipped to speak to the subject. James Forten was born free in 1766. His family had intimate contacts with Anthony Benezet, the Quaker who had agitated so forcefully against slavery during the 1770s. Forten attended the Quakers' African School for a brief time as a boy. In 1780, Forten volunteered to serve on a colonial privateer to aid the war effort. His service was short, as his vessel was captured and Forten would ultimately end his service on board a prison ship in New York harbor. Perhaps the most remarkable thing about Forten's service was his continued imprisonment, for his British captor (Captain John Bazely) had offered Forten freedom if he would return to England with Bazely's youngest son. Forten had clearly made an impression on the British naval officer, and the offer carried with it the implicit promise of patronage and advancement. But Forten refused. He had been captured in the service of liberty, he said, and he would not betray the interests of his country now. And so Forten spent seven months on a prison frigate in New York harbor before his release and return to his family. Forten would go on to be a successful sail maker and businessman in Philadelphia, where he kept abreast of issues pertaining to liberty and slavery in Pennsylvania and the United States.

What moved James Forten to public protest in 1813 was a bill before the Pennsylvania Assembly that would have forced black immigrants to the state to register or suffer deportation to and sale in southern states. *A Series of Letters by a Man of Color* announced a new kind of abolitionist pleading, one in which vocal people of African descent demanded that white Americans live up to the promises of human equality put forth in the Declaration of Independence. Forten staked a claim for citizenship as deep as that of any white man. "Many of our ancestors were brought here more than one hundred years ago; many of our fathers, many of ourselves, have fought and bled for the Independence of our country," wrote Forten. "Let the motto of our Legislators be: 'The Law knows no distinction.'"

Forten was not the first black man in America to demand equality, but he would become one of the most influential. His plain reading of the founding documents gave force to the notion that rights ought not to be divided across arbitrary racial lines and simultaneously gave the lie to those who claimed that nature had groomed darker-skinned people for subordination. Equally as prescient would be the different way he addressed his audience. The Pennsylvania Abolition Society spoke in deferential tones to elites. Forten spoke directly. "Yes, ye rulers of the black man's destiny," he said to the Pennsylvania legislators, "reflect upon this; our Children must be registered, and bear about them a certificate, or be subject to imprisonment and fine. You, who are perusing this effusion of feeling, are you a parent?" Here was a powerful sentimental appeal, calculated to stress the human connections between white and black, to bring them together. And although he formally addressed legislators, Forten's public letters also reached the people who elected them. It was a more democratic appeal than the Pennsylvania Abolition Society had hitherto adopted, and it would have its effect.

Slaveholders, too, pressed their rights on both the national and local stages. In 1796, slaveholders had protested the proposed federal antikidnapping law by invoking their rights. What was kidnapping, asked Maryland's congressional representative William Vans Murray? Was it kidnapping to steal a slave away from his master and spirit him to a free state? The question had drawn sharp responses from northern representatives, who rightly recognized it as a rhetorical deflection from the issue at hand. But Murray persisted. It was, in his estimation, just as much a violation of rights for an abolitionist to steal a slave as it was for a kidnapper to steal a free man. The Fugitive Slave Act of 1793, he continued, did not remedy the evil because recovery of monetary penalties under the law required that a claimant prove that the employer of a fugitive slave actually knew he was a fugitive slave. Murray moved a resolution that the House appoint a committee to look into whether a stronger fugitive slave act was needed, but the motion was tabled.

The problem was evidently real enough for slaveholders to continue to complain. In 1798, the Maryland House of Delegates adopted a resolution complaining that slaves were escaping into Delaware, New Jersey, and Pennsylvania, subjecting their owners to "great loss and inconvenience." The resolution authorized the governor and council to take measures with the governors of the neighboring states to correct the problem. Nothing came of it, though. So Maryland representatives continued to push their rights in Congress, where a special committee was eventually appointed, chaired by Maryland representative John Hopper Nicholson, who reported a bill in 1801. The proposal for an expansive federal law was certainly remarkable. It would require free blacks to carry certificates at all times attesting to their freedom. Anyone wishing to hire a person of color who was a stranger to them was required to advertise in two newspapers before doing so. And the bill had teeth. If anyone did employ a fugitive slave, regardless of their state of knowledge or intent, they were liable to the slaveholder for civil penalties of up to $500.

The bill brought acrimonious debate. Northern representatives invoked the same strict interpretation of federal power that had been deployed to defeat antikidnapping legislation half a decade earlier. It was wrong, they argued, to oblige northerners to advertise every time they employed a person of color. And they did not wish to compel blacks to carry about certificates everywhere they went. The debates are not reported in full, but the intrusion of Congress into the state domain of determining status clearly offended many. For their part, slaveholders complained that fugitives obtained open assistance from abolitionists and found ready employment in the states north of the Mason-Dixon Line. When fugitives were caught and returned, they regaled their comrades with stories of how well received and cared for they were, encouraging more to run away. In turn, slaveholders were forced to treat their slaves more severely. In short, slaveholders were arguing that the pretended philanthropy of abolitionists (and the indifference of northerners looking for cheap labor) actually hurt slaves.

This moral argument from slaveholders did not get much traction. And the real story was the change in political divisions. A scant half-decade before, northerners and southerners worried that an antikidnapping law unconstitutionally extended national power, and these constitutional scruples helped defeat the bill. But now, sectional interests drove the discussion. Southerners seemed oddly unfazed by allowing the national government to dictate employment relations and intrude on state-reserved regulations of people. The bill was defeated by only three votes in an ominously sectional ballot. Only seven northerners broke to vote for the bill, and one southerner (from North Carolina) voted against it. Slaveholders had flexed their muscles but did not prove quite strong enough to impose their will on Congress.

However, they did keep agitating for their rights. In 1815, Marylanders living on the border with Pennsylvania petitioned for state action to prevent their slaves escaping northward. The Maryland House of Delegates resolved to seek help from the Pennsylvania legislature, but the measure was defeated in the Maryland Senate. In the following year the measure was brought up again. The inconvenience had become so great, the legislature claimed, that silence in the face of it was improper if not criminal. The legislature thereupon ordered the governor to communicate the resolution to the bordering free states and seek for legislation remedying the problem. The Pennsylvania legislature shrugged it off, and in 1817 the Maryland legislature again demanded of its governor that a correspondence be established. Resurrected in this resolution was the notion that abolitionist enticement and harboring of fugitives made life more difficult for slaves back home.

At the same time, Congress again took up the Fugitive Slave Act. In December of 1817, Virginia representative James Pindall introduced a new fugitive slave bill to Congress. The bill asked for two major reforms. First, it sought authorization for northern judges and magistrates to issue arrest warrants for fugitive slaves. This was clearly intended to clothe slaveholders with official legal authority during arrest so they would not be exposed to charges of kidnapping or assault and battery. Its second reform was to take discretionary power away from northern judges. Under the bill, slaveholders could obtain certificates from their home-state courts after attesting to a runaway's status as a slave and location in a free state. The certificate then obliged — on pain of penalty — judges and magistrates in free states to issue arrest warrants and certificates of removal.

No other federal bill had attempted such an interpretation of the Constitution. The bill essentially forced the courts and officers of free states to be subordinate ministers of the commands of the judges of the slave states. As Pindall defended the bill over the next few months, he unfolded a rational defense of the bill's peculiar federalism. He began by reminding the body that they were not discussing the *general* right of Congress to impose duties on the state courts. Rather, they were discussing a very *specific* case. The fugitive slave clause, Pindall argued, directed the states to act. States acted through their officers. When representatives complained that Congress had no right to coerce state officers to act, Pindall replied that Congress had long instructed state officers to carry out certain federal laws. It followed that they could up the ante and put state officers under penalty.

But what of the rights of free blacks? From New Hampshire, Representative Clifton Clagett rose to remind Pindall that scrupulous enforcement of the fugitive slave clause might be necessary to carry out the terms of federal union, but that did not mean that Congress could run roughshod over the equally important Article I, Section 9 command that "the privilege of the Writ of Habeas Corpus shall not be suspended, unless when in Cases of Rebellion or Invasion the public Safety may require it." Free black citizens of New Hampshire (or any other free state), Clagett argued, would have no recourse to their own courts to prove their freedom under this new law. Slaveholders returned the fire, referring to their right to slave property as "inalienable" under the Constitution and suggesting that habeas corpus hearings that resulted in the freedom of alleged fugitives violated slaveholders' Seventh Amendment right to a jury in civil cases.

The debate would simmer for the next few months. Northern representatives and senators demanded some assurance that a stronger fugitive slave bill would protect against potential abuses by unscrupulous slavecatchers, but the more zealous among them moved amendments to the bill designed to destroy it. Even some free state representatives expressed exasperation at these tactics, one going so far as to admit that the prejudice against slavery was so great in some northern states that no jury could be trusted there to return a fugitive. One northern supporter of the bill stated that he did not believe it would suspend habeas corpus at all. Slaveholders once again proved united enough to force the bill through each house of Congress. Constitutional scruples, however, forced compromise in both, leading to the House and the Senate passing two different bills, each with a different antikidnapping provision attached. The two bills were never reconciled, and slaveholders again failed to change the terms of fugitive slave rendition.

Meanwhile, Pennsylvania abolitionists succeeded in obtaining a new and stronger antikidnapping law from their state legislature in 1820. Of course, the Pennsylvania Abolition Society had always lobbied the legislature, and this was not their first success in that measure, but the antikidnapping law of 1820 was its strongest victory to date. It defined as kidnapping the removal, by force or fraud, of any black person from Pennsylvania with the intent to make that person a slave. Such kidnapping was punishable by a jail term of from seven to twenty-one years and a fine of $500–$2000, one half of which was payable to the person "who shall prosecute" the case. The Pennsylvania Abolition Society, with its standing committee that inquired into every such removal, could now expect its expenses to be defrayed upon any successful conviction. The law further prohibited aldermen and justices of the peace (petty magistrates, in essence) from taking cognizance of fugitive slave rendition hearings under the Fugitive Slave Act of 1793. Judges and recorders could still conduct such hearings and issue certificates of removal, but they were now required to make a thorough evidentiary record of the alleged fugitive and the evidence used to prove his or her status as a slave, as well as recording the name and address of the person claiming his or her service.

This antikidnapping law was different because it amended the congressional act, albeit in a small way. It adopted the abolitionist argument that petty magistrates, some of whom could not even hear significant property claims, ought not to determine the momentous question of a person's liberty. The effect of the law would be twofold. It would protect free blacks from kidnapping, but it would also make fugitive slave reclamation more difficult. Slaveholders received the latter message loud and clear. Pennsylvania's antikidnapping bill was signed into law on March 27, 1820, and not a week later James Pindall — the representative from Virginia who had introduced a new fugitive slave bill in Congress in 1818 — requested that a copy of the act be laid before the House of Representatives and a select committee appointed to inquire into what federal law might be necessary to secure slaveholders their rights to fugitive slaves. Nothing would come of it. Two weeks later in the Senate, William Smith of South Carolina asked for a similar resolution ordering the Judiciary Committee to investigate the subject and return a bill if necessary. He was opposed by Pennsylvania's senators, who took some time to explain the particulars of the antikidnapping law. Another senator complained that it would be impossible to consider a complicated fugitive slave bill so late in the session. The Senate tabled Smith's resolution. Abolitionists had deployed every parliamentary tactic necessary to defeat a stronger proslavery fugitive slave bill from passing Congress in 1818 and 1820, and they would do so again two years later. As strongly proslavery as the federal government was, abolitionists could flex their muscles too.

This small abolitionist victory was all the more impressive given the energy slaveholders had expended. Maryland's congressional delegation departed for Washington in 1820 with explicit instructions from the Maryland legislature to seek a stronger fugitive slave law. Runaways, the legislature admonished its representatives, were harbored and protected in Pennsylvania. Slaveholders seeking to vindicate their constitutionally secured property rights found every legal obstacle raised in their path. The report charged further that when the law favored the slaveholder, abolitionists resorted to force. So too did fugitives, and they could now do so under cover of law.

Slaveholders were not dealing in hypotheticals. In 1820, a Baltimore slaveholder named Samuel Griffith located his runaway slave in Philadelphia. He went there with his overseer, Peter Shipley, and two other men to arrest his slave, who now went by the name of John Read. Read had lived in Philadelphia some two years and claimed to be a manumitted Maryland slave. He feared kidnappers, or so he made everyone aware, and frequently went about armed. At midnight on December 14, 1820, Samuel Griffith and his party claimed to be police executing a warrant and demanded entry into Read's home. Read told them to go away, rolled a cider barrel in front of the door, and drew his pistol. The party beat the door off its hinges, and Read warned them it would be life for life. They ignored the warning. Griffith was the first through the door. Read unloaded his pistol at point blank range on Griffith, mortally wounding him. Shipley raced in, and Read clubbed him in the head, dropping him to his knees. When Shipley struggled back to his feet, Read hit him again. Then Read fled to his neighbor's house. Shipley dragged himself to a home some one hundred yards away and prevailed upon the woman who lived there to let him in. He died eight days later from the bludgeoning Read had given him.

John Read would be indicted and tried for the murder of Samuel Griffith (his reputed owner) in May 1821. The judge in the case interpreted the Pennsylvania antikidnapping law of 1820 to prevent *any* forcible taking of someone out of the state without legal process. If it was the intent of Griffith to reclaim his fugitive and return to Baltimore without obtaining a certificate of removal, the judge said, then Read was acting to prevent a felony from occurring. The jury acquitted him of murder.

As shocking as Read's acquittal might have been for slaveholders, Read was not out of trouble just yet. In November, he was tried for the murder of Peter Shipley, the overseer who had accompanied Griffith. The judge in this case (who had, incidentally, been the prosecutor during the previous trial) offered a different interpretation of Pennsylvania law. He did not believe that the law set a kidnapper on the same footing with a slaveholder who was exercising a legitimate claim. The jury convicted Read of manslaughter and sentenced him to nine years in the penitentiary.

John Read's punishment afforded little comfort to slaveholders attempting to claim their fugitives. Slavecatchers reported increasing violence. In 1821, the Maryland legislature received several petitions complaining of Pennsylvanians' obstruction of fugitive slave reclamation. The committee on grievances and courts found true a petition from one of its very own members—a delegate from Baltimore County—who complained that his attempts at peaceable and legal fugitive slave rendition in York County, Pennsylvania, had met with threats of violence both private and public. Men bullied him. Civil authorities threatened him with fine and imprisonment under the 1820 law.

In the face of this official violence against its citizens, the Maryland legislature faltered. The house asked for official interposition, but the senate demurred. It preferred to send official requests to the Pennsylvania legislature for a new law. The Maryland legislature eventually chose this option, making requests of Pennsylvania, Delaware, and New Jersey. This was not the first time such a request had been made, nor would it be the last. In 1822, upon receipt of yet another petition complaining of interference with fugitive slave rendition, the Maryland legislature appointed a joint committee to communicate directly with Pennsylvania. The committee's report adopted the conciliatory and polite tone of petitioners asking for action from Pennsylvania. It referred to slavery as a calamity. Maryland deplored it as much as Pennsylvania, the report said, but until such time as the institution was abolished, Marylanders had just as much a right to slaves as to any other property. "The existence of our happy Union depends," admonished the committee's report, "in a great degree, on preserving harmony among its members."

The entreaty did not fall on deaf ears. The governor of Pennsylvania noted the problem in his annual address to the legislature, and by 1825 the Maryland delegates had been met with approbation in Delaware. There they secured a fugitive slave bill that explicitly sanctioned the congressional Fugitive Slave Act of 1793, made it a crime against the state to obstruct fugitive slave rendition, and admonished ship captains not to leave the state with fugitive slaves. The act further ordered that all suspicious people of color being found without a pass would be taken up and treated as runaways. These were significant new policies, and they put a much greater onus on free blacks than had hitherto been done. But such a law must be understood in context. Almost alone among the states, Delaware vigorously prosecuted kidnappers. And among their 1826 laws was a stronger antikidnapping provision. It increased the number of lashes kidnappers would receive to sixty (from thirty-nine) before they would stand for an hour in the pillory. True, kidnappers would no longer have their ears nailed down to the pillory, nor would they have to face having the soft part cut off, as they had under Delaware's 1793 statute. But they now faced a fine of $1,000–2,000 and imprisonment for three to seven years, after which they would be "disposed of as a servant, to the highest bidder, for the period of seven years."

Pennsylvania officers received the Maryland delegation as well, although both the Pennsylvania Abolition Society and a delegation of Quakers made clear their opposition to passage of any act that might make matters easier for slavecatchers. On February 4, a fugitive slave bill was introduced to the Pennsylvania legislature that would have kept the provisions of 1820 in effect while also providing a procedure for fugitive slave reclamation. The bill quickly became the most contentious issue in the session. Opponents attempted to kill the bill through postponement, and only narrowly failed. Perhaps realizing they did not have the votes to end the matter, abolitionists turned their efforts to securing favorable amendments. They succeeded in winning

{ *Chapter 4* }

the concession that the slaveholder's oath would not be admitted into testimony, which became part of the compromise bill that William Meredith introduced to the assembly on February 13.

Even the compromise made abolitionists uneasy, and they deployed all manner of arguments to defeat it – procedural, moral, and constitutional. They moved to postpone yet again. Failing that, they fulminated against slavery in general. Some abolitionists complained that Pennsylvania had no business legislating on the subject of fugitive slaves. The fugitive slave clause was Congress's province, they argued, and the state had no business interfering. William Meredith rose to defend his compromise measure. He skillfully deflected the moral problems, both apologizing to those among his constituents who adhered to antislavery convictions and testifying to his own antislavery credentials. Nonetheless, he understood fugitive slave reclamation as a duty of the state, mandated by the U.S. Constitution. To those who argued that Pennsylvania had no business interfering with congressional legislation, he answered that the Pennsylvania law of 1820 had already done so when it prohibited aldermen and justices of the peace from taking jurisdiction under the Fugitive Slave Act of 1793. Abolitionists could hardly endorse the 1820 law (as they had) and now denounce this bill as unconstitutional.

Meredith's support for the bill did not rest on power and duty alone, but also upon right and justice. If Pennsylvania neglected to legislate on the procedure of the rendition of fugitive slaves, this left the vague evidentiary standards of the Fugitive Slave Act of 1793 in place. "Does it much conduce to our honour as a sovereign state," asked Meredith, "that any individual should exercise the privilege of entering our territory and seizing any negro, perhaps a Citizen, detaining him in custody, and finally dragging him before a Judge, and all this without proof or process of any kind?" The Fugitive Slave Act, we will recall, allowed precisely this to occur when it authorized slaveholders to seize their fugitives anywhere they found them and then take them before a judge or magistrate to secure their rendition. Under the Pennsylvania bill, slaveholders would have to first obtain a warrant from a judge or justice of the peace. Once executed (with the assistance of the state's peace officers), the warrant was returnable only before a judge. Aldermen, justices of the peace, and other petty magistrates were admonished under pain of misdemeanor not to take jurisdiction under the Fugitive Slave Act of 1793 and were prohibited by the statute from issuing certificates of removal. Judges could issue certificates of removal once "proof, to the satisfaction of such judge, that the person so seized or arrested" was in fact the claimant's fugitive slave. The Quaker amendment, forbidding the slaveholder's oath from being entered into evidence, remained within the bill. Meredith was essentially arguing that putting slavecatchers under fair legal procedure was the most just option. "To the free negroes, Citizens of this State," explained Meredith, the provisions of the bill "give them what, to our disgrace be it spoken, they have never yet had, equal protection with ourselves, in relation to personal liberty."

Equal protection was a big rhetorical claim, but there was truth to it. The proposed bill changed the legal procedure of federal fugitive slave rendition in three major ways. First, it provided a process for securing arrest warrants. This gave legal assistance — and oversight — to slaveholders before they seized fugitives. Second, it gave judges the discretion to commit a fugitive to jail if there was any question about his or her status, thereby allowing the fugitive (and his or her friends) to gather evidence. Third, it excluded the slaveholder's oath as evidence. This forced the slaveholder to arrive with enough impartial evidence to prove his or her claim. The bill may not have satisfied those abolitionists who objected to *any* measure that supported the rendition of fugitive slaves, but it did provide free blacks more protection. Perhaps more importantly, Meredith's claim shunted the debate off the track of absolute morality and onto that of equal legal protection. If free blacks could claim the same measure of protection against slaveholders' claims as any other citizen could, then the law might in fact be just.

Of course, one might object that the Pennsylvania bill did not repeal the Fugitive Slave Act of 1793, and as such slaveholders could still seize alleged fugitives whenever they pleased, under cover of federal law. Meredith owned up to this. But he argued that, should the legislature pass the bill before it, the Fugitive Slave Act would fall into comparative disuse. "At present," Meredith explained, "the fair claimant and the kidnapper are obliged to proceed in the same way; both seize the negro wherever they can find him, and without any sort of process." By passing a law placing the arrest procedure under cover of state law, this left the claimant with two options: seize a fugitive alone, or seek state help. If one sought state help, then they would have to follow state law, subjecting them to somewhat more of an inconvenience given the stricter evidentiary requirements and the necessity of obtaining an arrest warrant. But the alternative was to forego the use of any state court, leaving slaveholders with only a skeletal federal judiciary to process a claim and issue a certificate of removal. Even worse, seizing an alleged fugitive without a warrant rendered the slaveholder vulnerable to a kidnapping indictment, the end of which was an expensive trial and the potential of serving seven to twenty-one years in prison. "The moment," Meredith explained, "that you give the real claimant a mode, by which he may with tolerable facility and convenience assert his claim in a regular course of law, he will be sure in almost every case to avail himself of it. . . . The kidnapper indeed will not be disposed to take this course." The bill, in short, promised to separate the kidnapper from the legitimate claimant, and to protect both the free black and the slaveholder in their legitimate rights.

Meredith's long speech before the Pennsylvania House of Representatives was received favorably, but it failed to convince abolitionists. The measure came to a vote three days later and passed by the scant margin of 44–39. The bill "to give effect to the provisions of the constitution of the United States, relative to fugitives from labor, for the protection of free people of color, and to prevent kidnapping," was signed into law a month later, on March 26, 1826.

The history that brought the Pennsylvania personal liberty law to passage stretched back far further than the bill's immediate legislative record and encompassed far more than merely an abolitionist desire to make fugitive slave reclamation more difficult for slaveholders. The statute was a reflection of two competing struggles for the protection of rights. On the one hand, slaveholders asserted their constitutional right to reclaim runaways. On the other, abolitionists demanded stronger protection for free blacks caught up by unscrupulous kidnappers. While the two issues might have been separate in theory, they were joined in practice. Neither the abolitionist nor the slaveholder position was completely coherent or unified. Both had their theoretical and constitutional inconsistencies. Nonetheless, in the various political clashes between these two contending forces we can witness the compromises struck between two sides of a ferocious rights struggle.

Slaveholders pushed Congress to protect their property rights by impinging on both the rights of free blacks and state sovereignty. On two separate occasions, slaveholders moved for the adoption of federal law that would have required blacks (free and fugitive slave alike) either to carry proof of their freedom or to make their case in a slave state. They also demanded that federal law greatly restrict the discretionary power of northern judges and magistrates, in essence curbing state sovereignty. This was a muscular argument for national authority to protect abstract rights. The implication was that, if the Constitution granted a right, then it contemplated the means for its enforcement. This interpretation required that a positive right be inferred from a clause that essentially worked in the negative. Strictly construed, the fugitive slave clause *prevented* states from freeing fugitives and *instructed* them to deliver fugitives to their masters. If that meant that Congress had to direct state officers, then it could do so. Not that slaveholders put all their eggs in the federal basket. Maryland sent frequent entreaties to its neighboring states of Pennsylvania, Delaware, and New Jersey to press the rights of their citizens. Marylanders kept a steady stream of petitions before their legislature on the subject. It was just such entreaties that resulted in a reformation of the law of Delaware and Pennsylvania in 1826.

Abolitionists white and black struggled for their rights as well. They petitioned their state legislatures and Congress, seeking protection from kidnappers. They pushed for legislation that would subordinate the right of slaveholders to their fugitive property to the right of free blacks to be secure in their persons. They also did little to hide their goal, which was to rescue as many people from slavery as possible, whether this meant protecting the free black from kidnapping or the fugitive from being reclaimed. On the federal level, they succeeded in forcing Congress to place antikidnapping provisions in any fugitive slave bill they considered. And at the state level, they realized the Antikidnapping Act of 1820. Within this context, many abolitionists genuinely felt that the Personal Liberty Law of 1826 was a surrender of principle.

In truth, Pennsylvania's 1826 law can be cast as either a personal liberty law or a fugitive slave law, depending on how one reads it. If one thinks in terms of its source of authority, then it reads both ways. The law was passed both to execute the fugitive slave clause of the U.S. Constitution and to fulfill the state's obligation to protect the liberty of its residents. This bifurcated justification reflected Pennsylvania's commitment to fulfilling both its obligations. The contours of the bill also respected the established procedure for fugitive slave rendition: a summary hearing to determine the status of an alleged fugitive followed, when appropriate, by issuance of a certificate of removal. Pennsylvania's law did modify federal law by refusing jurisdiction to its petty magistrates and setting evidentiary standards considerably higher than those of the Fugitive Slave Act. And it also defined kidnapping as the removal of someone from Pennsylvania's borders without first obtaining a certificate of removal. Each party, in short, got something out of Pennsylvania's Personal Liberty Law of 1826. It was a compromise between two contending rights movements and one that took seriously the constitutional framework within which these claims for rights were made.

CHAPTER 5

Black Sailors, Kidnapped Freemen, and a Crisis in Northern Fugitive Slave Jurisprudence

While immediate negotiations with neighboring Maryland produced Pennsylvania's Personal Liberty Law of 1826, the law itself belonged to a more general historical movement. In the 1820s, northern states began passing personal liberty laws that ramped up protections for their free black populations. This movement was both an indication of political success by abolitionists and a legitimate response to the problem of kidnapping. Personal liberty laws often rested on the dual authority of national and state constitutions, thus purporting to balance the duties of fugitive slave rendition and the protection of free blacks from kidnapping. Southern states also passed laws protecting their residents from an imminent danger. South Carolina would lead the section in 1822 in passing its Negro Seamen Act, a law which required that any black sailors coming into port be jailed for the duration of their stay. South Carolina passed the law on the basis of its sovereign power to protect its residents. Free blacks, South Carolina claimed, disrupted their social order, undermined slavery, and threatened the state with insurrection. South Carolina rested its position on the reserved, sovereign authority of any state to prevent what it considered to be a class of dangerous people from entering its borders. Other southern states followed suit.

Both these laws would be challenged in court in the 1820s and 1830s. The northern and southern defenders of state sovereignty responded acidly to claims that these laws violated constitutional integrity and national unity. The inability of a U.S. Supreme Court judge to persuade South Carolinians that their Negro Seamen Act was unconstitutional — and his virtual social banishment as a result of his attempt — underlined the acrimony. The northern personal liberty laws also threatened national unity. Whether the laws stood on solid constitutional ground or not, they had the practical effect of making life more difficult for slaveholders claiming their runaway slaves. It became more costly to transport the number of witnesses needed to prove a claim in Pennsylvania, and one had to risk a jury trial if seizing a fugitive in New York. Compounding this was abolitionists' earnest defense of every fugitive that aimed every available legal weapon against slaveholders. Laws that protected the liberty of free blacks could be exploited to protect fugitive slaves, and abolitionists defended both with zeal.

Two things made the 1830s and 1840s different from the first two decades of the nineteenth century. First, both abolitionists and slaveholders sharpened their arguments. Immediatism swept abolitionism, resulting in a movement that insisted upon calling slavery a sin, organized new societies directly devoted to action and confrontation, and demanded that all necessary constitutional weapons be turned upon slavery. Even though these immediatists conceded basic constitutional principles that protected slavery — for instance, abolitionists understood that constitutional arrangements prevented Congress from effecting a general emancipation — their new stance was militant enough to shock the consciences of slaveholders.

Second, judges became increasingly willing to speak out on constitutional issues. This had its greatest effect in northern courtrooms where slaveholders argued that the personal liberty laws impeded their rights. Abolitionists responded in kind, deploying arguments about the unconstitutionality of the Fugitive Slave Act. This was not necessarily new — lawyers had been putting forward these arguments in northern courts for some time. But judges' behavior changed. Where once judges largely deferred to legislatures and avoided confrontational issues, now they seemed more willing to weigh in on constitutional disputes. One northern judge declared that the personal liberty laws of the states were unconstitutional because only Congress could legislate under the fugitive slave clause. Another suggested that the Fugitive Slave Act was unconstitutional because Congress had no warrant to legislate under the clause. Still others simply moored themselves to the central issues in a given case without wading out into troubled waters. But whether cautious judges were the rule rather than the exception mattered little. The result was jurisprudential confusion by the close of the 1830s.

Pennsylvania was not alone among the states in passing laws that clarified state procedure in fugitive slave rendition. In the 1820s, New Jersey, Indiana, Delaware, and New York all passed such laws. These laws varied in their specifics. On one end of the spectrum stood the laws friendly to slaveholders. Delaware's law, highly influenced by the official delegation from Maryland, gave slaveholders security against abolitionists and required all blacks who were strangers to carry passes or risk being jailed and sold as a fugitive slave. On the other end stood the laws least friendly to slaveholders. New York's law, for instance, allowed alleged fugitives recourse either to habeas corpus or *de homine replegiando*, which had the potential advantage of offering a jury trial to alleged fugitives. Whether a jury was better than a judge or not for a fugitive was arguable, but the constitutional point was meaningful. A fugitive had the right to a jury trial before being taken from the state of New York. This was exceptional only insofar as it deviated from a strict interpretation of the Fugitive Slave Act of 1793, which had specified a summary hearing for fugitive slave rendition. Most states that had passed laws governing fugitive slave rendition had followed the congressional lead. Indiana, New Jersey, and Pennsylvania — the other states to pass laws in the 1820s — had all adhered to this interpretation. New York went further.

The same constitutional source that fed personal liberty laws also nourished illiberal laws restricting the rights of free blacks in North America. The states had, of course, long regulated their domestic relations along arbitrary lines, creating different laws to govern whites than those that governed others. But in the federal union, these domestic relations impacted more than just fugitive slaves. In 1822, South Carolina's Negro Seamen Act mandated that all black sailors who came into port, whether they were freemen or not, be jailed for the duration of their visit. The ship's captain was to pay all associated expenses with the lodging of his black seamen. If the captain refused, he faced a fine, and the black sailor faced enslavement.

It was not a fair law, and it had constitutional problems. Blacks could claim citizenship in some states, and at the very least ought to have had reciprocity in South Carolina through the privileges and immunities clause. Even if one overlooked Article IV, the Negro Seamen Act substantially burdened interstate commerce. Boston ship captains were now being taxed if they carried black sailors through the port of Charleston. And what of black British sailors? They were governed by treaties and, by the supremacy clause, treaties trumped state laws. Why pass a law so disagreeable to the provisions of the United States Constitution? In a word, fear.

The South Carolina legislature passed the Negro Seamen Act in the shadow of the fabled and failed Denmark Vesey conspiracy. Denmark Vesey was a free black, a carpenter, and a preacher. He had won a lottery in 1799 and used the proceeds to purchase his freedom and establish his own carpentry workshop. He later founded a black church and became a leader of Charleston's free black community. Free blacks like Vesey had been a growing part of the urban South in the early republic, even if they occupied precarious ground. Then the unthinkable happened — or at least was rumored to have happened. In 1822, several slaves confessed to their masters that Vesey and other free blacks had attempted to entice them into an insurrection. A wave of panic swept over Charleston. Subsequent trials before hastily established inquiry courts ended with the hanging of thirty-six blacks (including Denmark Vesey) and the banishing of forty-three more. But the fear of free blacks enticing slaves to insurrection lingered, and the Negro Seamen Act was its legacy.

The law underwent immediate challenge. Henry Elkison, a Jamaican-born, free black British subject jailed under the Negro Seamen Act, petitioned for a writ of habeas corpus returnable before the U.S. circuit court and Supreme Court Justice William Johnson. Elkison's lawyers contended that the law was unconstitutional because it violated the commerce clause. Lawyers for South Carolina argued that the sovereign state of South Carolina never surrendered such vital and paramount rights. If those rights conflicted with the treaty-making power of the federal government or with the commerce clause, then so be it. Justice William Johnson disagreed. In *Elkison v. Deliesseline* (1823), he gave his opinion that the Negro Seamen Act was in conflict with the U.S. Constitution and thus void. Nonetheless, he could not find a remedy for Henry Elkison. No federal law allowed him to grant a writ of habeas corpus to someone in state custody. In short, his ruling on the constitutionality of the Negro Seamen Act was unenforceable dicta.

Johnson had gone out of his way to avoid bringing the federal government and South Carolina into direct conflict. His ruling admitted the limited nature of federal authority and the great powers left the states under the Constitution. This did not assuage outraged South Carolinians. So fierce was the assault that Johnson, a South Carolinian himself who had read law in the office of Charles Cotesworth Pinckney, retired to Philadelphia rather than Charleston. South Carolina did revise its Negro Seamen Act in 1823, exempting free blacks serving on board warships, making exceptions for those shipwrecked, and moderating the penalties for free blacks whose captains did not redeem them from the sheriff (reducing the penalty from enslavement to corporal punishment). This revised Negro Seamen Act became a model for other states. Georgia passed its own version in 1829, and by 1840 North Carolina, Florida, and Alabama followed suit. Louisiana and Texas would both add their own versions before 1860, although by then the laws had largely fallen into disuse and several states (including South Carolina) had repealed the law.

The illiberal Negro seamen acts and the liberal personal liberty laws of the 1820s shared a common constitutional source: the power of the states to protect their residents, reserved to it explicitly by the Tenth Amendment. But each made a different peace with U.S. sovereignty. In the case of personal liberty laws, states had to contend with both the fugitive slave clause and a congressional law interpreting it. Congress had prescribed a summary hearing for slaveholders to obtain a certificate of removal, had extended jurisdiction to state judges and magistrates, and had left antikidnapping laws in the hands of the states. By the 1820s, the states had responded by providing their own summary remedies in the form of habeas corpus hearings that could protect against potential kidnappers. (New York was the exception, still allowing a jury trial.) This was the nucleus of a constitutional settlement in which congressional interpretation set a framework for state action. South Carolina, by contrast, claimed that only the state could determine where its sovereign limits lay. The Negro Seamen Act conflicted with the commerce clause and with the treaty-making power, but South Carolinians refused to admit that federal law or treaties trumped their sovereign right of self protection. Although South Carolina's supreme court used procedural technicalities in two subsequent cases to limit the law's effectiveness, the judges never addressed the constitutional issues. And the state's legislature and executive refused to submit to outside judgment on the matter.

Historical events conspired to harden South Carolina's position. Increasingly confident and righteous abolitionists heeded the call to action from men like James Forten (the black Philadelphian who had protested discriminatory bills by publishing *A Series of Letters by a Man of Color*) a decade before. These abolitionists tested the moral foundation of gradual abolition and found it soft. Their conversion to immediatism — the notion that slavery was sinful and should be immediately abolished — was varied and diffuse. Nonetheless, from such sundry conversions would be born a singular movement. In 1833, immediatists came together under the banner of the American Anti-Slavery Society (AASS). William Lloyd Garrison, publisher of the immediatist newspaper *The Liberator*, authored the society's declaration of sentiments. The declaration contemplated a moral assault on slavery based on moral suasion and political action. Convincing the public that slavery was a moral and spiritual travesty required a propaganda campaign, and publishing proliferated.

Abolitionists also changed their tenor. To win over the court of public opinion, abolitionists began building a case. Literally. They amassed evidence in the form of testimony and physical artifacts and presented them to the public as if it was a jury. Abolitionists prosecuted slavery mercilessly, giving the lie to the paternalistic protests of masters who claimed that they loved their slaves and that their slaves loved them. This was an aggressive rhetoric that abandoned politeness. It was a democratic rhetoric, too. Invoking metaphors of a public prosecution sought to put the whole institution on trial before We the People of the United States and to demand political action against slavery. The AASS admitted that its options were limited by the Constitution. Congress had no power to abolish slavery outright (only the states could abolish it within their own borders). But Congress did have power to make "all needful Rules and Regulations" for United States territories. This meant it could prevent slavery there. Article IV, Section 3, also gave Congress plenary power to admit new states, so abolitionists reasoned that Congress could refuse to admit new slave states. It could abolish slavery in the District of Columbia. More arguably, Congress could prohibit the interstate slave trade. These were all areas where the Constitution granted power to Congress, and abolitionists were erecting a muscular constitutional edifice from which to attack slavery at the edges of the slave states.

For slaveholders, such a call could not have come at a worse time. The Denmark Vesey conspiracy was followed by the revolt of Nat Turner of Virginia in 1831. Turner's band of rebels had executed whites in a rampage that seemingly came from nowhere, exciting slaveholders' fears that potential insurrection lurked just beneath still waters. A copy of *An Appeal to the Colored Citizens of the World*, written by David Walker — a free black — and published in Boston in 1829, turned up in Charleston. Walker's polemic denounced slavery in uncompromising terms and called on slaves to rebel. Added to this was the growing success of the antislavery movement in Great Britain. With the founding of the Society for the Amelioration and Gradual Abolition of Slavery in 1823, English abolitionists concentrated on undermining slavery by attacking its economic foundation. In addition to organizing massive petition campaigns, abolitionists attacked protective duties on sugar. And they flooded England with antislavery pamphlets after 1823, producing more than half a million in 1831 alone. The hammer finally came down on British West Indian slavery in 1833, when Parliament provided for a compensated, general emancipation. For southern slaveholders who had long identified with their British Caribbean counterparts and had believed that the right of property was sacred, this was an ill omen indeed. Faced with the example of the British parliament's naked deployment of power, U.S. slaveholders had reason to fear the worst.

It was in this context that fugitive slave rendition began to be viewed differently, even if the reality was that practice did not change much. Pennsylvania abolitionists had long used all available legal means to discourage slavecatchers, whether they pressed legitimate claims or not. And kidnappers were also clearly abroad in the border states. Stories abounded of men professing to engage young boys as chimney sweeps and then selling them; of enticing boys and girls onto ships where they were chained below deck for transport to slave markets; and of whole kidnapping rings working the docks in port cities. In 1828, Philadelphia's city council instructed the mayor to offer rewards for information leading to the prosecution of kidnappers and granted him a discretionary budget of $500 to combat "this outrage upon the rights of our free citizens." It produced results. Kidnappers were found, arrested, and bound over. Several ended up serving lengthy terms, although the ring's leader evaded capture. The mayor reported that ten victims had been restored to freedom.

The old trick of kidnapping under cover of fugitive slave rendition also persisted. A report to the Pennsylvania Abolition Society recorded the case of a free black nearly kidnapped by legal means. In 1830, the Recorder of Philadelphia granted an arrest warrant to a Marylander named Massey who had come seeking a fugitive slave. Or so he said. Massey and his brother arrested a woman and brought her to the recorder, who heard the case promptly and without giving the prisoner time to procure counsel. Under the Pennsylvania Personal Liberty Law of 1826, the slaveholder's testimony would not be entered into evidence. So Massey produced his brother, who swore he knew that the woman's mother had been a slave, for she had been the property of Massey's grandfather and then father. Massey's father had then gone bankrupt, and Massey's brother swore that he had purchased the woman at a sheriff's sale and then sold her to Massey. This testimony satisfied Pennsylvania's requirement that the slaveholder's own evidence not be admitted, and the recorder seemed disposed to grant the certificate of removal. But then a "coloured man of respectable appearance" testified that the prisoner's mother had been manumitted before the prisoner's birth. The recorder was not inclined to believe the word of this stranger, but he did grant a postponement, giving the alleged fugitive time to mount a defense. Application was made to the Pennsylvania Abolition Society, which procured her counsel.

At the next hearing, the prisoner's lawyer attacked Massey's seemingly strong case. He first objected to the claimant's evidence. The sole witness had, after all, sold the woman to the claimant, and he therefore had an interest in proving the title good. (If the title was bad, then he risked being the target of a lawsuit.) The recorder overruled the objection. The lawyer then produced a certificate of manumission for the woman's mother. The black stranger's story now had independent verification. The recorder examined the manumission and then handed it to the claimant. Was it genuine? Massey didn't know. Was that not his brother's signature witnessing it, he was asked? Massey prevaricated. He had an uncle of the same name, he said. Massey's lawyer attempted to argue that the manumission was issued after the woman at the bar was born, but the defense intimated that they had witnesses ready to testify as to her age and prove her free. The recorder thereupon granted a continuance to give Massey a chance to amass more conclusive evidence that the woman prisoner was in fact his slave. He never did. A few days later, Massey offered to sell the woman to abolitionists. Sensing his claims were bogus, they declined. When the recorder held the next hearing, Massey was nowhere to be found. The claim, it would appear, had been a scam.

That the unscrupulous might attempt such things seemed unremarkable to the Pennsylvania Abolition Society. More concerning was that the recorder had appeared to take these claims at face value. Facing an empty seat at the plaintiff's table, the recorder had declared that he had been ready to hand the woman over to the claimant on the strength of the evidence presented. The abolitionists, meanwhile, did some research. Massey's grandfather, it appeared, had left no slave to his son. No sheriff had sold off a slave of Massey's father to satisfy debts. The two men had concocted a fiction and very nearly succeeded in convincing a judge to extinguish a woman's inalienable liberty. "Comment is unnecessary," read the report to the society.

We should be careful of taking the report at its word. The report's comments were private, directed to the society, not a public accusation backed by courtroom evidence. Moreover, the bare face of the record indicates a more thoughtful court. The recorder had been cautious and forced the claimant to produce evidence. If he had wished to disregard the manumission or place the burden of proof further on the alleged fugitive to prove her freedom, he might have done it before granting a continuance. Instead, the recorder's behavior seemed to indicate that the system worked, that kidnappers might be distinguished from legitimate claimants.

There was evidence of successful rendition processes throughout the country and in multiple states. Judges seemed disposed to do their duty, to weigh evidence and grant legitimate claimants their fugitives. To take another example from Pennsylvania, consider the case of Charles Brown, a young boy claimed as a fugitive slave in 1835. The Recorder of Pittsburgh issued a written opinion in that case that illustrated this devotion to duty. The recorder expressed great sorrow in having to reduce a boy to slavery, and he confessed that he had been partial to the boy's case. But it did not avail the fugitive in the end. "I am bound by my oath of office to support the constitution of the United States, and the constitution of Pennsylvania," he explained, "not to let my feelings as a man interfere with my duties as a judge." Such a sentiment might give us the false impression that the fugitive's attorneys asked the judge to set aside the law in favor of humanity. They had not. They had instead argued every procedural and evidentiary point. They challenged the deed by which the slaveholder had given his agent power of attorney; they argued the claim was insufficiently supported and then objected to a continuance in order to procure more supporting evidence; they asked that witnesses shuttled in all the way from Maryland be disqualified because the claimant paid their travel expenses. They did, in short, what any good lawyer in a courtroom would do, which was to use all available legal tactics and tricks to secure the end goal for their client: freedom. In the end, they could not overcome the strength of the claim. Abolitionists' loss helped prove that the Pennsylvania Personal Liberty Law of 1826 could distinguish genuine claimants from kidnappers.

Even if Pennsylvania's law worked, its enhanced protections for free blacks had consequences. Attorneys for the claimant of Charles Brown complained mightily that they were forced to go to such great lengths to secure witnesses to make their case. This was, they warned, a subversion of constitutional rights. "We cannot fail of being convinced," said the attorneys, after quoting both the fugitive slave clause and the privileges and immunities clause, "that no impediment can properly be thrown in the way of the master of a fugitive slave, to recover his property, in a summary and speedy manner, by any act of a state legislature, at variance in its provisions with the constitution of the U. States and the acts of congress on this subject." This sentiment had been voiced before. A Philadelphia lawyer heard from his indignant Maryland client in 1829 that had he known how difficult it would be to recover his fugitives in the state, he would not have gone to the trouble and expense of hiring a lawyer to do so. A slaveholder pursuing his slaves in Pennsylvania in 1833 was stopped by a group of abolitionists who attempted to arrest him for kidnapping. The slaveholder sued in federal court, prompting a tirade from Supreme Court Justice Henry Baldwin about the indecency of equating a legitimate claimant of a fugitive slave with a kidnapper. Lawyers were coming around to the argument that slaveholders' rights were constitutional and paramount. If this was so, then no state could materially alter fugitive slave rendition procedure. By implication, the personal liberty laws that attempted to guard against fraudulent fugitive slave claims were void. It was a case where states' rights had to recede in favor of individual rights secured by the Constitution. But some public entity had to enforce this right against the states. Speaking from the floor of the U.S. Senate in 1836, John Pendleton King of Georgia put it rather bluntly. Slaveholders gained the right to their fugitive slaves from the Constitution, "and the slaveholder had a constitutional right to the whole power, moral and physical, of [the federal] Government to enforce it."

King's was an interesting way to render the power of government— as a force for the protection of rights—because it was the same justification offered by abolitionists, who had complained vocally about the "outrage upon the rights" of their free black citizens. In this manner, the question of who the Constitution empowered to pass fugitive slave legislation was recast. If the slaveholder's property right was paramount, then potentially any state law which complicated the matter was void. If the free person's liberty right was paramount, then the state could assert its full sovereign authority to protect its residents.

No state had gone further than New York in securing favorable legislation for its free black population, guaranteeing alleged fugitives access to the writ *de homine replegiando* with its guarantee of a jury trial. In 1834, a man named Jack was arrested in New York City as a fugitive. His lawyers sued out a writ *de homine replegiando*. The slaveholder demurred, claiming that Jack's claims to the writ were unsustainable at law, even before the issue came to a jury. In essence, the slaveholder argued that her right to Jack was guaranteed and governed by the Fugitive Slave Act of 1793 and that this automatically superseded any state-mandated procedure. The trial judge agreed and dismissed the case. Jack's lawyers appealed to the appellate division of the New York Supreme Court, which upheld the trial court. Associate Justice Samuel Nelson wrote the opinion.

Nelson's life had hitherto been unremarkable. He was born four years after the ratification of the Constitution, so he had no living memory of the document's adoption. Educated at Middlebury College in Vermont, he read law and entered private practice in New York. He was an office seeker. After serving briefly as a regional postmaster, he obtained a state circuit court judgeship in 1823. In 1831 he became an associate justice of the Supreme Court of New York and went on to be its chief justice in 1837. In 1845, Nelson became the only one of President John Tyler's six Supreme Court nominations to survive the confirmation process in the Senate. This last bit of trivia may be the most that distinguished Nelson. Not that he was incompetent by any stretch. He was a capable lawyer, and his jurisprudence bespoke of technical fluency. Philosophically he was a committed nationalist in the mold of John Marshall or Joseph Story, even if he lacked the former's grandeur or the latter's industry. He was instead a model of adroit mediocrity, and he issued few memorable opinions in his career. *Jack v. Martin* was one of those few.

Nelson situated the case as a conflict-of-laws case, thus making the question one of whether a certificate of removal could be interrupted by a parallel procedure by jury to determine an alleged fugitive's status. Undergirding his opinion was the assumption that concurrent powers tended to conflict, thus bringing disorder. This assumption showed little regard for the actual practice of fugitive slave rendition. Hitherto, slaveholders in New York had shown no reticence about using state law to recapture fugitive slaves. Disgusted abolitionists reported (in a typical story) that a Baltimore slaveholder had arrived in Kinderhook, New York, and used a habeas corpus hearing to secure a certificate of removal for a fugitive who had been two years resident in the state. But Nelson took no note of such practices. Instead he sought in the opinion to answer definitively whether the power to pass laws defining fugitive slave rendition lay with the federal or the state governments. He sided firmly with the federal government. His rationale was fairly simple. Powers could either be concurrent or exclusive. If exclusive, the matter was settled. If a power was concurrent, then any state law would be superseded should Congress legislate. Nelson made it clear that he believed the power exclusive in Congress. But even if it were concurrent, he reasoned, congressional law superseded New York law, and that ended the matter.

Nelson's reasoning was subject to the objection — raised, incidentally, by Jack's attorneys — that the Constitution had not given Congress authority to legislate. In other words, the power was, by implication, reserved to the states. To overcome this objection, Nelson looked to the clause's purpose. At the time of the Constitution's adoption, argued Nelson, slavery was on its way out in the North. It was "natural," he surmised, for the southern states to fear that northern states might "be tempted to adopt a course of legislation that would embarrass the owners pursuing their fugitive slaves, if not discharge them from service, and invite escape by affording a place of refuge." Slaveholders had already experienced such problems under the Articles of Confederation, and in any case the trouble generated over slavery in the Constitutional Convention "was well calculated to confirm [slaveholders'] strongest apprehensions." To remedy *this* evil, the fugitive slave clause was proposed. Its very existence implied a doubt on the part of the Framers that sovereign states would do so on their own. If this point was conceded, then the purpose of the clause was "palpable," and judges should construe it so as to guarantee that its purpose was carried out.

This jurisprudential approach gave the ambiguous text a definitive meaning. If the enforcement of the clause was left up to the states, then they might encumber slaveholders with lengthy procedural hurdles, in essence using the law to deny them their constitutional rights. Such an interpretation, Nelson surmised, was untenable. But Nelson was not content to sit back on the question of reasonableness. The text itself, he declared, mandated congressional legislation. The fugitive slave clause gave an unqualified command that the fugitive "shall be delivered up on claim of the party to whom such service or labor may be due." Since the states had already parted with the power to free fugitives upon arrival in their state, and because they might utilize state law to defeat the rights of slaveholders, the only body left was "Congress, where the rights and interests of the different sections of the country" were represented. There were other reasons that Nelson gave for his opinion. The Fugitive Slave Act of 1793, he reminded everyone, was a "contemporaneous exposition of the constitutional provision," and we should hesitate some forty years out to question those who had a more intimate knowledge of the Constitution itself.

Federal exclusivity had big theoretical consequences, the most momentous of which was throwing the antikidnapping laws into doubt. It was "plausible" to Nelson that kidnapping under cover of the Fugitive Slave Act could occur. But this proved only "the defectiveness of the law of Congress, not the authority of the State." Anyone concerned with this situation, Nelson concluded, should petition Congress to amend the Fugitive Slave Act rather than try "to amend it by state legislation." The states might still punish kidnapping, but not if the kidnapper used federal legal process.

Nelson's opinion required a finding of congressional exclusivity, a difficult task given that the fugitive slave clause had no congressional grant. To prove his point, Nelson relied on reason and inference. He followed the simple rules of statutory construction in much the same way Justice William Tilghman of Pennsylvania had two decades earlier. Both justices considered the fugitive slave clause vital and the faithful exercise of it paramount. But Tilghman's historical interpretation had justified a shared-power approach that protected free blacks' liberty as well as slaveholders' rights. Nelson's history precluded any state involvement on the principle of national exclusivity. Even if the text of the Constitution did not explicitly grant power to Congress, reason dictated it. Even if it were a concurrent power — and Nelson clearly did not believe that it was — the simple fact that Congress had legislated preempted the states. Not surprisingly, Nelson's ruling was celebrated in the south. *The Mississippian* lauded the "important decision" that declared New York's law to be "unconstitutional and void, on the ground that the state legislature could not prescribe another mode of ascertaining the title of the master than that directed in the act of Congress." The *Richmond Enquirer* complained that some southern papers were inflaming public opinion by refusing to report that the judges of the north were faithfully upholding the Constitution against northern personal liberty laws.

But *Jack v. Martin* was extraordinary, not ordinary, and this cannot be forgotten. Most judges did not even consider the possibility of throwing out state personal liberty laws. Supreme Court Justice Smith Thompson considered the very same law shortly after the New York Supreme Court did, in *In re Martin* (although of the same name, the case was unrelated to *Jack v. Martin*). While he explicitly rejected the arguments of counsel asking him to strike down the Fugitive Slave Act of 1793 as unconstitutional, he also refused to pass judgment on New York's personal liberty law. He noted that state laws providing for the specific mode of fugitive slave reclamation were, provided they were in conformity with the act of Congress, perfectly legitimate.

Furthermore, Nelson's opinion was undermined on appeal. In the state of New York's judicial hierarchy, the state's supreme court sat beneath the Court for the Correction of Errors (CCE), a body that consisted of the Senate and either the chancellor (if the case was appealed from the supreme court) or the justices of the supreme court (if the case was appealed from the chancery). The body voted on the outcome but did not provide an "opinion of the court." Any opinions were delivered seriatum. The CCE affirmed the supreme court's ruling, but the two opinions delivered contradicted each other. Senator Isaac Bishop's written opinion largely accepted Nelson's reasoning about national exclusivity in fugitive slave reclamation, although he fully expected the reclamation process to include fair proceedings before state judicial officers who could protect free blacks from kidnapping.

In another written opinion, Chancellor Reuben Walworth rejected Nelson's instrumentalist reading of congressional exclusivity. The Constitution certainly had not expressly given the power to Congress, nor could it be inferred from the "mere fact that it may be more convenient that Congress should exercise that power, than that it should be exercised by the State Legislatures." In Walworth's reading, the fugitive slave clause acknowledged the reality of the common law right of recaption, which he supposed universal in the states, all of which (excepting Massachusetts) still suffered slavery at the time of the Constitutional Convention. It just was not controversial. What else, he asked, explained the unanimity of the delegates on the adoption of the fugitive slave clause, especially in the face of resistance to the other clauses protecting slavery? Walworth settled on the position that had been sustained by courts throughout the 1810s and 1820s — the power was concurrent, and both federal and state law might govern procedure. In the present case, however, the defendant's legal admission that he was held as a slave by the laws of Louisiana defeated his claim. In short, the chancellor said that the New York Supreme Court had made the right decision for the wrong reasons.

At least one northern court in the 1830s came close to declaring the Fugitive Slave Act of 1793 void, although it stopped short. In New Jersey, Alex Helmsly was apprehended as a fugitive slave after an arrest warrant had been issued under the state's personal liberty law. He sued out a writ of habeas corpus heard by Chief Justice Joseph C. Hornblower, who remanded the prisoner with instructions to the sheriff to bring the fugitive back when the full court was in session. In the meantime, another court issued to the slaveholder a certificate of removal for Alex Helmsly, although that court refused to issue certificates for Helmsly's wife and children. Then, in the February 1836 term, the full bench of the New Jersey Supreme Court heard the petition for a writ of habeas corpus as *New Jersey v. Sheriff of Burlington* and released Alex Helmsly on the grounds that the proceedings under which he had been arrested were irregular. In his unreported opinion, Chief Justice Hornblower denied Congress had constitutional warrant to legislate on fugitive slave rendition. His reasoning was largely structural. Given that the first two sections in Article IV articulated four principles of comity, it was notable that Section 1 (the full faith and credit clause) contained a grant of congressional power while Section 2 (the privileges and immunities clause, fugitives from justice clause, and fugitive slave clause) did not. The natural inference was that it was intentional both times — the Framers anticipated a uniform rule in one case and not in the others.

Chief Justice Hornblower had exposed the structural deficiencies of Congress's authority, but he did not stop there. He fortified this analysis with practical reasoning. The full faith and credit clause required that states recognize "the public Acts, Records, and judicial Proceedings of every other State." Congress was given the power to "prescribe the manner" in which those official acts would be received. To Hornblower, it made practical sense to have a uniform rule. Otherwise, one state could prescribe how its acts would be received in other states, which was of course an absurdity. The same was not true, Hornblower reasoned, regarding the three clauses in Section 2. Privileges and immunities were local by nature, and a uniform rule passed by Congress could not govern them all. Likewise, the act of arresting and delivering up fugitives (from justice or labor) would necessarily involve state officers. The federal government could not direct state officers (they were, after all, not agents of the federal government). It therefore made sense that these matters of comity were left to the states to govern.

Although impossible to prove, it is highly probable that New Jersey Chief Justice Hornblower had read New York Chief Justice Nelson's opinion in *Jack v. Martin*, which had given the opposite rationale for the Framers' intent and the desirability of a uniform rule. Hornblower's arguments were not without their own problems, but they were a sufficient counterweight. Nonetheless, we must not make too much of it. Hornblower himself hastened to add: "It is not my intention to express any definitive opinion on the validity of the act of Congress." The Fugitive Slave Act was not even before the court, as the proceeding in question was held underneath the New Jersey personal liberty law. Hornblower's long opinion was therefore dicta. The fact that the other judges on the court concurred but delivered their opinions seriatim leads one to believe that he did not command a majority for his dicta. But we should also not make too little of it either. Hornblower's opinion exposed the gaps in Nelson's reasoning. And against Nelson's flat assertion that the individual states might "encumber" or "embarrass" slaveholders' rights if legislation was left to them, Hornblower reminded everyone that it was a person's liberty that was at stake. Counsel for the slaveholder argued that cases of mistaken identity or kidnapping could be properly handled before courts in slaveholders' home state, and he cited Chief Justice Tilghman's opinion in *Wright v. Deacon* (1819) in support. Hornblower left no doubt about his feelings on the matter. "So long as I sit upon this bench," snarled Hornblower, "I never can, no, I never will, yield to such a doctrine." His words are worth quoting at length:

> What, first transport a man out of the state, on the charge of his being a slave, and try the truth of the allegation afterward — separate him from the place, it may be, of his nativity — the abode of his relatives, his friends, and his witnesses — transport him in chains to Missouri or Arkansas, with the cold comfort that if a freeman he may there assert and establish his freedom!

There could be no doubt about Hornblower's sentiments regarding the sanctity of freedom, even if he could not reach the legal conclusion that he wanted in this habeas corpus hearing.

By 1836, three interpretations of the fugitive slave clause were at war in northern courts. The first was the one steeped in tradition. It regarded fugitive slave rendition as a concurrent power in which state officers, directed by state legal procedure, might operate under congressional interpretation of the fugitive slave clause as requiring a summary hearing to grant slaveholders certificates of removal. State and federal judges had largely accepted this interpretation and had demonstrated respect for state protections of free black populations. Abolitionists had developed a second interpretation. Seeking to protect free blacks and fugitive slaves alike, they strictly construed the Constitution to deny congressional authority to pass fugitive slave legislation. This would leave the execution of the clause in the hands of the states, where abolitionist influence could produce legislation less favorable to claimants. A third, proslavery, interpretation advanced congressional exclusivity, based on the following series of propositions: the Constitution cemented a union by introducing compromise among the various states; maintenance of the union depended upon faithful execution of the Constitution's terms; it could not be presumed that the free states would faithfully execute the fugitive slave clause, hence its addition in the federal Constitution. If one accepted these premises, then it was rational that the Framers (and hence the Constitution itself) contemplated federal exclusivity in fugitive slave rendition. This proslavery interpretation could take a second line of reasoning. If one assumed that the power was concurrent, then the supremacy clause meant that congressional legislation preempted any state regulations.

Each of these interpretations was flawed. The abolitionist interpretation embraced the constitutional principles of strict construction and states' rights — firm ground given the rise of states' rights ideas nationally in the Age of Jackson. Nonetheless, abolitionist jurists had never successfully explained why a congressional law which had been in operation for decades was so clearly unconstitutional. The proslavery position rested upon a constitutional jurisprudence of reason and inference. But this position had to reason around the fugitive slave clause's lack of a grant of congressional power. It also had to explain why a power which had been concurrently exercised for so long was, in actuality, exclusive. The traditional interpretation enjoyed the weight of authority and practice. It admitted to a flexible federalism that allowed Congress to set interpretive rules within which the states could act. This had long governed constitutional practice, long enough to be its own kind of practical jurisprudence. But for all its merits, this position was undermined by constitutional objections raised on either side of it.

There were other stakes in the 1830s. With their Negro seamen acts, slaveholding states had also rested on their sovereign authority to deny entry to black sailors, whether or not this violated the commerce clause or the treaty clause. The fact that the personal liberty laws also rested upon the sovereign state's police power raised a disconcerting parallel between the two. With sectional friction on the rise in the 1830s, the old conflicts over fugitive slave rendition took on new meaning, and judges became bolder in their judicial pronouncements. But they were not able to resolve the sectional conflicts with their actions.

CHAPTER 6

Arresting Margaret

While the jurisprudence over fugitive slave rendition was fracturing in the North, the central figure in the case of *Prigg v. Pennsylvania* was living in relative freedom as a free black, first in a slave state and then in a free state. Margaret (Margaret Morgan after she married the free black Pennsylvanian Jerry Morgan) had never been treated as a slave. She had lived peacefully, if not also painfully aware of the disabilities that her skin color imposed upon her in the free American republic. Her rights, privileges, and duties were defined not by liberal theory or democratic citizenship but instead by her status. And status was left to the states to determine. For Margaret, being born in the slave state of Maryland made all the difference. Maryland law defined her, constrained her, and ultimately doomed her to bondage.

Nonetheless, her story is more complicated than such a simple assessment allows. Maryland law admitted the presence of both black slaves and free blacks. It made provisions for manumission. Maryland's courts protected free blacks and granted petitions for freedom. The situation may not have been rosy — far from it — but it was also not hopeless for blacks with claims to freedom. Slaveholders depended upon the law to maintain their property, and this sometimes meant being taken to court by their slaves who sued for their freedom. Slaveholders always had the upper hand, but they did not always win.

Slaveholders had to know the law in the same way that any layperson has to have a fundamental grasp of the rudiments of law in order to conduct business in day-to-day life. Nonetheless, few laypersons followed the official reports of Maryland's Court of Appeals, kept up with the legal digests, or read statutes carefully. Much of the law discussed in this chapter may have been foreign to the principal characters. But they nonetheless knew the law — or thought they knew it — and their behavior often reveals this. The historian's task is to elucidate both realities—both the law as it existed before Margaret's arrest and the ways in which people's perception of the law (even when wrong) guided their actions.

A quick word about this chapter's title is in order. "Arresting Margaret" suggests a legitimacy about her removal to Maryland, a legitimacy strongly disputed by the state of Pennsylvania and by abolitionists ever after. But we must distinguish between Margaret's arrest and her removal to Maryland. Margaret was arrested by a warrant properly issued by Pennsylvania law. She was removed by force, and her captors did not have a certificate of removal from a federal or state court. Her removal might still have been an abduction or might have been her captors exercising a constitutional right by themselves. But in the end, Margaret's dilemma was the same one that was posed over and over again by the fugitive slave clause's operation—what separated a fugitive slave rendition from a kidnapping?

Her name was Margaret, but we know little about her. We do not know when she was born or how she was raised. This much is sure: her parents were the slaves of John Ashmore of Harford County, Maryland. Born in 1760, Ashmore was a prosperous mill owner and farmer. He enlarged his holdings in Harford County and rubbed shoulders with many of the older, established slaveholders, including the Prigg and Forwood families. We don't know what kind of man Ashmore was, but we do know that he allowed two married slaves to live in relative freedom on his estate in their old age. Unexpectedly, the wife bore a baby girl. Her parents—still slaves by law—named their daughter Margaret and raised her in freedom.

In 1821, the sixty-year-old Ashmore began distributing his property. He sold his considerable estate to his daughter and her husband, Nathan Bemis, for $1000 and "the consideration of natural love and affection." Excepted from the sale were household furniture and slaves. His neighbor and justice of the peace for Harford County, Edward Prigg, witnessed the deed. Prigg also attested that he and another justice of the peace examined Margaret Ashmore, John's wife, "apart from and out of the hearing of her husband," to determine whether she agreed to relinquish her dower rights in the property that John was transferring. She agreed, and the deal was struck. John Ashmore also continued freeing his slaves. In 1821, he sold two of his slaves and manumitted another. In 1822, Ashmore manumitted four more slaves. Then in 1824, at the age of 64, John Ashmore died without a will. His estate was inventoried after his death and was found to contain only two slave boys. The state did not inventory Margaret's parents or Margaret among John Ashmore's possessions at the time of his death. He had, simply put, never claimed her as a slave.

We do not know where Margaret lived prior to 1832. An attorney sympathetic to her claims of freedom would later state that she had lived with her parents on land owned by John Ashmore — land that he had sold to his daughter and her husband, Nathan Bemis, in 1821. She likely continued to live there even after she married Jerry Morgan, a free black from Pennsylvania. In the 1830 census, Jerry Morgan was listed as a head of household in Harford County, Maryland, with a wife and two children. Jerry's affection for Margaret might be judged by his willingness to live as a free black in a slave state, where his person was decidedly less secure than it ought to have been. But it may have been a safer decision than we know. Harford County, Maryland, had a sizable and growing free black population. The number of free blacks living there doubled between 1790 and 1800, and nearly doubled again between 1800 and 1810. The percentage of blacks who were free also rose steadily during this period, rising from 18 percent in 1790 to 33 percent in 1810 to 41 percent in 1830. And the trend continued. By 1860, more than 67 percent of Harford County's black population was free. In the legal borderlands, freedom and slavery coexisted.

We are a little more certain about when Margaret moved to Pennsylvania. Margaret's parents died in 1832, and she thereafter repaired with her husband and children to Pennsylvania. They settled just across the border in York County, where Jerry Morgan had been born. A full year later, she bore another child in Pennsylvania. Up until this point, neither John Ashmore nor anyone from his family had attempted to exercise any dominion over Margaret (or at least left no legal record of such an attempt). But in 1837, John Ashmore's widow, Margaret Ashmore, determined otherwise. She enlisted several neighbors, including her son-in-law Nathan Bemis and long-time friend Edward Prigg (now a constable for Harford County), to go to York County, Pennsylvania, and bring Margaret Morgan and her children back to Maryland. We do not know why Margaret Ashmore suddenly laid claim to Margaret Morgan as her property. Perhaps it was a sudden decision, or one that took many years to germinate and come to fruition? The records do not tell us.

Margaret Morgan had a significant claim to freedom under Maryland law. Her parents had been released from service by John Ashmore, a fact verified by his failure to account for Margaret or her parents in any of his transactions and by the state of Maryland's failure to do so when he died intestate. The U.S. census taker in 1830, who also was the county sheriff, listed her as free. But as significant as these facts may have been, they were not dispositive. John Ashmore may have released Margaret's parents from service, but he failed to manumit them formally. Manumission was not difficult in Maryland, but it did have to meet several requirements. Slaves had to be under forty-five years of age, healthy, of sound mind, and able to provide food and clothing for themselves. In addition, a master could not free a slave if it would prejudice the claims of creditors. These were reasonable conditions in a slave state. The first four requirements prevented slaveholders from hiding behind "humanitarian motives" for casting off their slaves in old age or because they failed to be of any more use for the slaveholder. The last requirement protected society's financial health, albeit at the expense of Maryland's black residents.

John Ashmore had not had any trouble with creditors, or if he had, they had not filed suit against him. So why had he not manumitted Margaret's parents? After all, he had made arrangements for his other slaves. It is likely that they were older than forty-five when he came to the decision to manumit them, or perhaps they were not of ample physical or mental strength to pass the legal requirements for manumission. John Ashmore may have fully intended that Margaret's parents and their child should be free. But his intentions may not have lined up with Maryland law.

Unfortunately, John Ashmore's intent did not matter. The Maryland courts had not been friendly to freedom petitions that argued intent over the letter of the law. Those masters who did not strictly conform to the manumission statute left their former slaves in the penumbra of freedom. They might live free, but if they were challenged at law it was highly unlikely that a court would concede their liberty.

Nonetheless, Margaret Morgan had one other claim to freedom. She had relocated to Pennsylvania in 1832. If her mistress, Margaret Ashmore, had known she did so and had not stopped her, then this could be interpreted as consent. This question, however, still further depended on location. If Margaret Ashmore *had* consented, then Margaret Morgan was certainly free by Pennsylvania law, as Pennsylvania did not suffer nonresidents to import slaves into the state. If Margaret Ashmore had *not* consented, then she was a fugitive slave by Pennsylvania law.

But what of Margaret Morgan's child who was born on Pennsylvania soil? Both Pennsylvania and federal judges had held that the children of fugitives were not fugitive slaves. A strict, literal reading of the fugitive slave clause combined with the application of the notion of birthright citizenship (operative in Pennsylvania) meant that Margaret's child was governed by Pennsylvania law and was free. Against this position, one could argue that the fugitive's status was determined by the fugitive slave clause and that the clause clothed Margaret in her slave status wherever she was. As such, the laws of Maryland governed her and her issue, and Margaret and this child were thus the property of her mistress. This is certainly plausible, but it ran against prevailing precedent. More to the point, it admitted an inroad on each state's right to determine the status of its residents. It was a dangerous path. Venturing down it might lead slaveholders to one day have to face down abolitionists who could use the same logic to undermine slavery in the slaveholding states. Anyone perplexed by this need only wonder how the privileges and immunities clause might operate if free states began granting free blacks full citizenship and demanding that these rights be respected by slave states.

What mattered more than Margaret Morgan and her Pennsylvania-born child's legal status was who got to determine it. In Pennsylvania, her claims were strong. In Maryland, less so. True, some of the border slave states had long made it judicial policy to grant petitions for freedom on the grounds that masters had voluntarily taken their slaves into free states or free territory. Doing so meant that the slave became free. This was an application of the *Somerset* principle, but the remarkable fact is that slave states recognized it. Missouri's courts, for instance, followed this policy, and a few years after the conclusion of the *Prigg* case, a slave named Dred Scott petitioned for his freedom in St. Louis. It is no small fact of history that Dred Scott's petition was initially granted, only later to be overturned by the Missouri Supreme Court, which was eager to end the practice of applying the *Somerset* principle.

But whatever the law in Missouri or in other slave states, it was not the law in Maryland. Sojourning to Pennsylvania, even with her master's consent, could not make a slave free. So said the Maryland Court of Appeals in *Davis v. Jacquin & Pomerait* (1820). The slave petitioning for freedom claimed that his residence in Pennsylvania had made him free by Pennsylvania law. The appeals court shrugged. It might be so, but Maryland law allowed residents to travel and return with their slaves. "Where there is no constitutional barrier," said the court, referring to the U.S. Constitution, "we are bound to observe and enforce the statutory provisions of our own state."

This prohibition, however, was not as absolute as it appeared. In the June term of 1837, the Maryland Court of Appeals opined that there were cases in which residence in a free state might free a slave. In *Bland v. Beverly*, a slave (Beverly Dowling) struck a bargain with his mistress to purchase his freedom for $200. He worked for extra wages and had already paid $173 to his owner, Sophia Bland, when he traveled to New York on his own to work as a waiter on a steamboat. When he returned, his mistress refused to accept the last payment of $27 and instead declared him a runaway and sold him to Austin Woolfolk of Baltimore. Dowling sued. The court sided with him, instructing the jury that the master's actions implied consent for him to travel to New York and that therefore he had become free by New York's laws. The jury obliged and freed Dowling. The Maryland Court of Appeals upheld the order, and Beverly Dowling was free.

Bland v. Beverly might have offered Margaret Morgan some hope, but the facts did not exactly fit her case. Beverly Dowling had made a deal with his mistress, and she had acted in bad faith. The trial judge and the Court of Appeals had clearly wanted to hold Beverly Dowling's mistress to her word but could not because slaves could not enter into contracts. The judges faced a dilemma — how could evidence of the contract be admitted if the contract were not recognizable by law? The answer was to focus on Sophia Bland's consent to allow Dowling to travel to New York. Why had she done so? So that Dowling could earn the rest of the money to pay her off. The previous payments from

Dowling to Bland (totaling $173), as well as her allowing him to work for wages at all, became evidence of her consent. And if she had consented to his leaving for New York on his own, then she had relinquished her property right. It followed that Beverly Dowling was no runaway.

This was the critical point. The Court of Appeals made clear in its ruling that the relevant law was a Maryland statute preventing the importation of new slaves into the state. In short, the Maryland Court of Appeals was not admitting the principle that travel to a free jurisdiction automatically made someone free. Instead, it defined a limited case in which a slaveholder's consent to allow a slave to depart might result in relinquishing the property right. In the November term of 1837, the court clarified its ruling in *Bland v. Beverly* as applying only to *permanent* departures. Temporary sojourners were protected by Maryland law if they returned with their slaves. The bare fact of travel to a free state did not bestow freedom by Maryland's laws.

Importantly, these cases were adjudicated after Margaret Ashmore sent Edward Prigg and his party out to claim Margaret as a fugitive slave. They were not aware that her claim might be jeopardized by that case, although they were doubtless conscious that Margaret Ashmore's claim would be threatened if it could be proven that she had (even tacitly) consented to Margaret Morgan's leaving the state of Maryland.

Still, Margaret had yet another claim to freedom. She could have argued that John Ashmore *had* manumitted her parents and that the court must presume a deed of manumission even though one did not exist. After all, John Ashmore had allowed them to live in freedom and had never claimed her, and neither had his widow, at least not until she sent slavecatchers into Pennsylvania. The Maryland Court of Appeals had ruled in *Burke v. Negro Joe* (1834) that a jury could presume a deed of manumission if the facts fit a certain pattern. The petitioner, Negro Joe, established that his parents and grandparents had both been free, although a deed of manumission could not be produced. The court agreed. But the burden of proof was substantial. The court made clear that "going at large and acting as free for any length of time, will not *per se* be a sufficient foundation" for a claim of freedom. After all, a slave might have run away and lived as though free without the knowledge of his master. Rather, the court rested on the facts that three generations of Joe's family had acted as free while living *within three miles* of the owner who had manumitted them. When the original owner had died, there was no claim made upon the free black family. But this was still not enough. The long passage of time with no prosecution of the former slave's masters for allowing slaves to wander about and act as if free was the final piece of evidence required. The Maryland court further clarified in *Wilson v. Ann Barnet* (1836) that the law would not presume the consent of a master to manumission unless proved by external evidence.

It is not a stretch of our historical imagination to say that Margaret Morgan had a significant claim to freedom, as did her children, by both Pennsylvania and Maryland law. Margaret Morgan's claim was strong in Pennsylvania. In Maryland, it was less so, if only because the burden of proof on Margaret to establish her freedom was substantial. Margaret Ashmore, or at least Nathan Bemis, Edward Prigg, and the other slavecatchers who went to retrieve Margaret Morgan as a fugitive slave, knew that her claim was weaker in Maryland. Their actions confirm this suspicion.

In February 1837, Edward Prigg and his party crossed into York County, Pennsylvania, to retrieve Margaret Morgan and her children. That so many traveled on behalf of Margaret Ashmore made sense. The Pennsylvania Personal Liberty Law of 1826 required that proof to the satisfaction of the judge be presented to issue a certificate of removal and prevented the slaveholder's testimony from being entered. A plethora of witnesses, all of whom were tied to the Ashmore family but had no direct interest in the property claim, would help make the case. The party applied to Thomas Henderson, a justice of the peace in York County, for an arrest warrant. Henderson issued a warrant directed to Constable William McCleary, and the whole group then arrested Margaret Morgan and her three children. Jerry Morgan, protesting the arrest of his wife, accompanied them back to town. The arresting party returned Margaret and her children before Henderson. If Henderson made the writ returnable before him, then he had made a potentially fatal error. Pennsylvania's personal liberty law disqualified him from actually issuing a certificate of removal. Only a judge in a court of record could do that, and JPs and other petty magistrates did not preside over courts of record. It is also possible that Henderson had made the writ returnable to a judge of a court of record and pointed out that Prigg and his party had brought the fugitive slaves to the wrong venue. Either way, he refused to continue.

The progress of events from that point on is hazy. One account had Prigg and his party promising that they would take the matter before a judge of a court of record the next morning. They convinced Margaret's forlorn husband to attend to his affairs at home and join them in court the next day. Once he was gone, they stole away in the night to Maryland. Whether this was true or not, one fact was indisputable. Prigg and his party declined to follow either the procedure laid out in the Pennsylvania personal liberty law or that in the Fugitive Slave Act of 1793. They simply carried Margaret and her children out of Pennsylvania. But why would they have followed the law to a point and then not followed through? Perhaps they had misunderstood Pennsylvania's personal liberty law and believed that a local justice of the peace could issue certificates of removal. Perhaps they believed that Henderson would do so under the Fugitive Slave Act of 1793, although to do so would have made him liable for a misdemeanor and fine under Pennsylvania law. Perhaps Henderson had been willing to do so if the matter were handled quietly, but Jerry Morgan prevented him. This is eminently plausible, if we assume that Henderson knew the law. Whatever the case, Prigg and his party sensed trouble. With Jerry Morgan protesting his family's freedom and with the delay imposed by having to go before a judge thus giving Jerry time to assemble a case and enlist the support of abolitionists, Margaret Ashmore's tenuous claim would be scrutinized before a Pennsylvania judge. They decided in the end not to risk it. They took Margaret and her children to Maryland under cover of darkness and without a certificate of removal.

Once in Maryland, Margaret Morgan pressed her freedom claim before the Harford County Court. The case was initiated in May, and a jury was impaneled on August 28. The trial record is sparse. We do not know anything about specific testimony, although a dozen witnesses appeared for the slaveholder. It does not appear that Margaret was represented by counsel. Even if she was, the law was fairly well against her. Without a formal emancipation, she was still a slave. There was some question, of course, about whether her mistress had consented to her leaving for Pennsylvania, but the case law that would be of most help to her (*Bland v. Beverly*) had just been adjudicated, and the report was yet to be published. On August 30, a jury determined in the end that she was a slave by the laws of Maryland. Margaret thereafter disappears from the historical record, with abolitionists later reporting that she and her children were sold further south.

If we are to historicize rights and do so properly, we must consider the context in which claims to those rights are raised. Margaret Morgan's legal rights in America flowed from her status, not from her U.S. citizenship or any abstract notion of natural law. Her status was either that of a free black woman of Pennsylvania residence or a fugitive slave under the law of Maryland. Put another way, she was a Pennsylvanian only if her mistress, Margaret Ashmore, had relinquished her property right in her, and this could only be established by proving that her mistress had consented to her travel to Pennsylvania. If it was so, then Pennsylvania had a legal interest in her continued residence. After all, she had married a Pennsylvanian and had had a child in Pennsylvania. So her status was key, and her status came down to a simple question: did Margaret Ashmore consent to Margaret Morgan's departure for Pennsylvania?

A court of law and a jury in Maryland decided this question. This was irregular, if only because Edward Prigg removed her from Pennsylvania without legal process. Both federal law and Pennsylvania law required a certificate of removal to transport fugitive slaves across state lines, and that could only be obtained from a judge in Pennsylvania. Prigg had clearly not wanted to chance a hearing in the free state, and so he and his party took matters into their own hands. They may have justified breaching Pennsylvania law on the grounds that they were enforcing the constitutionally-guaranteed rights of their employer, Margaret Ashmore. They might have rationalized this with the slave's freedom claims in mind, if the thought ever crossed their minds. Margaret Morgan, after all, would receive due process in Maryland in the form of a jury trial. She was, after all, a Marylander by birth and her status (they may have reasoned) ought to be determined in Maryland's courts.

There is also the matter of Margaret Morgan's child. Established law recognized birthright residence for Pennsylvanians, and the children of fugitives had never been considered fugitive slaves by the courts. The claim of Margaret Morgan's child to freedom was strong, and her Pennsylvanian residence entitled her to Pennsylvanian protection. Even if one allows that Margaret was legally a fugitive slave, it is no stretch to say that her child, unnamed in the records, was abducted. But for the unnamed child the narrative ended here with the tragic silence that consumed many Americans living in the age of slavery. For Edward Prigg and the others in his party, however, the story was just beginning.

CHAPTER 7

Arresting Edward Prigg

Shortly after Edward Prigg and his party returned to Maryland with Margaret and her children, the sheriff of York County arrived with arrest warrants for the lot of them. It was illegal in Pennsylvania to remove someone, as a fugitive slave, by force or fraud from its jurisdiction without first following the procedures laid out in Pennsylvania's Personal Liberty Law of 1826. The arrest warrants were at first declined by Maryland's governor on the grounds that they had not been founded upon an indictment by a grand jury. This was quickly remedied, as the grand jury found true bills on each of the defendants. Warrants for their arrest followed, and the governor of Pennsylvania made his request to the governor of Maryland according to the dictates of the 1793 congressional statute regulating fugitive criminal rendition — the same statute that contained the provisions for fugitive slave rendition.

Pennsylvania's quick action came at the behest of the aggrieved. Jerry Morgan may have been reluctant to travel to Maryland to see after his captive wife and children, but this was not due to any coarseness on his part. He took the ferry north to Harrisburg and personally appealed to the governor of Pennsylvania, begging him to use his state resources to save his family. The call prompted action, but Jerry Morgan would not live to see it. Returning to York via a canal boat destined for Columbia on the Susquehanna River, he suffered the loss of his jacket by one of the boat hands. His jacket contained his papers. Being unable to produce any identification when asked, Jerry was seized and bound, suspected of being a fugitive himself. Having just lost his wife and children, Jerry Morgan had reached the end of his tether. He bolted when they approached the lock gate in Columbia and leaped for the wall of the lock. He didn't clear the wall. He fell backwards into the water and was dragged under the boat. Being bound, he could not pull himself to safety, and he drowned. Jerry Morgan's story ended in true tragedy. Despite being born free and living in a free state, he was in the end a victim of the color line that ran through every corner of the American democratic republic.

Pennsylvania's extradition demand put Maryland officers in an awkward position. To ignore it invited retaliation by Pennsylvania and other free states, which might begin blocking fugitive slave requests. To comply was to risk conceding that the free states could interfere with Marylanders' constitutional rights. After all, Edward Prigg and his party believed that they had merely been carrying out the provisions of the fugitive slave clause. How could a slaveholder who was exercising the constitutional right to recapture fugitive slaves face state prosecution for those actions? But there did not appear to be an easy way to resolve the problem. The normal course of the legal process could potentially leave the matter before the courts of Pennsylvania, an unacceptable venue for a final decision from Maryland's perspective. Executive interference with criminal extradition – a process proscribed by the U.S. Constitution and regulated by federal law – risked the charge that Maryland was flouting the very Constitution under which it was demanding its rights.

Arresting Edward Prigg proved to be more difficult than Jerry Morgan and his friends had hoped, but it was not impossible. Ultimately, Maryland's Assembly negotiated for his surrender and for a resolution of the case in the U.S. Supreme Court. Many histories of *Prigg v. Pennsylvania* pass over this portion swiftly, ignoring the details of how the pro forma case created by a Pennsylvania statute came to be. But the context is important. Perhaps most directly, it reveals how constitutional crises were navigated in this period. Resolution in the courts was not the first thought of any of the parties, nor had the fugitive slave controversy up until this point found any resolution in the courts. The legislature had been the preferred forum. Once again, it was a legislature that would seek to resolve this controversy – by suggesting that the matter be referred especially to the *federal* courts. If both states could agree upon this course, the Supreme Court could prove to be the very forum in which the question could be answered. But this solution made the details important for a second reason – both sides needed to control the narrative in order to make their specific constitutional arguments. The spate of legislative activity between 1837 and 1839 that turned the arrest warrants for Edward Prigg and party into *Prigg v. Pennsylvania* was a contest for the high constitutional ground. It was a contest that Maryland largely won.

Marylanders registered outrage at Pennsylvania's attempt to arrest Edward Prigg and his associates in 1837, and why not? Had Prigg not merely executed rights guaranteed by the U.S. Constitution? Was this anything but another example of the infidelity of the free states when it came to carrying out the Constitution's bargains? From the halls of the Maryland Assembly came a chorus of denunciations matched by private conversations around the state.

The shrill pitch of this reaction to Pennsylvania's simple extradition request must be understood within the twin contexts of national contests over slavery and a local politics steeped in crisis. Recall that the American Anti-Slavery Society (AASS) had formed in 1833 and begun its propaganda campaign against slavery. Since part of its goal was to convince southerners that slaveholding was a sin, it sent many of its pamphlets and papers southward in the U.S. Mail. Southerners were shocked. They gathered by the hundreds outside post offices. In August 1835, residents of Charleston, South Carolina, established a committee of safety of twenty-one citizens who met with the postmaster and received guarantees that no abolitionist tracts would be delivered. In North Carolina, a crowd took it a step further when it broke into the post office and burned the papers. The same occurred in Richmond, Virginia. In Georgetown, a mob hunting for a mulatto (said to have spoken ill of a white man's wife and daughters) found abolitionist papers in the home of a man thought to be harboring him. The homeowner was committed to jail, but likely for his own protection, as the mob ransacked his house, and the militia had to be called out.

The outrage was not confined to mob action. The Charleston committee of safety, established in 1835, was headed by a respected judge. In Frederick County, Virginia, a grand jury issued a presentment against all the members of the New York Antislavery Society "and especially Arthur Tappan." The grand jury considered the abolitionist association "an evil of great magnitude, tending to disturb our peace and to excite insurrection among our slaves, injuring the right of property guarantied by the constitution of the United States, and endangering the lives of our citizens." The grand jury further recommended that its judges and magistrates practice "unceasing and increasing vigilance in the detection of all fanatical emissaries." By February 1836, five southern legislatures had passed resolutions essentially demanding that the northern states restrict abolitionist speech. Andrew Jackson raised the specter of slave insurrection in his 1836 annual address to Congress, requesting that the post office be protected from abolitionists' fanatical schemes.

These were official pronouncements, and they cohered into a constitutional argument. Invariably, they referred to the Constitution as a compact amongst independent sovereignties. This was not particularly new, nor controversial — yet. Slavery was a local institution, regulated by the independent states. The Constitution had left it so. Upon this point, even the AASS agreed. But thereafter their constitutional visions parted company. The AASS argued that Congress held plenary authority over slavery in the territories, slavery in the District of Columbia, the admission of new slave states, and the interstate slave trade. Their pamphlets and petitions called for action in these areas. Responding to the abolitionist mail campaign of 1835, southern legislatures argued that the terms of union precluded such powers. The Constitution, they said, respected slavery, and slaveholders entered the compact with the understanding that their property would be protected. It would, therefore, be a violation of the Constitution's "implied conditions" to abolish slavery in the District of Columbia or in any U.S. territory.

This proslavery constitutionalism was taken one step further. The implied conditions of union not only restricted congressional power, but also enjoined *positive duties* upon the free states. Central to this was the problem at hand — abolitionist pamphlets. The legislature of Alabama complained in 1836 of the "millions" of pamphlets scattered southward by abolitionists; South Carolina called it a "torrent." Along with Virginia, North Carolina, and Georgia, all demanded that northern legislatures suppress abolitionist societies. As South Carolina put it in the resolutions they sent to northern states, the formation of abolition societies is "in direct violation of the obligations of the compact of union." North Carolina invoked the "duty" which was binding upon free states to suppress abolitionists. "The constitution which unites us," North Carolina went on to conclude, "cannot be supposed to have lessened our mutual obligations." Georgia's legislature admonished northern states that "the perpetuity of this glorious Union is only to be ensured by a strict adherence to the letter of Constitution, which has guaranteed to us certain rights with which we will suffer no power on earth to interfere."

Georgia had taken this argument too far. No strict, textual reading of the Constitution could produce the duty of states to suppress abolitionists. As many of these resolutions made obvious, their positions depended upon a reading of the *implied* rather than *express* conditions of union. Slave states generally fell back on the notion that the Constitution's original meaning prevented an antislavery reading of federal grants of power. This was how the South Carolina legislature could resolve that congressional abolition of slavery in the District of Columbia would be "a violation of the rights of the citizens of that district, derived from the implied conditions on which that territory was ceded to the general government." These same implied conditions meant not just that northern abolitionists had no right to use Congress to try to end slavery, but that northern states were obligated to *stop* abolitionists from trying to do so. The abolitionists' "incendiary publications," southern states charged, disrupted their peace and security. While none of them despaired of their slaves' loyalty and passivity, "we do ask, and think we have a right to demand," said North Carolina, "that others shall not teach them evil."

Slaveholders did not rest in relying upon the goodwill of their sister states. They took their cause to Congress, where they demanded in 1836 that the post offices not be used to distribute abolitionist pamphlets and that Congress stop receiving abolitionist petitions. This ignited a firestorm of protest. Were not speech and petitioning sacred rights guaranteed by the First Amendment? The protest against these southern demands came from the early republic's great luminaries. Daniel Webster, Henry Clay, and John Quincy Adams all registered their dissent. John C. Calhoun of South Carolina put the demands in the starkest of terms: No one had a right to unsettle a state's domestic institutions. Abolitionist rhetoric threatened the internal security of southern states by inciting slaves to rebellion. No First Amendment right could rest on such foundations, argued Calhoun, as there was no express or implied national right to threaten the very peace and stability of a sovereign state. The result of all this trouble was a mixed bag: Congress did not pass a law touching on the abolitionist use of the mails, but the House did institute a procedural rule in May of 1836 that automatically tabled antislavery resolutions without reading them into the record. John Quincy Adams protested, but slaveholders quickly called the question in order to end debate, leading Adams to inquire of the House on May 25, 1836, "Am I gagged or not?" The name stuck. The Senate followed the House in adopting its own Gag Rule.

This was the immediate national context of the York County Sheriff's presentation of the warrant for the arrest of Edward Prigg, Nathan Bemis, Stephen Lewis, and Jacob Forwood in February 1837. What might in another age have been a routine rendition request suddenly became a matter of intense political scrutiny. For the state's governor, Thomas W. Veazey, handling the rendition request would require caution and fortitude. In the face of abolitionist pamphlets raining down on the South and the outrage upon southern honor in the halls of Congress, Veazey stood as a firm proponent of slavery and slaveholder's rights. But Veazey, an elder politician with a long and distinguished Maryland pedigree, did not confuse fortitude with recklessness. He was well aware that to refuse the rendition request outright would invite a constitutional crisis.

He had experience with such crises. When the rendition request arrived from Pennsylvania in February of 1837, Veazey was fresh from handling Maryland's constitutional debacle of 1836, which arose over a problem of apportionment in the legislature. The Maryland Constitution of 1776, still in force, gave the counties equal representation. This did not bode well for the northern counties, where a swelling population found itself underrepresented in the assembly. A convention of mechanics, laborers, and artisans in Baltimore met in 1836 and declared that the people could change their government at any time, effectively claiming that they could nullify the state constitution and adopt a new one. This claim rattled the state's elite, especially coming as it did on the heels of the violent Baltimore bank riot of 1835. Events in 1836 promised more of the same when the September senatorial elections returned (potentially) a 100 percent Whig senate, despite the Democrats having won the popular vote.

How it came to this was a result of the Maryland Constitution, which required the appointment of senators by electors who themselves had been elected by the people. (This system was, incidentally, the inspiration for the electoral college established by the U.S. Constitution.) In 1836 in Maryland, malapportionment meant that a clear Democratic electoral victory resulted nonetheless in a small Whig majority of electors. This small majority of Whigs could then appoint *all* of the senators. In September, Democratic electors made clear their intent to boycott the senatorial electoral college in order to deny it a quorum. Without a quorum, the thinking went, the college could not appoint a senate. Without a senate, the assembly could not sit, a governor could not be appointed (the assembly appointed the governor), and government in essence would devolve to the people, who could call a constitutional convention.

It was politics by crisis, a risky move by any measure. And the Whigs gave as good as they got. Governor Veazey (still in office until the assembly and senate were supposed to be seated in the December sessions) tarried just long enough after to allow two intervening elections to be held in November, one for the Maryland House of Delegates (the lower body of the assembly) and one for the president of the United States. Both returned Whig victories as the electorate punished the Democrats for their radical tactics. The day following the November elections, Veazey issued a proclamation decrying the Democrats' move as disorderly and unconstitutional and tending towards "CIVIL WAR." He then called the newly elected House of Delegates and the previous year's senate into a special session in order to run the affairs of government. The Democratic press assailed him as a "despot" and "King Veazey," but found its audience chilly. Public opinion was clearly against the Democrats and their tactics. The electoral loss had broken the spirit of resistance, and the Democrats relented. They came to the college and elected a new senate. The crisis was over.

In hindsight, Veazey's actions appear both calculated and decisive, and chroniclers have often been kind to him. But a more honest interpretation of the crisis would take into account Veazey's own uncertainties and anxieties. Veazey was conscious of the high stakes and aware that if the popular winds had blown in another direction, then his proclamation may not have worked. He was also clearly stung by public criticism, especially that which accused him of tyranny. As a

Whig, Veazey believed firmly in legislative supremacy. References to "King Veazey" recalled contemporaneous Whig denunciations of "King Andrew" Jackson. They cut him to the quick. When the Whig Party moved to defuse the constitutional issue by suggesting its own reforms in the 1836-1837 session, Veazey signaled his support. But even this was tepid. Veazey believed himself a ministerial agent of government, not an energetic leader.

Only months removed from that constitutional debacle, Veazey was suddenly faced with another potential crisis when warrants were presented for the arrest of Edward Prigg and his party in February 1837. His handling of it exposed the same trepidation. Veazey's first move was delay. He submitted the matter to his attorney general, who gave him grounds for refusal. As the arrest warrants had not emanated from a grand jury indictment, it appeared that Veazey could stand on solid ground in refusing to execute the warrants. But Pennsylvania responded by bringing the alleged kidnapping to the grand jury, which returned true bills. On March 20, 1837, Pennsylvania's governor appointed Adam Klinefelter, sheriff of York County, as the agent of Pennsylvania to retrieve the fugitives from justice and return them to Pennsylvania for trial. He arrived and delivered the warrants, sojourning a while with Sheriff John Carsins before he returned. The local paper was generous to the Pennsylvania sheriff, noting his gentlemanly deportment. But there could be no doubt about the effect of his arrival. "Pennsylvania," the *Baltimore Chronicle* noted, "is about to bring the matter to a crisis."

The warrants now followed true bills found by a grand jury. Maryland's attorney general reported back to Veazey that the executive had no discretion in the matter. Pennsylvania's rendition request met the legal requirements under federal law. Maryland's governor swore an oath to uphold the U.S. Constitution and was required to arrest the men and turn them over to Pennsylvania's agents. But Veazey again delayed. He sent a deputation to Pennsylvania governor Joseph Ritner asking that the request be withdrawn to avert the crisis. Governor Ritner in turn delayed action until the Harford County Court decided the freedom petition of Margaret Morgan. But when a jury declared her Margaret Ashmore's slave on August 30, 1837, the rendition request was repeated. Governor Veazey would have to make a choice.

Veazey's actions thus far were within the scope of limited executive action that comported with his constitutional scruples. But he was now without any other recourse, short of violating his oath to support the U.S. Constitution. And so he dutifully ordered that the defendants be arrested, although the warrants were not quick to appear. The arrest warrants had still not run when the assembly inaugurated its annual session on December 25, 1837. A special committee was appointed the next day to investigate Pennsylvania's rendition request. On January 6, 1838, the committee reported back its recommendation that a deputation be appointed to repair to Pennsylvania's capitol and demand the dismissal of the indictments as well as more favorable laws for slavecatchers. From the committee's report came a view of the facts different than the view from Pennsylvania. "The only offence alleged against the citizens demanded," read the report, "was the arrest and bringing into Maryland certain slaves which had absconded from Margaret Ashmore of Harford county." Edward Prigg and his party had attempted to follow Pennsylvania law by obtaining a warrant for the fugitives' arrest and had sought a certificate of removal, but the justice of the peace "refused to act further in the case." Without recourse, they returned to Maryland. There the fugitive slaves had their due process. Margaret Morgan and her children filed their petitions for freedom in Maryland, and a judge and jury declared them to be slaves.

This narrative emphasized the slavecatchers' lawfulness. Prigg and party had made a good faith effort to follow Pennsylvania law, yet they were still indicted. Their actions were in accord with the provision of the Constitution guaranteeing slaveholders their slaves, should they seek refuge in a free state. Finally, Maryland law gave recourse to blacks protesting their freedom. They could have their claim decided by a jury. Courts (and juries) had not been hesitant to grant petitions for freedom when the law warranted them. But a court and jury judged Margaret Morgan and her children slaves. These facts — this narrative — established the procedural integrity of Prigg's actions, making clear that the only question was whether the free states would have the power "to nullify that Article of the Federal Constitution which recognizes the relation of master and slave, and guarantees the right of property in persons held to service."

The Maryland Assembly received the committee's report favorably, if somewhat critically. Even the committee's membership moved to soften its provocative language. The suggestion arose that a neutral arbiter might be required to solve the problem. One proposal was to surrender Edward Prigg and his associates and to have the state represent them in their defense in such a way as to raise a constitutional issue. It would then be possible, under Section 25 of the Judiciary Act of 1789, to remove the case by writ of error to the U.S. Supreme Court. Surely the state of Pennsylvania would allow Prigg and his associates to remain at large on bail during the proceedings, under the promise that they would surrender themselves if they lost the case before the Supreme Court. This alternative aroused the interest of legislators, although they ultimately rejected it. Either they were concerned with the possibility of committing themselves to the surrender of Edward Prigg and his associates, or there were doubts that the U.S. Supreme Court's jurisdiction could be established simply on a constitutional defense against state law.

In the end, the assembly adopted the suggestion, but on modified terms. The final resolutions approved by the legislature laid out a strong constitutional position. Maryland resolved that the right of fugitive slave reclamation predated the Constitution and that the Constitution itself merely recognized and guaranteed that right. As such, the right could not be "abridged, restrained or embarrassed by the legislation of any State in the Union." Pennsylvania's Personal Liberty Law, the Maryland legislature claimed, did precisely this — it abridged, restrained, and embarrassed rights belonging to the citizens of Maryland. "In order to maintain inviolably that equality of privileges and immunities," the legislature continued, "the National Judiciary ought to preside" in all cases when citizens of one state were opposed to another. Moreover, when two states disagreed about the true meaning of the Constitution, or when there was any collision between state laws and the U.S. Constitution, it was only natural that the question be resolved by the Supreme Court, "which, having no local attachments, will be likely to be impartial between the different States and their citizens."

Despite inviting the Supreme Court to settle the matter, the Maryland legislature made clear its view of the limits of national power. Noting that the Constitution did not invest any court with original jurisdiction to determine this kind of case, the resolutions concluded that there was no way to resolve the current impasse "without withdrawing the protection due to every citizen" of Maryland. Therefore, the governor (who, the legislature felt, had himself behaved in a restrained, commendable, and constitutional manner) was authorized to appoint a commissioner to travel to Harrisburg and "endeavor" either to procure a dismissal of the charges or to have the matter referred to the Supreme Court of the United States without compromising Edward Prigg's rights.

Such was Maryland's constitutional position. It declared that the right of reclamation was a natural, proscriptive right that was *confirmed*, not created, by the Constitution. Pennsylvania's laws violated this right of Maryland's citizens, and a Pennsylvania court could not be the final judge in such matters. The only proper recourse was to the U.S. Supreme Court, which could settle the constitutional question but (presumably) would have no power over Maryland's citizens themselves. This was part a hedging of bets but also part constitutional position. Maryland, like Pennsylvania, was making a constitutional stand on its duty to protect the liberty of its citizens against unwarranted power.

The resolutions passed the Maryland Assembly on March 7, 1838, and the governor took action, appointing James Meredith as a commissioner with the consent of the senate. He departed for Harrisburg, arriving on Thursday, April 12, where he took up residence at the modestly elegant Wilson Hotel. From there he wrote the Pennsylvania governor's office to announce his arrival and seek an audience. Governor Ritner did not tarry. His secretary wrote back the next day offering him an 11:00 appointment, "if it suit your convenience." Meredith assented, met with the governor, and presented his commission, complete with instructions and the Maryland Assembly's resolutions. The meeting apparently went well, and the governor's secretary wrote the next day to inform Meredith that he would move "with as little delay as possible." However, some delay would be inevitable. It was already Saturday, and the Pennsylvania legislature was due to adjourn the next Tuesday. There would be no time in the session to deal with this matter. "Should it meet the views of your State, and suit your own convenience," wrote Burrows, the governor's secretary, then the governor would bring the matter to the next session of the legislature, due to convene on the first Tuesday of December in 1838.

So Meredith and Maryland could expect immediate action, in eight months' time. This was hardly the response Meredith craved. "Yielding my personal wishes to the opinion of His Excellency," Meredith agreed not to press the matter with the Pennsylvania Assembly before its adjournment. But he made clear his expectations. Considering the matter "as opened and pending," Meredith would return as Maryland's accredited agent in December, "relying on the assurance you have been kind enough to give me, that the subject will be brought to the notice of the Legislature of Pennsylvania in the annual executive message." This prompted a testy reply from the governor's secretary. The matter was not pending or open – it had not yet been broached with the legislature – and the governor was not reserving a space in his annual message for the Maryland commissioner. He might, of his own mere motion, choose to bring the matter up in a special message to the legislature. It was a terse reminder to Meredith that he could make requests, but not demands, of the Commonwealth.

In the end, however, Pennsylvania and Maryland sought the same goal: resolution. At the next session, the Pennsylvania legislature largely agreed to Maryland's offer to allow the Supreme Court to adjudicate the matter. They did so by passing a public law on May 22, 1839. The statute began with the fiction of "voluntary surrender" of one or more of those indicted for kidnapping. The surrender would result in their immediate release on recognizances in the amount of $1000, along with a promise to abide by whatever decision the court reached. Section 2 of the law authorized the attorney general of Pennsylvania to collaborate with defense counsel to agree to a written statement of facts. These would be entered into the record in the form of a special verdict. From there, the case would be taken by writ of error to the Pennsylvania Supreme Court for the middle district. From there, a writ of error would take the case before the Supreme Court of the United States.

It was a useful format. Three of the jury's findings read into the official record the entirety of Pennsylvania's 1780 gradual abolition act, the 1788 revisions to the gradual abolition act, and the Personal Liberty Law of 1826. This unambiguously made their constitutionality an issue. The rest of the jury's findings laid out the facts of the case. By cooperating on deciding the facts of the case rather than contesting them, a clear statement of the law could be achieved. Or so went the hope. It may be useful here simply to list all the agreed-upon facts:

1. Margaret Morgan was the legal property of Margaret Ashmore of Maryland.
2. Margaret Morgan fled from Maryland to Pennsylvania.
3. Edward Prigg was the legal agent of Margaret Ashmore when he crossed into Pennsylvania and applied for a warrant for Margaret Morgan's arrest.
4. T. Henderson (Pennsylvania JP) issued a warrant for Margaret Morgan's arrest returnable before him.
5. A Pennsylvania peace officer executed the warrant and returned with Margaret Morgan and her children.
6. T. Henderson refused to take further cognizance of the case.
7. Prigg then removed Margaret Morgan and her children from Pennsylvania to Maryland without a certificate of removal.
8. One of the children removed as a fugitive was born in Pennsylvania.

These, of course, were not *all* the facts. What of Margaret Morgan's claims to freedom? Certainly they were not insignificant, especially those which had tended to establish her freedom. But they had been adjudicated and settled in a Maryland court. Given that Margaret Morgan's status would have been determined by the laws of Maryland, this was as close to finality as one could expect. And to admit that Margaret Morgan was, by the laws of Maryland and the U.S. Constitution, a fugitive slave was to thrust to the center one particular legal issue: could Pennsylvania dictate the procedure and evidentiary requirements for fugitive slave rendition? By deciding the facts in this way, the courts could potentially sidestep the issue of a *doubtful* case. Margaret Morgan's was no case of mistaken identity; the Supreme Court would be free to decide the legal issue without worrying about shades of gray. But the presence in this statement of facts of the child, born on Pennsylvania soil, suggests that the attorneys had agreed to complicate the matters slightly. It was not just Margaret Morgan's *admitted* status as a fugitive slave that would concern the Court. Her child, after all, had never fled from one state to another, and Pennsylvania law regarded her as free.

Maryland won another contested point handily. The special verdict declared that T. Henderson had issued a warrant returnable before him and then refused to take cognizance of the case after the warrant was executed. But Pennsylvania's personal liberty law did not allow justices of the peace to issue certificates of removal. If Henderson did in fact issue such a warrant returnable to him, then it was invalid under Pennsylvania's law. If it was returnable before a justice in a court of record, then he had not "refused" to take part in the case. Which was it? The facts as stated in the special verdict supported Maryland's narrative, likely at Maryland's insistence. The state's position had been that Prigg was merely executing a constitutional right and that Pennsylvania was obstructing it. They had buttressed this position repeatedly with a narrative that emphasized Prigg's good faith effort to follow the law. Although it had relatively little legal import (and this might explain why Pennsylvania's attorney general did not press the point), it had real value to Maryland's constitutional narrative. And they wrote this narrative into the legal record, despite whatever had really happened.

Crisis was the watchword for Maryland politics in the late 1830s. The antibank riot, brinksmanship over the state's undemocratic constitution, and national angst over the surge of abolitionist activity had raised the state's collective blood pressure. A reluctant governor had declined to act decisively, leaving the matter for the legislature. The Maryland Assembly had not failed Prigg, taking a muscular constitutional position that asserted a new and potentially decisive reading of the fugitive slave clause. It was based on a particular narrative, one that recast constitutional history and emphasized certain facts of Margaret Morgan's arrest. Theirs was a narrative of ancient rights, secured (not created) by the Constitution. It built upon a proslavery constitutional narrative that had been established in the wake of abolitionist efforts to turn what available weapons the federal government had (e.g., plenary power over Washington, D.C., and the territories) against slavery. Against this position, the slave states had invoked the notion of *implied* conditions. If one conceded that the Constitution was a compact amongst sovereign states, then the slave states had entered believing that slavery would be protected. By situating the fugitive slave clause as securing rather than creating slaveholders' rights, Maryland was weaving Prigg's story into a national narrative.

Maryland's success was reflected in the official record, and in particular in how they portrayed facts. By the agreement of both of the states, Margaret Morgan's status as a fugitive slave was conceded. Maryland also contended that Prigg had made a good-faith effort to follow legal procedure, a fact that added weight to Maryland's claims that their citizens' rights were disturbed by Pennsylvania's laws. This was more fiction than fact, given that Prigg and his party had neglected to go before a judge to obtain the certificate of removal. These were significant victories for Maryland, at least in terms of casting the narrative in a pattern best suited to its case. Pennsylvania had complicated this matter only a little. By insisting that at least one of Margaret Morgan's children had been born in Pennsylvania, the Commonwealth had stood by the principle that all those born in Pennsylvania were free, or at least to be determined free or not by their laws. And now the case was to repair to Washington, D.C., for final adjudication before the bench of the Supreme Court.

CHAPTER 8

Before the Court

The Supreme Court of the antebellum era was not quite the Supreme Court of today. It did not occupy its own building; rather, it met in the North Wing of the Capitol, in a half-moon-shaped chamber directly below the floor of the Senate. In this cellar-like room, which one writer compared to Milton's "lower deep," the Supreme Court justices met and conducted business in the cold winter months from January to March. The back walls of the room formed a half-circle, and spectators entered at the back of the curve. Pillars supported the ceiling above, obstructing views. Along the flat wall sat the slightly elevated bench, and behind it were three windows that backlit the justices, making it difficult to tell what expressions they made during oral arguments or the reading of opinions. Between the bench and the spectators was the "pit," the place where lawyers would argue cases before the Court. Once visitors had been admitted and the Court was ready to be called to order, the justices entered. They each walked to a row of pegs next to the bench (there being no separate robing room in those days) and, in full view of the audience, they donned their robes and shuffled to their seats.

Unlike our Supreme Court justices today, those of the antebellum era had no staff to research difficult questions or provide draft opinions. The work of the justices was done by the justices themselves, and often in short order. Decisions had to be issued in weeks or even days following oral arguments, as the justices met together in Washington only for the short period between January and March of each year. This was in keeping with Washington's status as a transient city, one that supported not just the itinerant Supreme Court justices but also the congressmen and their families who arrived for the legislative session and the traveling circus of lobbyists and office-seekers who trailed them. But while representatives and senators returned to their homes,

Supreme Court justices repaired to their respective circuits where they sat as circuit court judges for at least two sessions a year, usually in May and November, but varying by circuit. The circuits reflected the nation's political geography. In 1842, this favored the South, as five of the nine judicial districts were composed of slaveholding states. The chief justice, Roger B. Taney, was himself a former slaveholder.

Given the furor stoked by the militant abolitionists after 1833, few could mistake the import of *Prigg v. Pennsylvania*. Most of the fury over slavery and national politics was vented on the floors of the U.S. House and Senate, although it often blew through the other democratic venues of the republic: state legislatures, mass meetings, and into the pages of the partisan press. The Supreme Court, by contrast, was a place where collegiality tempered sectarian loyalty and reason trumped political will. Such was the promise of the law as an objective arbiter among warring interests. The case of *Prigg v. Pennsylvania*, however, threatened to infect the law with the ill politics that accompanied slavery. If the justices had any doubt of this, they were relieved of it when counsel for the state of Maryland gravely informed the Court that "it would perhaps be not too much to say, that the case was one of vital interest to the peace and prosperity of the Union itself."

Confronting the Court was essentially the same question that had vexed Congress in 1793 and every state legislature and court thereafter: what separated kidnapping from legitimate fugitive slave rendition? The accommodation that had been formed in Pennsylvania allowed for the operation of two different standards. In federal courts, slaveholders could bring in a fugitive without having obtained an arrest warrant, invoke the Fugitive Slave Act with its low evidentiary threshold ("proof to the satisfaction of such judge or magistrate either by oral testimony or affidavit taken before and certified by a magistrate of any such state or territory"), and receive a certificate of removal. To avail themselves of state courts, Pennsylvania law required slaveholders to obtain an arrest warrant, appear before a judge of a court of record, and provide two witnesses, neither of which could be the actual slaveholder, to receive the same certificate of removal. Anything less than this, Pennsylvania defined as kidnapping. These laws had operated in tandem for over a decade when the case reached the Supreme Court, and one option would have been to leave the system in place. There were other issues to consider, however. If Pennsylvania could add evidentiary requirements to the summary hearing for fugitive slave rendition, could states (as New York and New Jersey had) also require a jury trial? These and other questions made *Prigg v. Pennsylvania* a momentous case when it reached the Supreme Court docket in 1842.

Prigg v. Pennsylvania was the first fugitive slave case to arrive before the Supreme Court. As such, there was no case on point to provide guidance. Nonetheless, the Court had heard cases that concerned slavery both directly and indirectly. It had tried freedom suits for blacks and prosecutions of slavers who violated the U.S. ban on the international slave trade. There had also been several cases that touched on the powers of both the states and the federal government in relation to matters of race and slavery. These cases did not provide a definitive answer to the fugitive slave question, but they did offer clues to what the Court would do in *Prigg v. Pennsylvania*.

One principle constantly reaffirmed by the Supreme Court in these cases was that slavery was a status affixed by state law, one in which federal law and Constitution did not touch unless absolutely necessary. Of the half-dozen freedom suits that had arrived before the Supreme Court before 1842, all but one arrived by virtue of the Supreme Court's appellate jurisdiction over the Washington, D.C., district federal court. Only *LaGrange v. Chouteau* (1829) came on writ of error from a state supreme court. The slave in that case had claimed freedom by having passed into territory originally governed by the Northwest Ordinance of 1787, thus making him (his lawyers claimed) free forever. A jury had ruled otherwise in Missouri, and Chief Justice John Marshall had refused to rule on the merits, instead dismissing the case on the grounds that there was no substantial "federal issue" to justify taking jurisdiction under the twenty-fifth section of the Judiciary Act of 1789 (which extended the Supreme Court's jurisdiction over state supreme courts when federal statutes, treaties, or the Constitution was involved). Marshall's denial of jurisdiction read the law narrowly to avoid controversy and affirmed that a Missourian's status as slave or free was an issue for Missouri's courts.

The Supreme Court had also proven willing to enforce the United States' 1808 ban on the international slave trade, although once again the Court attempted to steer clear of controversy. Somewhat counterintuitively, the Court had become more stringent even as the issue of slavery became more sensitive. Chief Justice John Marshall had read the law in a prohibitively narrow way in 1813 to prevent federal officers from prosecuting slavers who had outfitted for the trade but had not yet sailed. Marshall strained to reach this ruling, and the Court overruled him in *The Emily and the Caroline* in 1824. But even when prosecuting the slave trade vigorously, the Court hardly took on the antislavery mantle. It risked offending too many. Justice Joseph Story had discovered this in *La Jeune Eugenie* (1822), an opinion he issued while riding circuit. He took the opportunity in that case to commit to the official record a condemnation of the slave trade as inhuman, against Christian morals, against the law of nature and the law of nations. Marshall warned him about the perils of offending powerful constituencies, and Story sat silent in *The Antelope* (1825) when Chief Justice Marshall held that the slave trade was not contrary to the law of nations. This public humiliation likely stuck with Story.

Joseph Story was not the only Supreme Court justice to enrage slaveholders. Justice William Johnson had done so on circuit in the case of *Elkison v. Deliesseline* (1823), a case discussed in detail in Chapter 5. Johnson, we will recall, had declared that South Carolina's Negro Seamen Act conflicted with both the commerce and the treaty clauses of the Constitution and was thus void. South Carolina had rested upon its sovereign police power to protect its people. The public defense of the law (and vilification of Johnson), insisted that free blacks were a class of people too dangerous to admit into South Carolina. The law's defenders also made clear that South Carolina would not tolerate outside interference when it came to determining the limits of its own sovereignty. In this way, issues of race were recast as issues of state sovereignty and states' rights.

Because South Carolina had rested on its sovereignty, cases which touched upon the limits of the states' police powers took on a special significance. In *Gibbons v. Ogden* (1824) the Court invalidated a monopoly given by New Jersey to a steamboat line operating solely on waterways within its borders because, among other reasons, it conflicted with congressional licensing laws. Despite this strong nationalist ruling, the Court took care to clarify that the opinion in no way conflicted with the reserved police power of the states, although the

Court did not elaborate on the extent of those reserved powers. And *Gibbons v. Ogden* belonged to a number of opinions that marked the high tide of the Marshall Court's nationalism. Beginning in the late 1820s, the Court's nationalism ebbed in favor of a more robust states' rights jurisprudence. It was a development that dispirited John Marshall in the last years of his tenure. The ascendency of Roger B. Taney to the chief justiceship after Marshall's death in 1835 signaled the demise of Marshall's grand nationalist vision. The police powers doctrine received a muscular articulation in *New York v. Miln* (1837), in which Justice Philip Barbour declared for the Court that New York quarantine laws did not run afoul of the commerce clause. All matters of internal police, wrote Barbour, "are not thus surrendered or restrained." When a state passed laws to regulate the health, welfare, and morals of its residents, its authority was "complete, unqualified, and exclusive." If a state could pass quarantine laws that interfered with interstate commerce on these grounds, it was not too difficult a move to argue that the southern Negro seamen acts (which also interfered with the commerce clause, among other things) would also be constitutional. Even in cases with no direct relation to that subject, slavery exerted a powerful influence.

The Supreme Court directly addressed slavery in two cases during the 1841 term. The cases demonstrated a desire on the part of the Supreme Court justices to reach a consensus on slavery, as both cases were decided by significant majorities on neutral constitutional principles. The celebrated *Amistad* case, made difficult by jurisdictional complications, nonetheless posed a simple question—could Africans not held properly as slaves (for they were kidnapped in an illegal trade) exercise their natural right to self-defense and kill their captors? Despite the political emotion the *Amistad* case evoked, the Court handled the case dispassionately. Justice Joseph Story wrote the opinion for the 8–1 majority declaring that the Africans were not slaves and could not be held as such. To draw in the southern members of the majority, his narrow opinion eschewed rhetorical embellishment about slavery and avoided collateral issues. *Amistad* was a lesson in how the narrow construction of legal issues could avoid controversy, achieve consensus, and accommodate both moderate antislavery and proslavery interests.

It proved a brittle accommodation. In the same term that the

Supreme Court decided with near unanimity the *Amistad* (1841), it fractured over the case of *Groves v. Slaughter*. The case involved a simple debt. Robert Slaughter sued Moses Groves for refusing to pay on a promissory note that had been issued for the sale of slaves in Mississippi. Groves refused to pay because Mississippi's 1832 constitution (while allowing slaves to be imported for use as laborers) prohibited "the introduction of slaves into this state, as merchandise, or for sale." The federal circuit court in Louisiana disregarded Groves's argument and ordered him to pay up, and he promptly appealed to the U.S. Supreme Court. Justice Smith Thompson — a New Yorker appointed by James Monroe — delivered the opinion of the Court, a tepid piece of writing that accepted the defendant in error's arguments that the constitutional provision banning the introduction of slaves into the state for sale required legislation for it to take effect. Because Mississippi's legislature had never passed such a law, Thompson reasoned, Groves was obligated to honor the notes. It was a transparent way of sidestepping the issue of whether the state could ban the introduction of slaves into the state for any reason.

It was John McLean in *Groves* who opened a Pandora's box. McLean was the son of New Jersey farmers who moved west to Ohio while McLean was a child. McLean grew up a frontier pragmatist, and he had a penchant for resorting to "plain meaning" as an interpretive style. He was not quite an abolitionist, but he was no sympathizer with slavery either. And he disliked concealing his moderate antislavery sentiments. Thompson's effete opinion in *Groves* irritated McLean, who wrote a concurring opinion just to state for the record that he believed that states could ban the interstate slave trade without running afoul of the commerce clause. McLean spent some time reaffirming his belief that the commerce clause gave Congress an exclusive right to regulate interstate commerce, although this did not mean (for McLean) that Congress had the power to ban the slave trade. He took time to distinguish the international from the interstate slave trade and to separate slaves from the normal flow of commerce. Because slavery was local in nature and because states had the power to protect themselves from the "avarice" of slave traders and the "inconveniences and dangers of a slave population," the states could ban the trade. McLean went further: "The right to exercise this power, by a state, is higher and deeper than the Constitution." It was a matter of self-preservation: "a law vital to every community, and especially to a sovereign state." Slavery, McLean was saying, was a special kind of evil.

Although McLean had hinted that congressional power did not extend to banning the interstate slave trade, his concurrence nonetheless alarmed Chief Justice Roger B. Taney. While Taney agreed with McLean that slavery was local and that the states could regulate the trade, he clarified in his own concurrence that Congress could *not* prohibit the trade. Taney's emphatically proslavery stance in *Groves* is not easily explained. Taney was once a slaveholder, but in 1818 he had emancipated seven of his slaves. In 1820, he (with his younger brother) then emancipated two slaves held by his father, and he would manumit two more over the next several years. During the Missouri crisis, Taney had been in the Maryland senate, where he opposed a resolution demanding that Missouri be admitted as a slave state with no restrictions. This was a bold, if only moderate, antislavery stand. Also, as a lawyer, he had gained notoriety by defending a Methodist minister who had attacked slavery during a revival sermon. A grand jury indicted the minister for inciting insurrection. Taney's defense of the minister was legally skillful, but Taney did not shy away from the issue of slavery, which he attacked as unjust. He won an acquittal for his client. Thereafter, however, Taney's antislavery feelings abated, although we are not entirely sure why. He rose in the political ranks, and his support for Andrew Jackson landed him the position of attorney general. In 1832, he wrote an opinion in favor of the constitutionality of South Carolina's Negro Seaman Act by referring to blacks as a degraded class who could claim no rights except those explicitly conceded by the state. He carried these views with him to his appointment as chief justice of the Supreme Court, and his concurring opinion in *Groves v. Slaughter* announced a clearly proslavery stance.

None of the other justices outright concurred with Taney's opinion, but Henry Baldwin went even further in articulating a proslavery jurisprudence. Born in 1780 in Connecticut, Baldwin attended Yale and graduated at the age of 17. He made a fine career for himself in law and showed promise for a political one as well, being elected to the House of Representatives in 1816 and serving three terms until ill-health kept him from seeking reelection in 1822. He remained connected to politics, and Andrew Jackson rewarded him with a nomination to the Supreme Court in 1830. In 1833, he suffered a nervous breakdown that forced him to miss the Court's term that year, and he was never after the same. He feuded with his colleague Joseph Story, whose prodigious learning and revered stature Baldwin found threatening. It was Baldwin who was the lone dissenter in the *Amistad*, arguing in that case that the Africans did not have any rights that the white man was bound to respect. In *Groves v. Slaughter*, Baldwin attacked John McLean for trying to separate slaves from commerce, which he believed impossible if a state recognized slaves as property. It followed for Baldwin that a state might prohibit slavery but could not prohibit the slave trade. Thus, Mississippi could not both *allow* the introduction of slaves and *prohibit* their sale. (It was all or nothing, for Baldwin.) But even those states that did prohibit slavery could not, Baldwin argued, ban the interstate slave trade. A slave trader going from Maryland to Missouri, for example, could travel with a coffle through Ohio. The slave trader could not sell his slaves in Ohio, for Ohio did not recognize slaves as property, but Ohio law could not prevent the slave trader from passing through or free the slaves in transit. Baldwin took this one step further. Should Congress (which could apparently treat slaves as articles of interstate commerce) choose to ban the slave trade, Baldwin signaled that he would regard it as an explicit violation of both the privileges and immunities clause and the Fifth Amendment's due process clause.

This was further than any southern justice was willing to go. By Baldwin's logic, slave states could not regulate the commerce in slaves, which would constitute a serious blow to their sovereignty. Chief Justice Taney might have preferred other company in his concurrence, but none was to be had. Joseph Story and John McKinley of Alabama both dissented, although they failed to provide a written opinion to the reporter. Nonetheless, their stated reason was that the notes were void, clearly signaling that they felt the Mississippi Constitution ought to be construed according to its plain meaning. Story and McKinley also joined Thompson and Wayne in concurring with the majority that the clause in the Mississippi Constitution did not conflict with the U.S. Constitution's commerce clause. On this point, the Court seemed to be in round agreement, with only Baldwin dissenting from this holding.

What did *Groves* decide? On the one hand, the Court had definitively settled that the states could ban slavery within their borders, and (although Baldwin disagreed and Taney was silent on this point) that states could prohibit slave traders from coming within their borders. The Court also signaled that Congress could not prohibit the interstate slave trade, but only Taney and Baldwin explicitly said this was so. McLean hinted in his position that Congress could not prohibit intercourse in goods between the states, but he also reasoned from the position that slavery was a special kind of evil. It would not be too far a step from this to reason that the United States might find it conducive to the general welfare to ban the interstate slave trade, and it was likely this implication that drove both Taney and Baldwin to make explicit their belief that Congress could not regulate the interstate slave trade. While the fact that other judges chose to avoid the issue indicated a desire for consensus, the fault lines on the Court were showing.

The lessons from the Supreme Court's slavery jurisprudence before *Prigg v. Pennsylvania* are complex and not always intuitive. The Supreme Court proved ready and willing to enforce the ban on the international slave trade, even when the Court held a southern majority. The most vocal defender of slaveholders' rights was no southerner, but instead Connecticut's Henry Baldwin. By contrast, John McKinley of Alabama and Anthony Wayne of Georgia had refused to signal that they would rebuff any attempt by Congress to outlaw the interstate slave trade. The rise of states' rights jurisprudence suggested that the Court would receive the Negro seamen acts favorably. However, if the states had the power to guard against the introduction of free blacks, then by analogy they also had the power to pass personal liberty laws which protected free blacks' liberty. These divisions proved contentious, and the unnecessary concurrences in *Groves* betrayed the deep disagreements spawned by slavery and the Constitution.

Such was the Court that counsel for Maryland and Pennsylvania faced when they arrived on February 8, 1842, to argue *Prigg v. Pennsylvania*. Each state sent two attorneys, and the four of them would take up three full days of oral arguments. For the plaintiff in error, Jonathan Meredith and John Nelson appeared, both representing Maryland through Edward Prigg. Pennsylvania sent its attorney general, Ovid F. Johnson, and a deputy attorney general, Thomas C. Hambly, to argue its side.

Jonathan Meredith's argument for Maryland offered a northern rather than a southern position. In fact, he drew his argument entirely from Samuel Nelson's *Jack v. Martin* (discussed at length in Chapter 5), which he proclaimed was "entitled to the most attentive consideration of the Court." Following Nelson, Meredith put forward an originalist argument that explained the textual ambiguities of the fugitive slave clause. Meredith asked rhetorically: why was the clause in the Constitution at all? Because, he went on to explain, "public opinion in the northern section of the country, had materially changed with regard to the policy and humanity of a system that had unfortunately been fastened upon the colonies by the power of the mother country, without regard to their interests and in defiance of repeated protests." Slavery was an evil, Meredith contended, and northern states had undertaken to end it. Pennsylvania passed an act for its gradual abolition in 1780. That same year, continued Meredith, Massachusetts emancipated her slaves by the Declaration of Rights in the state's constitution. In time, all the New England states would follow. But the southern states had not, and to come into the union they had required security for their property. They came willing to compromise, however. In exchange for giving Congress the right to prohibit the Atlantic slave trade after 1808, the North protected slavery where it existed. Such was the intent of the Framers and "undoubtedly, was the confidence of the whole south." In short, both the original intent and the original understanding of the fugitive slave clause contemplated federal enforcement of the clause, because "its whole purpose might be defeated" were enforcement left to the individual states.

This was an argument developed by a northern jurist, to be sure, but one that supported the proslavery outcome of negating the states' personal liberty laws. Despite being proslavery, it was not in concert with the southern position articulated in the wake of the abolitionist mail campaign of the 1830s. Meredith did not rest southerners' claims to fugitive slaves on implied conditions of Union, or on a property right paramount to the Constitution. This argument had been reflected in Maryland's official response to Pennsylvania's extradition demand for Edward Prigg and his associates, when the Maryland legislature declared that Marylanders' right to their fugitive slaves predated the constitutional grant. The distinction may seem academic, but it carried with it a refutation of the antislavery principles that accompanied *Somerset v. Stewart*. Meredith never mentioned it. It is possible (even likely) that his colleague John Nelson did, but Nelson never submitted his argument to the reporter and there is no extant copy.

Pennsylvania's attorneys followed separate tracks in their arguments. Thomas Hambly endorsed the abolitionist argument that a strict textual interpretation of the fugitive slave clause gave no authority to Congress to legislate, nor gave the slaveholder a direct, immediate, and unqualified right to recaption. Hambly provided an amusing, if morbid, illustration of why this could not be so. What if, on the streets of Philadelphia, a man from Virginia and another from South Carolina simultaneously claimed the same man as their fugitive slave? Should they "execute the judgment of Solomon?" A judicial hearing was required to decide whose was the true claim. And because the fugitive slave clause did not give power to the federal government, the principle of strict construction reserved the power to hear fugitive slave claims to the states. As for the idea that it would be more expedient to have one national rule rather than multiple state rules for rendition, Hambly admonished the justices that "we must take the Constitution as we find it! Our duty is to construe, not to legislate." Following Hambly's argument, the Court was duty bound to strike down the Fugitive Slave Act of 1793. This was a bold request. Not only had the Supreme Court traditionally steered clear of striking down federal law, but the Fugitive Slave Act had been passed by a Congress that boasted both framers and ratifiers of the Constitution and signed into law by George Washington. Surely contemporaneous exposition of the Constitution by the Founders themselves was due respect and deference. Hambly met the argument with contempt. "If there be any one thing in this country entirely loose, uncertain, and vacillating, it is legislation," he snarled, "and whenever the judicial exposition of our highest Courts becomes so wavering and uncertain as to bear comparison with our legislation, we shall truly be the pity and contempt of all civilized nations."

Hambly was not content to rest solely on the principle of strict construction. He argued trenchantly that Pennsylvania's Personal Liberty Law of 1826 was in concert with the spirit of the Constitution. "In the non-slaveholding states the presumption is, that every man is a free man until the contrary be proved," Hambly told the Court. "It is like every other legal presumption, in favour of the right." This was true in criminal prosecutions as well as debt cases. Slaveholders' claims to their runaways were no different. They had to be proven. Hambly frankly acknowledged that slaves were not parties to the Constitution, but this was beside the point: "Pennsylvania says: Instead of preventing you from taking your slaves, we are anxious that you should have them; they are a population we do not covet, and all our legislation tends toward giving you every facility to get them: but we do claim the right of legislating upon this subject so as to bring you under legal restraint, which will prevent you from taking a free man."

Ovid F. Johnson, Pennsylvania's attorney general, spoke next. He argued for a preservation of the status quo that allowed both the federal and state governments to render fugitives in accordance with congressional interpretation of the clause, and left to the states the ability to protect their residents from kidnapping. Johnson argued that this was more in keeping with traditional constitutional practice. Against Jonathan Meredith's (and really, Justice Samuel Nelson's) originalist argument, Johnson offered one of his own. "Had the southern states demanded more than this simple guarantee," Johnson pointed out, "had they required that the right of the states to prescribe the mode of surrendering up fugitive slaves should be yielded to Congress exclusively; we know not but it might have jeoparded the formation of the Union itself." Here was a clever rhetorical reversal of the notion that the fugitive slave clause constituted a fundamental article of union. If it was in fact so necessary a bargain, then it followed that one ought to be faithful to its exact text.

The heart of Johnson's argument lay in his understanding of federalism. Against the strict separation of sovereign powers, he allowed that the Founders had envisioned a system of concurrent authority. In this case, "The acts of Congress and of Pennsylvania form together a harmonious system, neither jarring nor conflicting in any part of its operation." Arriving at this conclusion depended upon an evolving constitutional jurisprudence. The Fugitive Slave Act of 1793 clearly contemplated state action in fugitive slave rendition, but it had since been settled by the Court that Congress could not compel state officers. The states had legislated in the interim to enforce the fugitive slave clause. Provided state law did not conflict with the Fugitive Slave Act, Johnson concluded, both congressional and state law were con-

stitutional. Johnson cited one more pertinent reason for the constitutionality of Pennsylvania's law. Congress's Fugitive Slave Act gave
the slaveholder a remedy if his property were taken from him, but it
was "silent as to the rights of negroes wrongfully seized." Clearly, it
was up to the states to protect free blacks, whose right to liberty was
every bit as strong as slaveholders' right to their property. Or so Pennsylvania argued.

Thus ended oral arguments. Chief Justice Roger B. Taney assigned
the opinion of the Court to Joseph Story. Likely he chose Story
because it would be advantageous to have a northern justice issue an
opinion that many contemporaries would consider proslavery. Story
had also issued the opinion in *The Amistad* and had succeeded in that
opinion in drawing together all elements of the Court. Likely, it had
been clear at the time of the opinion's assigning that all the justices
agreed that Pennsylvania's law should be struck down as unconstitutional. Perhaps it was less clear that the justices would disagree over
the reasoning, for Taney himself would come to regret assigning Story
the opinion.

CHAPTER 9

Deciding *Prigg*

Justice Joseph Story read his opinion in open court on March 1, 1842, not three weeks removed from the conclusion of oral arguments. He began by candidly acknowledging that "few questions which have ever come before this Court involve more delicate and important considerations; and few upon which the public at large may be presumed to feel a more profound and pervading interest." His next paragraph warned away those who might read too much into the opinion. "We shall limit ourselves to those considerations which appropriately and exclusively belong to it," said Story, "without laying down any rules of interpretation of a more general nature." If Story read this portion of his opinion aloud, hearts likely fluttered in the audience. Someone was going to be offended. Exactly who was cleared up a few minutes later, when Story said that the fugitive slave clause was so vital to southern interests at the time of the framing and ratification of the Constitution "that it cannot be doubted that it constituted a fundamental article, without the adoption of which the Union could not have been formed."

Supporters of Pennsylvania's position (if they had ever allowed themselves any hope) likely felt their hearts sink at this point, for Story's short invocation of "historical necessity" signaled acceptance of Jonathan Meredith's argument that the moral arc of history had doomed slavery in the North prior to the adoption of the Constitution. The implication was that the free states could not be trusted to return fugitives. And this meant that the Founders must have contemplated federal enforcement of the fugitive slave clause. Any hopes that *Prigg v. Pennsylvania* would be a triumph for freedom, along the lines of Story's own opinion in the *Amistad* case, were dashed.

But Story's was not the only opinion in *Prigg v. Pennsylvania*. Six other justices entered the fray, leaving only two silent. Nine justices agreed that Pennsylvania's Personal Liberty Law of 1826 was unconstitutional, but they disagreed sharply as to why. Some of their disagreements would be on pedantic points of doctrine and interpretation, others on more fundamental issues of federalism. The rupture was visible. The Court would leave unresolved the issues of slavery and the Constitution that it had promised to solve when it took the case.

Story's opinion for the Court attempted a grand logical solution to the riddle of slavery, freedom, and constitutional rights. He faced a formidable challenge. The slaveholders claimed a constitutional right to fugitive slaves. Abolitionists demanded strict construction of the fugitive slave clause in order to empower the states rather than the federal government. Free blacks' liberty was imperiled if no law protected them from kidnapping. Unionists rightly recognized the explosive potential of the situation. This was especially true given the rise of states' rights in constitutional thinking, politics, and jurisprudence. If Justice Story was to salvage a truly national Union on consistent principles, he would have to reconcile these competing claims and do so logically and consistently.

Story had invoked the notion that the fugitive slave clause was historically necessary for union, but he nonetheless ticked through all the other reasons why the Fugitive Slave Act was itself constitutional. The passage of a law not four years after the consummation of the Constitution, a law signed by none other than George Washington himself, was as close to contemporaneous exposition as one could get. The long acquiescence of the country to the Fugitive Slave Act was another mark in its favor. Likewise, every court before which it had appeared sustained its constitutionality. But even these proofs were, for Story, gratuitous: "Our judgment would be the same if the question were entirely new, and the act of Congress were of recent enactment. We hold the act to be clearly constitutional in all of its leading provisions." Story's was a position dependent first and foremost upon logic and reason.

Of all the questions Story was addressing, what clearly concerned him the most was securing the high ground for congressional power to legislate. Having given practical evidence of the Fugitive Slave Act's constitutionality, Story next provided theoretical proofs for national exclusivity. The fugitive slave clause, argued Story, created "a new and positive right . . . confined to no territorial limits, and bounded by no state institutions or policy. The natural inference deducible from this consideration certainly is, in the absence of any positive delegation of power to the state legislatures, that it belongs to the legislative department of the national government, to which it owes its origin and establishment." Story then put this another way. It would be a "forced construction" to assume that the Framers meant to leave the enforcement of a national right to the states. In keeping with his own rules for constitutional construction (as he elucidated in his widely read *Commentaries on the Constitution*), Story turned to the object and purpose of the fugitive slave clause, which required "that it should be controlled by one and the same will, and act uniformly by the same system of regulations throughout the Union." Without a uniform system, the mode of recovery would differ from state to state. One state might require more proof than another; one state might have a summary hearing while another might refuse remedies altogether. "Consequences like these must have been foreseen as very likely to occur in the non-slaveholding states," Story proclaimed. There was but one conclusion: "construe the right of legislation as exclusive in Congress, and every evil, and every danger vanishes."

Story supplied one caveat to this rule of national exclusivity: it was not meant to interfere with the police power of the states, which had never been surrendered to the United States. The police power allowed the states "to arrest and restrain runaway slaves, and remove them from their borders, and otherwise to secure themselves against their depredations and evil example, as they certainly may do in cases of idlers, vagabonds, and paupers." States could pass these laws but could not interfere with the "just rights of the owner [of fugitive slaves] to reclaim his slave."

The internal logic of Story's opinion was sound, if one accepted his premises. The right of slaveholders to their fugitive slaves was now completely grounded in the Constitution and had no basis in natural law or the law of nations. From this right, Story reasoned, slaveholders had the power to seize fugitives wherever they found them (within the United States) and to compel them to return to their home state. This was a straightforward reading of the common law right of recaption. Story then used the common law to limit this right by requiring that seizures be conducted "without any breach of the peace or any illegal violence." No one in 1842 could have imagined that fugitive slave reclamation could be conducted without breach of the peace, both because fugitives resisted being forced back into slavery and because abolitionists protected fugitives. Put another way, slaveholders might have the right of recaption, but it was fairly useless in the face of resistance. In order to avoid the private violence that accompanied recaption, slaveholders would have to rely upon publicly authorized uses of violence. But which authority took precedence in the system of dual sovereignties? Story had labored to show that the design and purpose of the constitutional right to fugitive slaves demanded that Congress exercise the right. Congressional exclusivity was reasonable if one accepted that the historical basis for the fugitive slave clause was to restrain abolitionist sentiment in the free states. But this was also a clever way of stating that slavery had no basis in natural law but could only be supported by express recognition in the Constitution. Thus, *Somerset v. Stewart* undergirded Story's reasoning, and he duly cited the case. But *Somerset* was a prop for Story, deliberately placed to convince slaveholders how dependent they were on constitutional guarantees for their property. It also lent weight to his instrumentalist reading of the Constitution. If a uniform, national rule better effected the enforcement of a constitutional right, then it took precedence. And if it worked here, it might work elsewhere — despite Story's disingenuous claim that he was not laying down any general rules of interpretation. Story was elevating his nationalist jurisprudence on the backs of fugitive slaves.

Congressional exclusivity raised the problem of whether or not Congress could direct state judges to take jurisdiction in fugitive slave rendition hearings. Story disposed with this problem rather casually in a statement that revealed another point of unanimity on the Court. While disagreement existed as to whether state judges were bound by the act of Congress to take jurisdiction "none is entertained by the Court that state magistrates may, if they choose, exercise the authority unless prohibited by state legislation." In short, Congress could extend jurisdiction to state judges to hear rendition cases but could not compel them to hear cases. State judges and magistrates could take jurisdiction unless forbidden to do so by state law. This at once dismissed abolitionist arguments that the Fugitive Slave Act was unconstitutional because it compelled state officers and legitimated all the rendition proceedings that had taken place at the state level, some under the aegis of state law. It reassured stalwart defenders of states' rights that Congress could not compel state officers to enforce federal law. But it nonetheless maintained congressional supremacy and thus took a significant power away from the states.

A second problem lay in his treatment of the state's police power. Story treated the subject gingerly, leaving space for the state to act against the "evil example" of runaways by arresting or deporting them. But this threw into doubt the constitutionality of state laws friendly to slaveholders seeking fugitive slaves. It also sidestepped the question of kidnapping. Nowhere did Story attempt to distinguish between a state's appropriate use of the police power to protect free blacks from kidnapping and inappropriate interference with fugitive slave rendition. Story chose to meet this problem by ignoring it.

In summary, Story's opinion made the following points. First, slaveholders' right of recaption of their fugitive slaves was guaranteed by the Constitution. They could seize their fugitives anywhere, with or without a warrant, and no power could prevent them from doing so. (They did, however, have to do so without breaching the peace.) Second, the power to enforce the fugitive slave clause lay exclusively with Congress. Third, the states could not interfere with or even enforce the fugitive slave clause through legislation. It followed that Pennsylvania's Personal Liberty Law of 1826 was unconstitutional and void. Fourth, states could pass laws restraining and/or expelling fugitive slaves by virtue of their police power, provided they did so under their reserved rights to police their populations rather than under warrant of the fugitive slave clause. Fifth, Congress could not compel the states to enforce the Fugitive Slave Act, but state officers could take jurisdiction under it if they so chose.

However much a victory for Maryland this was, the Maryland-born Chief Justice was unhappy with Story's reasoning. Like Story, he reasoned from the constitutional right of slaveholders to their fugitives, although he put it in much stronger terms. A slaveholder had, by the fugitive slave clause, "a right, peaceably, to take possession of him [a fugitive slave] and carry him away without any certificate or warrant from a judge of the District or Circuit Court of the United

States, or from any magistrate of the state; and whoever resists or obstructs him is a wrongdoer: and every state law which proposes directly or indirectly to authorize such resistance or obstruction is null and void." The constitutional right was paramount, and neither Congress nor the states could ever take it away. More to the point, Pennsylvania's law was unconstitutional because it *required* a slaveholder to obtain a certificate before leaving the state. Like Story, Taney made no distinction between the slaveholder who obtained a certificate of removal from a federal court and one who exercised the right of recaption and carried the fugitive back without a certificate, provided it was done peaceably. A strict reading of Taney's opinion might suggest less of a commitment to this qualification, as it was difficult to presume that any seizure of a fugitive slave could be done without violence, unless carrying someone away in manacles chained in a wagon could be considered peaceable. But this was a difference in degree, not in logic, and up to this point, Taney and Story were in agreement.

Where Taney broke with Story was over Story's holding of congressional exclusivity. The language of the Constitution, Chief Justice Taney argued, did not prohibit the states from enforcing the master's right to his fugitive slaves. The states were "forbidden to make any regulation that shall impair [the master's right]," Taney explained, "but there the prohibition stops." Against Story's constitutional construction that placed so much emphasis on the *object* of the clause, Taney substituted a textual rule: "the words of the article which direct that the fugitive 'shall be delivered up,' seem evidently designed to impose it as a duty upon the people of the several states to pass laws to carry into execution, in good faith, the compact into which they thus solemnly entered with each other." Taney also rejected Story's assertion that because the slaveholder's right stemmed from the U.S. Constitution, it could be upheld only by the federal government. "There are other clauses in the Constitution in which other individual rights are provided for and secured in like manner," said Taney, "and it never has been suggested that the states could not uphold and maintain them." By way of example, Taney pointed to the contracts clause, which prevented states from impairing contractual obligations but did not prevent them from enforcing them. In fact, the states were obligated to uphold private contracts; Taney implied by analogy that the states were also obligated to provide for the rendition of fugitive slaves.

Taney's opinion reached further, into the practical consequences of congressional exclusivity. The very nature of fugitive slave reclamation depended upon cooperation from state officers. Not only were the jails and courtrooms necessary in order to secure the body of fugitives, but a slaveholder would stand powerless without the aid of state law enforcement to guard his property if abolitionists were determined to harbor or rescue fugitives. Against this, the Fugitive Slave Act of 1793 was little comfort. "Now," remarked Taney, "in many of the states there is but one [federal] district judge, and there are only nine states which have judges of the Supreme Court residing within them. The fugitive will frequently be found by his owner in a place very distant from the residence of either of these judges." Without state assistance, in other words, slaveholders faced perilous odds in the free states. There were further problems. The Fugitive Slave Act did not provide for arrest warrants, a necessity if fugitives were being harbored inside citizens' homes. And the Fugitive Slave Act of 1793 clearly "counted upon the cordial co-operation" of state authorities.

One might argue here that Story's opinion left a little leeway for the states to pass laws to aid fugitive slave reclamation, under their police power. But Taney exposed the problem with Story's reasoning: "The fugitive is not always arrested in order to prevent a dangerous or evil-disposed person from remaining in her territory. He is himself most commonly anxious to escape from it. . . . He may sometimes be found travelling peaceably along the public highway on his road to another state, in company with and under the protection of a white man who is abetting his escape." The police power, in other words, was a sandy ground upon which to lay a foundation for assistance in the rendition of fugitive slaves. Why not plant it in the firm soil of the fugitive slave clause, which states had been doing for the better part of half a century? Provided that state laws were "not in conflict with the remedy provided by Congress," Taney saw no constitutional impediment.

Taney's opinion provided a pole for dissent. He essentially agreed with all of Story's points, save the conclusion Story reached on congressional exclusivity. Other justices weighed in. Justice Peter Daniel of Virginia — a states' rights stalwart — concurred with Taney that states held concurrent power to pass laws aiding in fugitive slave reclamation, although he was silent on the subject of whether the fugitive slave clause was self-executing. Justice Smith Thompson also rejected the notion of congressional exclusivity. He laid out several scenarios in which state legislation would be appropriate. Thompson refused to enlarge on the point, leaving open the question of whether federal law preempted state law (thus immediately negating it) or whether the states could pass laws concurrently. It was a tepid opinion by Thompson, mirroring his approach in *Groves v. Slaughter* a year earlier. Only Justice Anthony Wayne concurred fully with Justice Story's opinion of the Court. Catron and McKinley chose to remain silent, and scholars have debated ever since whether this meant they fully concurred with Story's opinion or just with the central holding that the Pennsylvania personal liberty law was unconstitutional.

Henry Baldwin proved a loose cannon. Again. He, too, agreed that Pennsylvania's law was unconstitutional, but (as the court reporter recorded from Baldwin's oral remarks at the reading of opinions) "he dissented from the principles laid down by the Court as the grounds of their opinion." Baldwin reportedly declared that the clause was self-executing and that once Congress legislated, that legislation preempted the states. However, Justice Anthony Wayne (and a lawyer who attended the reading of opinions) reported that Baldwin also held that both federal and state law were unconstitutional because the clause was self-executing. These two stances were contradictory, and Baldwin filed no written opinion to clarify his meaning. This fit Baldwin's erratic jurisprudence.

Justice John McLean of Ohio wrote a spirited dissent. But his dissent did not accept Pennsylvania's position, nor did it accept the abolitionist argument that the Fugitive Slave Act of 1793 was an unconstitutional exercise of authority by Congress. On the contrary, he concurred with Story that the power to pass laws enforcing the fugitive slave clause was exclusive in Congress. The focus of his dissent was the apparent agreement among the justices that a state could not punish kidnapping as an offense. "Can the master seize his slave and remove him out of the state in disregard of its laws," asked McLean rhetorically, "as he might take his horse which is running at large?" No! A slave was "a sensible and human being," subject to local law. "The state may protect him against all the world except the claim of his master," McLean continued. "Should any one commit lawless violence on the slave, the offender may unquestionably be punished; and should the slave commit murder, he may be detained and punished for it by the state." The state's right to do so, added McLean, could be "in disregard of the claim of the master."

McLean was putting the rights of the master up against the sovereignty of the states, and in this sense he was dissenting not so much from the holdings of the Court as from the reasoning that elevated the slaveholders' rights above all others. Against Taney's position that the clause was self-executing, McLean maintained that slaves, just like anyone else, were subject to the laws of the jurisdiction in which they found themselves and that this would necessarily prohibit a slaveholder from merely seizing a person upon a naked claim. Against Story's opinion of the Court, McLean held that there were legitimate exercises of the police power that might interfere with the master's right: for instance, punishing a fugitive slave for murder superseded the master's right to take hold of the fugitive. And should a master be mistaken in his claim—should he seize a freeman claiming that the freeman was his slave—then he was liable to state charges of kidnapping. This meant, for McLean, that in the case before him both parties were at fault. The justice of the peace to whom Edward Prigg brought Margaret Morgan was "bound to perform the duty required of him by a law paramount to any act, on the same subject, in his own state." But the justice of the peace's refusal did not in turn justify Edward Prigg's actions: "he should have taken the fugitive before a judge of the United States, two of whom resided within the state." And the failure to do so, McLean was saying, could be legitimately punished as a crime by Pennsylvania.

McLean's opinion was hardly a victory for abolitionists, especially if judged against the antislavery jurisprudence of the 1840s. But he was the only judge who took seriously the problem posed by kidnapping. Again, the bare act of removing someone against her will across state lines to reduce her from freedom to slavery could be either a kidnapping or a rendition. McLean hammered home the fact that none of the other judges gave this any consideration. The bench spoke only to the rights of slaveholders and not those of free blacks. Even McLean spoke only obliquely about the rights of free blacks by invoking the power of individual states. To this he added a provocative point: the states might resist the Supreme Court by continuing to enforce their personal liberty laws in defiance of *Prigg v. Pennsylva-*

nia. Even if the Supreme Court demanded to review such a case, "the supreme court of a State may refuse to certify its record on a writ of error to the Supreme Court of the Union under the 25th section of the Judiciary Act." The Supreme Court had encountered precisely this resistance before. In fact, it had faced significant resistance to its decisions in every decade since the Constitution's adoption. This was a fundamental problem in a constitutional system where dual sovereigns claimed authority. "But resistance to a constitutional authority by any of the state functionaries should not be anticipated," McLean commented, "and if made, the Federal Government may rely upon its own agency in giving effect to the laws." The final solution would thus be a matter of power rather than legal authority. McLean would prove prescient in this regard.

With McLean's dissent recorded, the justices were done speaking about *Prigg v. Pennsylvania*. The case had been decided.

By the time the opinions had been issued in *Prigg v. Pennsylvania*, the fault lines that had been evident in the Court in *Groves v. Slaughter* of a year earlier had deepened. This time it was Story rather than McLean who braided Lord Mansfield's *Somerset v. Stewart* into his opinion. *Somerset* had grounded slavery's existence in naked power rather than natural property rights. So too did Story refer to fugitive slave recaption as "a new and positive right" granted by the Constitution, independent of any other legal source. Slaveholders owed the continued existence of this right to the Constitution and to Congress.

Although Story denied that he was laying down general rules of interpretation for other cases, it is hard to imagine that he did not have a few related issues in mind when he wrote *Prigg v. Pennsylvania*. At the heart of his opinion was the notion that Congress's power could be extended on the basis of expediency rather than a strict reading of the text. If a uniform rule was *desirable*, Story was saying, then Congress ought to have the authority to pass a uniform rule. But the logic of his opinion went in another direction as well. He had argued that the fugitive slave clause fully contemplated national supremacy. When a power belonged to Congress, it necessarily blocked any concurrent legislation by the states that touched the same subject, essentially voiding such laws. By analogy, the Negro seamen acts had regulated interstate commerce by jailing northern sailors of African descent when they entered southern ports. But if the power to regulate interstate commerce was exclusive in Congress — and no one could deny that it was — then the Negro seamen acts would, by analogy, be unconstitutional. Of course, the Negro seamen acts had found their basis in the reserved police power of the states. But Story's opinion made an allowance for regulations of police, provided they did not interfere in an area in which federal power was exclusive. Clearly the Negro seamen acts did not meet this standard. More to the point, black sailors could seek habeas corpus protection in federal courts if jailed by a southern law that purported to regulate interstate commerce.

Whether Story wrote *Prigg v. Pennsylvania* with this analogy in mind is not provable, but his singular focus on congressional exclusivity and its implications for the limits of state sovereignty supports the reading. But the point was also subtle enough that most of the other members of the Court missed it. After all, John McLean — the most openly antislavery justice — carved out a larger space for state sovereignty that would have undermined application of the *Prigg* principle to black sailors in southern ports. And McLean's dissent further exposed the silent racism upon which Story's opinion was founded. Story could elevate the slaveholder's right of warrantless recaption, the summary hearing, and the weak evidentiary standards of federal law only by denying that free blacks had rights. But Story never made this denial explicit. He simply ignored their rights. For his part, McLean did as well, but he at least insisted that the states had the power to punish those who did not even submit to the minimal legal process required by federal law.

Taney's opinion supporting the concurrent authority of the states to pass fugitive slave laws refuted Story's claim of exclusivity, but it did not entirely refute Story's constitutional reasoning. He did reference the "compact" among the states, which placed obligations upon the federal and state governments alike. This signaled an acceptance of the southern position that the implied conditions of the Constitution prevented action against slavery (for instance, banning it in the territories or in the District of Columbia), but Taney did not explicitly say so. Nor did Taney enjoy support from the southern bloc of justices. Only Justice Daniel of Virginia sided with him. Both John Catron of Tennessee and John McKinley of Alabama were silent, and

Anthony Wayne of Georgia sided with Story. On the Supreme Court at least, Taney's was not the "southern" position.

In all of the sixty-six printed pages of the judges' opinions on *Prigg v. Pennsylvania*, one universal silence was observed. Not one justice dealt with the relevant fact of Margaret Morgan's child who was born in Pennsylvania. Story recited the facts of the case, noting that Margaret's children had been removed, but there his discussion ended. Not one justice addressed the question of what to do with a child born in the state of Pennsylvania to a fugitive slave. Both Margaret Morgan and her children had been taken against their will from a state of freedom to one of slavery. It is eminently possible that Margaret Morgan was by law a fugitive slave, and thus her removal a legal one, while the removal of her Pennsylvania-born child was done without law and was therefore a kidnapping. One might argue that this was the central question in the case, at least for the free blacks and fugitive slaves whom the decision would most directly affect. Slaveholders might have argued that the fugitive slave clause affixed the status of slavery to fugitives no matter where they ran and that this necessarily meant that their children would be subject to the law of the state from which they ran, and thus counted as slaves. But slaveholders did not even bother to make this argument, and the justices were silent on the question. By this silence, the law made a slave of the child.

CHAPTER 10

After the Court

John Quincy Adams spent March 10, 1842, puzzling over *Prigg v. Pennsylvania*. The ex-president then serving as a congressman from Massachusetts recorded no kind words for the Supreme Court in his diary. The case was "seven judges, every one of them dissenting from the reasoning of all the rest, and every one of them coming to the same conclusion—the transcendent omnipotence of slavery in these United States, riveted by a clause in the Constitution that persons held to labor escaping from one State to another, shall be delivered up on the claim of the person to whom labor is due." Adams was no mean rhetorician; his hyperbole was intentional. It had the effect of pointing out that all the justices of the Supreme Court—no matter if they were northern or southern, for or against slavery—were ready and willing to interpret the Constitution in a way that reaffirmed the "omnipotence of slavery."

Adams's take on the Supreme Court may have been unkind to the justices, but it also predicted the upheaval that the case would cause. The Court had attempted to resolve a constitutional question that had bedeviled America for half a century: how does one negotiate the difference between kidnapping and fugitive slave reclamation? Slaveholders and free blacks had previously sought rights in petitions to their legislatures and in suits before the courts. The answer had been to divide kidnapping from rendition conceptually and to require that status determination occur in the state where the alleged fugitive was found. The result may not have been tidy, but it did allow the states some latitude in determining what evidence was necessary to prove status, as well as balance constitutional duties to protect both property and liberty. In place of this, *Prigg v. Pennsylvania* served up a new set of principles. From now on, any attempt to stall fugitive slave rendition amounted to the denial of a constitutional right held by slaveholders. States were forbidden to interfere with the process. Kidnapping might still be defined as a crime, but no person claiming a fugitive slave could be charged with it.

But Adams also put his finger on one of *Prigg v. Pennsylvania*'s enduring legacies: confusion. Not everyone interpreted *Prigg* the same way. Amongst abolitionists, *Prigg v. Pennsylvania* had different effects. Some could not help but draw the obvious conclusion — that the Constitution protected slavery and was more an obstacle than a help in the drive to abolish slavery. Other abolitionists, just as committed to slavery's eradication, took umbrage at the Supreme Court's unsettling of the law. Still others found ways to comply with the new constitutional regime that still allowed them to hinder slaveholders in their hunt for slaves. Some slaveholders heralded the decision as a vindication of their rights. Others were suspicious. Many Americans who did not count themselves in either of these camps hoped the decision would be acquiesced to. But the most enduring contemporary reaction to *Prigg v. Pennsylvania* was confusion. Some judges were clearly uncertain what the Supreme Court's ruling meant. Many people continued to ask state courts to interpose themselves for the protection of residents, and the courts still did. Although the Supreme Court justices repeatedly upheld the ruling, signs of discontent with the nature of Story's opinion emerged. When Congress took up the issue in 1850, the debates revealed just how contentious the decision had been. Even the new Fugitive Slave Act of 1850, written in conformity with Story's opinion in *Prigg*, carried the seeds of doubt with it. It withstood federal judicial scrutiny in the 1850s, but was collapsing under the weight of extrinsic challenges.

Three days after the announcement of the decision in *Prigg v. Pennsylvania*, the *National Intelligencer* printed an unnamed lawyer's analysis of the opinion. The lawyer broke down the opinion into five major points. First, the fugitive slave clause constitutionalized the right of recaption. Second, the clause contemplated congressional legislation to make the delivery of fugitives more effective. Third, once Congress legislated, it preempted any state legislation on the subject. Fourth, the power of legislation was exclusive in Congress. Fifth, the states could, by their reserved police power, "take up runaway slaves, and guard against their misconduct or depredations." The lawyer also summed up the various concurrences. It was a straightforward analysis and, even if abbreviated and blind to nuances, essentially accurate. Newspapers throughout the country reprinted the *National Intelligencer* article, making it the standard for popular interpretation of *Prigg v. Pennsylvania*.

Abolitionists reacted swiftly. "The effect of this decision seems to be," declared the *Boston Courier* in a widely reprinted article, "to deprive the States of all power of affording protection to its colored free citizens." Any white kidnapper, the paper proclaimed, could now seize a black person, appear as a witness for himself, and then drag that person beyond even the borders of the United States without the benefit of trial by jury. "It is not so much against the power of taking away in this manner an *actual fugitive slave*, fully proved to be such, that complaint is made," explained the *Courier*, "as the manifest injustice of *deciding* whether a man IS free or a slave, upon such dangerous evidence, by such a summary process, and without the intervention of a jury." This, the abolitionist sheet concluded, violated the Fifth Amendment's guarantee of due process. The *New York Spectator* drew further implications. *Prigg* affected every man in the free states, and there was not a single person "whose personal liberty is not invaded and endangered by it." The author noted wryly that the Constitution made no distinction of color, so if a free black might be carried away by the law, so might Justice Story himself. There was a whiff of revolution in the way abolitionists were now asserting rights for free blacks. True, the tactic was old. James Forten's letters protesting the Pennsylvania registration law of 1813 (examined in Chapter 4) had asked legislators to imagine registering their own children — in short, to not divide privileges arbitrarily by race. Yet this went further. Abolitionists had divined a colorblind federal Constitution and were now judging Story's opinion by this standard.

Rights danced with power as well. *The Philanthropist* of Cincinnati crisply observed that "the decision of the court makes a wreck of state sovereignty." Without the power "to throw around their citizens the bulwarks of habeas corpus and jury trial," the abolitionist paper noted, then "every citizen of every state is to be placed at the sole discretion of Congress." Fighting the logic of *Prigg v. Pennsylvania* meant arguing that the Court got federalism wrong. The decision invalidated every state's antikidnapping law, insofar as a kidnapper could merely claim the legal cover of fugitive slave recaption and thus gain immunity from any state law. Part of Justice Story's essential logic had been that state laws were invalid because they might impede slaveholders' rights, thus defeating the constitutional guarantee. Abolitionists now in turn insisted that it was each state's right — duty, actually — to protect its citizens from potential kidnapping in order to fulfill constitutional guarantees to liberty. At issue was not only the extent of rights but the powers of both the federal and state governments.

Such arguments convinced many abolitionists of what they had already strongly suspected — that the Constitution was incurably proslavery and that disunion was the only remedy. Before encountering the opinion in *Prigg v. Pennsylvania*, John Quincy Adams (the ex-president had served as a representative from Massachusetts since 1831) was fresh off a colossal fight in the U.S. Congress that stemmed from an antislavery petition that residents of Haverhill, Massachusetts, had given to him. Adams introduced the petition on January 24, 1842. All petitions touching on the subject of slavery were, by the Gag Rule adopted in 1836, tabled without referring the petitions to a committee, printing them, or discussing them. Northern Democrats supported the Gag Rule as a means of getting the volatile issue of slavery out of the room. Most northerners in 1836 were hostile toward abolitionists anyway, so they made an easy target. But John Quincy Adams believed the Gag Rule an unconstitutional usurpation of the cherished First Amendment right to petition. He became its implacable foe, repeatedly attempting to subvert it by reading petitions when he had the floor during debate in the House of Representatives. This was precisely what he did on Monday, January 24, 1842. But the petition from Haverhill was different. It called for a dissolution of the union.

The House was stunned. James A. Meriwether of Georgia said such a petition ought not to be allowed within the walls of the House. Addressing the Speaker of the House, George Washington Hopkins of Virginia asked if a motion to burn the petition was in order. Adams's opponents immediately suggested that he be censured for bringing so clearly unconstitutional a petition before the body. In their estimation, this was the logic of abolition fully played out. Abolitionists, they felt, petitioned every year for deliberately unconstitutional acts to be taken by Congress against slavery. Here was but one more that specifically called for what slaveholders warned about: the dissolution of the Union. It was as if the petitioners from Haverhill had handed slaveholders their own best argument against Congress receiving abolitionist petitions. But Adams welcomed this fight. He stood upon the right to petition and refused the gag. On February 7, 1842 — the day before the Supreme Court heard oral arguments in *Prigg*, Adams's opponents admitted defeat and tabled the motion to censure him for introducing the Haverhill petition.

The Haverhill petition reveals that many abolitionists had come to the conclusion, in advance of *Prigg v. Pennsylvania*, that the Constitution was incurably proslavery. It was in February of 1842 that the antislavery hero Wendell Phillips thundered at an audience in Boston's Faneuil Hall that the Constitution was really "the South Carolinians' charter of safety." By April of 1842, abolitionists, including William Lloyd Garrison, were openly calling for dissolution of the Union. In 1843 and 1844, the American Anti-Slavery Society radicalized, adopting the slogan "No Union with Slaveholders." *Prigg* had provided the last bit of evidence to confirm their view of the Constitution, but it cannot be thought of as the primary reason for driving abolitionists to disunion. By 1845, Wendell Phillips had published *The Constitution: A Proslavery Compact*, which provided naked extracts from James Madison's notes of the Convention to demonstrate just how frankly the Founders had discussed, compromised on, and ultimately protected slavery.

At the other end of the abolitionist spectrum was Lysander Spooner, who also published in 1845 his radical text *The Unconstitutionality of Slavery*. It was a sophistic work that employed all manner of logical flaws to "prove" that the fugitive slave clause did not actually require the return of fugitive slaves. Intermittently employing textualism, natural law, and originalism, Spooner confidently concluded that people "held to service" were servants only and that slavery could not pass as a condition from parents to children. In Spooner's constitutional universe, there were no slaves. Such utopianism had no need of *Prigg v. Pennsylvania*, and it is likely for this reason that Spooner did not bother even to address the case, let alone dismiss it.

Prigg radicalized abolitionists in still another way. Story's opinion had allowed that state magistrates could hear fugitive rendition cases under the Fugitive Slave Act of 1793 unless expressly prohibited by state law but that Congress could never compel state officers to enforce the Fugitive Slave Act. Joshua Giddings, a representative from Ohio, grasped the implications of this immediately. Writing under the pen name *Pacificus, a Whig from Ohio*, Giddings began by admitting that it had always been presumed by Ohioans that they were bound to execute the fugitive slave laws. *Prigg v. Pennsylvania* corrected this misapprehension. State officers should *never* interfere with a slaveholder's recaption. Should a fugitive slave exercise his natural right of self-defense and turn on a slaveholder, argued Giddings, no Ohio law could prevent it. "If the slave, in defending himself, kill his master," Giddings explained, "it is a matter in which we have no concern." Even better, Ohioans were "under no constitutional, legal, or moral obligation" to aid the master in his act of recaption. Giddings's analysis descended into absurdity—of course Ohio law would take cognizance of murder within its borders, and nothing in *Prigg* could justify such a conclusion. But Giddings's other proposition was spot on. State officers could refuse to enforce federal law. The state legislature could forbid its officers from enforcing the Fugitive Slave Act.

And so they did. Massachusetts led the way with the passage of its "Latimer Law" in 1843. Named after George Latimer, a fugitive slave seized in October 1842, the law withdrew all state cooperation for the rendition of fugitive slaves. Latimer's arrest had outraged abolitionists, who publicized the fact that George Latimer was being held in a *city* jail. By withdrawing state support for fugitive slave rendition, the Latimer Law followed the logic of Story's opinion. Pennsylvania would follow Massachusetts's lead in 1847. Ohio repealed its law that aided fugitive slave reclamation but did not forbid its officers to participate in fugitive slave rescues. These were responses that made fugitive slave reclamation more difficult by withdrawing state support. Even in Ohio, where state officers were not specifically prohibited from assisting slaveholders, they also could not be penalized for refusing to act. Thus could opponents of slavery both obey the terms of *Prigg v. Pennsylvania* and carry on their fight.

There is evidence that Justice Story fully understood the implications of his decision and that he knew his opinion would result in the withdrawal of state resources from fugitive slave reclamation and therefore make life more difficult for slavecatchers. He admitted as much in a letter—written not two months after he delivered his opinion in *Prigg*—to Georgia senator John Macpherson Berrien, chair of the Senate Judiciary Committee. He suggested in his letter that the federal government should step up its general provision for federal law enforcement by allowing federal judges to appoint commissioners who could act in all cases where the enforcement of U.S. law was left to state officers. Story specifically mentioned to the Georgia senator that these commissioners could handle fugitive slave cases, a clear carrot to bring a slaveholder in line with expanding federal authority. Story's suggestion was not immediately taken up, but it would become pivotal when a new fugitive slave law was discussed in 1850. More immediately and publicly, however, there were implications for *Prigg v. Pennsylvania* regarding black sailors. A petition praying for relief from the Negro seamen acts of the southern states reached Congress in 1843 and was sent to the Committee on Commerce. The majority report argued that *Prigg v. Pennsylvania* adopted the doctrine that "the police power of the States can never justify enactments or regulations, which are in direct, positive, and permanent conflict with express provisions or fundamental principles of the national compact." Put another way, if slaveholders' rights protected by the Constitution could not be abridged by the free states, neither could free blacks' rights be abridged by the slave states. Late in the session the committee offered resolutions decrying the Negro seamen acts as unconstitutional, but the House of Representatives declined to adopt them. But broaching both these subjects—the expansion of a federal bureaucracy to enforce the fugitive slave clause and the unconstitutionality of the Negro seamen acts—indicated that *Prigg* had radical potential.

For their part, federal judges dutifully obeyed *Prigg v. Pennsylvania*. In the May 1843 term, John McLean—the lone dissenter from the *Prigg* decision—heard a suit initiated under the Fugitive Slave Act of 1793 by Wharton Jones, a Kentucky slaveholder, against John Van Zandt. Van Zandt ran a station on the Underground Railroad in southern Ohio and had been long helping fugitives to find their way further north to Canada. It had surprised no one when he was eventually hauled into court for these actions. Jones sued for the value of two lost slaves and for the amount recoverable under the Fugitive Slave Act of 1793—in all, $1700 (approximately $50,000 today). Van Zandt was a poor farmer with little income. Satisfying this debt would have meant losing everything. Faced with imminent ruin, Van Zandt appealed for help and found it in the antislavery lawyer Salmon P. Chase of Cincinnati. Chase had converted to abolitionism in the 1830s, at a time when such principles brought real danger. He once blocked the doorway of a building to prevent a mob from attacking the abolitionist printer James Birney, who was sheltered inside. Menaced by a leader of the mob who growled at Chase that he would answer for his actions, Chase replied that he could be found at any time. And he could. He defended fugitive slaves in court often enough to earn the title "attorney general of runaway negroes" from Cincinnati's black community. He defended white abolitionists as well, honing his antislavery constitutional arguments in state courts. Chase agreed to defend John Van Zandt, and the case ultimately reached the Supreme Court of the United States in 1847.

Chase's brief to the Supreme Court ran over 100 pages and was a splendid example of moderate antislavery constitutionalism. Unlike the radicals who either turned away from the Constitution's compromises with slavery or refused to acknowledge them, Chase confronted them directly. He declared that the constitutionality of the Fugitive Slave Act was still an open question, given that the statute had not technically been before the Court in *Prigg v. Pennsylvania*. Chase went further, attacking the decision's authority. "In no former case," remarked Chase, "has so great a diversity of views marked the reasonings by which the several judges of this Court have reached their respective conclusions." Chase then attacked warrantless recaption, characterizing it as "subversive of the sovereignty and independence of the states." Further, the Fugitive Slave Act endangered the Fourth Amendment's protection against unreasonable search and seizure, the Fifth Amendment's guarantee of due process, and the Sixth Amendment's guarantee of a jury trial in all criminal matters. He applied rules of strict construction to demonstrate that the fugitive slave clause did not authorize Congress to legislate, and he blended higher law arguments with constitutional construction with surprising elegance. There were things, Chase argued, that legislatures could not do—they could not abrogate contracts, they could not make darkness light or light darkness, they could not make a man a judge in his own cause, and they could not make men into things and things into men.

Against Story's assertion that a uniform rule in fugitive slave rendition was desirable and constitutional, Chase countered that the Fugitive Slave Act violated too many fundamental principles to be law.

Chase's argument was to no avail. Justice Levi Woodbury wrote the decision in *Jones v. Van Zandt* (1847), which unanimously upheld *Prigg v. Pennsylvania* in its entirety and dismissed Chase's arguments without so much as a nod. *Prigg* had withstood the abolitionist assault in the highest court of the land. For his part, Chase would not give up. As he wrote in a private letter, if the federal courts continued to entertain their proslavery construction of the Constitution, then "it must be dragged out, and denounced before the people." Chase was essentially arguing for an appeal from the Supreme Court. "If the courts will not overthrow it," he reckoned, "the people will."

Some people did resist *Prigg v. Pennsylvania*. Several states refused to repeal their laws protecting alleged fugitives. New York prominently maintained its personal liberty law. It was not a decisive act, as the public debate in the wake of *Prigg v. Pennsylvania* generally accepted that New York's law was in conflict with the Supreme Court's ruling. Nonetheless, supporters of the Court's position were unable to win repeal of the law there. The same was true in New Jersey, leaving state judges in confusion. The *Pennsylvania Inquirer and National Gazette* reported in 1843 that counsel for a fugitive slave requested a jury trial in New Jersey. The slaveholder's lawyer objected, citing *Prigg*, but the judge did not believe he had the power to overturn an act of the state legislature. The jury trial proceeded, although it should be noted that the jury returned the fugitive to the slaveholder, or so the paper reported. In New York, a habeas corpus hearing in 1846 resulted in the freeing of an alleged fugitive. Within these pedestrian operations of the law, *Prigg v. Pennsylvania* exerted no influence. People continued to turn to state law to determine procedures for fugitive slave rendition. State judges executed that law. These judges were hardly radicals — they simply were uncertain about the precise meaning of *Prigg* and whether it could actually supersede fundamental law.

Slavecatchers found little solace in *Prigg v. Pennsylvania* in the wake of concerted resistance. When Missouri slavecatchers in Iowa seized several fugitive slaves in 1848, they found themselves resisted by a mob. Despite their invocation of the right of recaption as articulated by Justice Story, they were forced to submit to a local habeas corpus hearing, and the fugitives were released. When a Kentucky slaveholder traveled through Indiana with fugitives he had seized in Michigan, he too found himself before a state court in a habeas corpus hearing, which ended with the fugitives' release. In both cases, the slaveholders sued for the lost value of their slaves, and in both cases they had enormous difficulty recovering those losses. Even more importantly, state judges clearly had no problem interposing habeas corpus proceedings during fugitive slave rendition, in spite of *Prigg*.

Prigg v. Pennsylvania was, by 1850, a failure. Some respected it, others did not. The Supreme Court unanimously upheld *Prigg* and repeated its holding that state laws interfering with recaption were necessarily void. State judges nonetheless equivocated in their reading of the case, unwilling in many cases to abrogate fundamental guarantees of liberty and to void state law. Moreover, compliance with the opinion had the ironic effect of defeating the fugitive slave clause's purpose. In the states where fugitives were most often to be found, the states had withdrawn official support for slaveholders seeking their fugitives. Southerners fulminated. Wild calculations of the monetary losses suffered by slaveholders circulated. Legislatures remonstrated. However proslavery *Prigg v. Pennsylvania* actually was, southerners cared not. With their constitutional rights being flouted, they hardly saw the Supreme Court's friendly ruling in *Prigg* as a victory.

Agitation over the fugitive slave question was but one mark of a political crisis that by 1850 threatened the Union. The massive gains in western territory won by treaty with Britain and war with Mexico had raised the specter of slavery moving westward. Abolitionists demanded that Congress exclude slavery from this new territory, and slaveholders retorted that any such exclusion was an unconstitutional denial of their equal rights. Meanwhile, news of gold strikes in California drew thousands of Americans west, only a handful of whom owned slaves. By 1850, Californians were demanding admission to the Union as a free state, mooting the question of whether Congress might ban slavery in that territory. The state of Texas pressed its territorial claims to the land adjacent to the full length of the Rio Grande, thus promising to extend slavery's empire westward yet further. Abolitionists still pressed for the end of slavery, or at least the slave trade, in Washington, D.C., the prospect of which greatly offended southern politicians loathe to give ground on even trifling issues. Predictably, the two great national parties — the Whigs and the Democrats — showed signs of cracking along sectional lines. Fistfights attended congressional sessions, and on the eve of the 31st Congress's meeting in December 1849, delegates from southern states planned to hold a convention in Nashville, Tennessee. Secession would be on the table.

Such were the circumstances under which the 31st Congress fashioned the Compromise of 1850. The Compromise was a balancing act, opening some territories to slavery while leaving others free of it, adjusting Texas's border and admitting California as a free state, banning the slave trade in Washington, D.C., and amending the Fugitive Slave Act of 1793. After Henry Clay's initial failure to roll the various provisions into one compromise package — the "omnibus bill" — the pieces were separated and passed individually. In truth, a new fugitive slave act had been on the table much earlier. James Mason of Virginia introduced it on January 4, 1850. His bill extended jurisdiction only to federal officers, including nonjudicial federal officers such as clerks, commissioners, marshals, and postmasters. It doubled the penalties for obstruction, and it authorized arrest warrants.

From the start, *Prigg v. Pennsylvania* framed the discussion of the new bill. Mason's bill promised to repeal that portion of the Fugitive Slave Act of 1793 which had granted jurisdiction to state officers. Although this accepted in theory Story's opinion in *Prigg v. Pennsylvania*, southern senators repeatedly drew distinctions. The fugitive slave bill did not extend jurisdiction to state officers because Congress could not direct them, explained James Mason. But he insisted that this did not relieve the obligation on all states to return both fugitives from justice and fugitive slaves under Article IV. *Prigg v. Pennsylvania* had not relieved the states of that obligation, argued Mason, both because the issue had not been properly before the Court and because Supreme Court judges "have not the power" to relieve the states of their constitutional obligations. The latter point may have been true in the world of antebellum constitutionalism, as the Supreme Court was certainly *not* the final word on the Constitution's meaning (although some tried to argue that it was). But Mason's former point was dead wrong. The issue of state obligation to enforce the fugitive slave clause *had* been before the Court, and Story's opinion had in fact relieved the northern states of their obligations. True, state officers could take jurisdiction (except where state law prevented them from doing so) under the

Fugitive Slave Act of 1793 in accordance with Story's opinion, but they could not be compelled to do so. So Mason was wrong on that score. But he was right to point out that *Prigg* had become a means for northern states to repudiate their obligations under the fugitive slave clause.

Prigg v. Pennsylvania served as cover for northerners in one other important way. Those members of Congress who sought a resolution to the fugitive slave question but did not wish to appear entangled with slavery could now claim the Supreme Court had settled the matter. Daniel Webster allowed that he did not regard *Prigg* as a "fortunate" decision, as he personally believed the clause directed the states and not Congress. Nonetheless, the Supreme Court had so decided, and Webster stood ready to accept the decision. Other northerners indicated their assent as well. Interestingly, this question split southerners. Andrew Butler of South Carolina and James Mason of Virginia both vigorously denied the right of the Supreme Court to divest the states of their constitutional duties. George Edmund Badger, a North Carolina Whig, attacked them both, outlining as sturdy a defense for Joseph Story's finding of congressional exclusivity as had been made. For northerners eager to avoid the issue, this took the abolitionist argument — that Congress had no authority to legislate — off the table. *Prigg* proved good cover at least.

Not all northerners hid behind *Prigg*. Salmon P. Chase, the attorney who had argued so potently against the constitutionality of the Fugitive Slave Act of 1793 and who was now a senator from Ohio, refused the shelter. One senator accused Chase of authoring resolutions at a public meeting in Ohio that repudiated the fugitive slave clause in favor of the higher law. Chase vehemently denied the allegation, reaffirming his belief that all clauses of the Constitution ought to be enforced. Chase pointed out that before *Prigg* "every State, I believe, had legislated upon the subject, and very little complaint had been made of difficulties in the way of the reclamation of fugitives." Chase traced the difficulties in northern states back to the seizure of fugitive slaves without process. James Mason hotly answered that under *Prigg* it was perfectly lawful to do so. "I know that it has been so decided," retorted Chase, "but I think the decision wrong."

Still other northerners attempted to work within *Prigg v. Pennsylvania* to satisfy antislavery constitutional demands. In January, William Seward of New York offered his own version of a new fugitive slave bill that offered federal remedies of habeas corpus and trial by jury to alleged fugitives. This was an attempt to wed *Prigg*'s logic of congressional exclusivity to antislavery constitutionalism, which admitted the duty of returning fugitives but insisted that the slaveholders' rights did not trump guarantees of liberty to northern free blacks. And as abolitionists now labored to prove, color could be a thin dividing line between freedom and despotism. John Parker Hale illustrated the difficulty. "Any man that wants a victim," he thundered from the floor, might simply purchase an affidavit (they were for sale in slave as well as free states), and then "he may go . . . into your house or into mine—he may seize your wife or child, and upon an *ex parte* affidavit, taken behind our backs, hundreds and thousands of miles off, the wife of your bosom or the children of your love may be wrenched from your protection, and upon the strength of this *ex parte* affidavit, hurried off—" At this point, Andrew Butler of South Carolina, unable to take any more, interrupted. "Blacks," admonished Butler, attempting to remind the Senate that the fugitive slave clause comprehended a class of persons not included among "We the People." But Hale refused the distinction. "Sir, it does not say blacks, but anybody; and I have seen some that are holden as slaves, that it would be very difficult to tell by their complexions what their parentage was." Was it too much to ask, continued Hale, that the bare protection of habeas corpus and trial by jury be extended to protect cases of mistaken identity and outright kidnapping?

For the southern ultras, the answer was yes. Northerners repeatedly tried to add habeas corpus and trial by jury protections to the fugitive slave bill, but to no avail. Even a compromise proposed by Henry Clay promising a jury trial in the slaveholder's home state was rebuffed. To extend to fugitive slaves any constitutional protection admitted too much. Just as abolitionists had used the color line to show how the Fugitive Slave Act threatened the liberties of whites as well as blacks, slaveholders held fast to their position that any acknowledgment of black rights, no matter how spare, threatened their property and their society.

The final form of the new fugitive slave bill consolidated into law *Prigg v. Pennsylvania*. It repealed that part of the 1793 law that extended jurisdiction to state officers. It authorized the appointment of commissioners by federal district court judges to hear fugitive slave cases.

It prohibited "any molestation" of fugitive slave rendition by state law, in essence invalidating habeas corpus hearings and antikidnapping laws. But the bill innovated on *Prigg*'s principles as well. It authorized federal judges and commissioners to issue arrest warrants for fugitives, and it specified the threshold of evidence required to prove a fugitive's status, which amounted to proof of ownership, proof of escape, and some intimation of where the fugitive was, sealed by a court of record in the slaveholder's home state. Alleged fugitives were prevented from testifying on their own behalf in rendition hearings, giving the summary hearing a truly *ex parte* feel to it. And the bill innovated in one further way. Although Congress could not compel state officers to enforce federal law, Congress could still act directly upon the people of the United States. The bill did so by explicitly authorizing federal officers "to summon and call to their aid the bystanders, or posse comitatus of the proper county, when necessary to ensure a faithful observance of the [Fugitive Slave Act]." The bill then commanded all citizens of the United States "to aid and assist in the prompt and efficient execution of this law, whenever their services may be required."

On September 18, 1850, President Millard Fillmore signed the new Fugitive Slave Act into law. At that point, *Prigg v. Pennsylvania* ceased to be novel, as it was the innovations of the new law that roused the most indignation. In public meetings across the North, the Fugitive Slave Act of 1850 was condemned as immoral, un-Christian, and unconstitutional. Meeting after meeting pledged to seek repeal of the law and to protect fugitives at all costs. Such pledges carried weight. Fugitives arrested under the new law were rescued in Boston, in Syracuse, and in Christiana, Pennsylvania. This open flouting of the law moved pro-Union northerners to histrionics. President Fillmore asked for clarifying legislation allowing him to deploy the armed forces to return fugitive slaves, and the government charged rescuers with treason. These prosecutions came to nothing — treason proved too hefty a charge to sell to juries — and the government's overreaction only prompted more direct resistance.

Outright defiance was a form of protest that carried substantial risk. But abolitionists also promised to fight the law in Congress and in the courts, and they made good on this. The arrest of the fugitive slave Thomas Sims in Boston on April 3, 1851, presented such an opportunity. Sims was jailed in the jury room of the U.S. courthouse, a necessity given that Massachusetts had withdrawn the use of its jails as well as its officers from the enforcement of the Fugitive Slave Act. Fearing a rescue attempt (the fugitive slave Shadrach had been rescued from this same building only two months previous), federal marshals wrapped the courthouse in chains and stationed armed guards at the doors. Lawyers for Sims sought every remedy, including petitioning the Supreme Judicial Court of Massachusetts for a writ of habeas corpus. After first denying the petition, Chief Justice Lemuel Shaw reluctantly agreed to hear arguments. Sims had attracted an impressive cadre of volunteers for his defense, including Senator Robert Rantoul. After hearing arguments on Monday morning, April 7, the Massachusetts Supreme Judicial Court refused the writ. Sims's case rested on the notion that the warrant issued by the U.S. commissioner was unconstitutional and void, which presupposed that Congress lacked the authority to pass fugitive slave laws. Against this proposition, Shaw cited *Prigg v. Pennsylvania*, which "deliberately settled" the question in favor of the Fugitive Slave Act's constitutionality. Shaw allowed that there had been disagreement on the Court and that "some of the judges were of opinion, that the state legislatures might make laws on the subject," provided they did not impede rendition. This nod to Taney's dissent, however, did not touch the case before them. *Prigg* "appears to us to be authoritative and decisive, and it was so considered by the supreme court of the United States in the case of *Jones v. Van Zandt.*"

Prigg v. Pennsylvania would continue to be cited in this way—as the definitive proof of the constitutionality of the federal law. Federal judges in 1851 were also nearly universal in their approbation of the 1850 act. Peleg Sprague, judge of the federal district court of Massachusetts, asserted that *Prigg v. Pennsylvania* decisively proved that Congress could authorize U.S. commissioners to exercise a summary jurisdiction under the Fugitive Slave Act of 1850. Supreme Court justices Samuel Nelson, Robert C. Grier, and Benjamin Robbins Curtis defended the new Fugitive Slave Act on circuit, both by citing *Prigg v. Pennsylvania* as holding that Congress held the ultimate power to pass fugitive slave laws and implying that Congress alone had the right to determine those laws' substance. Only one doubt surfaced about *Prigg v. Pennsylvania*'s holdings. While charging the grand jury in the northern district of New York, Justice Samuel Nelson mused that "opinions were expressed in the case of *Prigg v. Pennsylvania*, that the power of congress to provide the mode of surrendering up the fugitive under the constitution was exclusive," while others believed that the power was concurrent with the states. "Whether the one or the other shall finally prevail," surmised Nelson, was not a subject upon which he should offer an opinion. These were strange and telling words given that Nelson had himself authored the exclusivity argument in *Jack v. Martin* (1834) that guided Justice Joseph Story's opinion.

In *Moore v. Illinois* (1852), the Supreme Court took by writ of error a case of the Illinois Supreme Court. Richard Eels was convicted under the Illinois criminal code of "harboring and secreting a negro slave." His lawyers contended that the law, which explicitly punished the act of harboring a slave or servant "owing service or labor" conflicted with the Fugitive Slave Act. This applied the logic of *Prigg v. Pennsylvania* rather severely. Justice Robert Grier wrote the opinion of the Court, noting the distinction between passing laws that aided fugitive slave reclamation and those passed under the general police power. States could expel fugitive slaves from their borders, as Story had said. Presumably, under that same power, states could also punish people for harboring fugitive slaves. John McLean dissented, trenchantly asserting that it was unjust to face punishment under two statutes for the same criminal act. If a power was exclusive in Congress, McLean argued (albeit by referencing his 1847 dissent in *Fox v. Ohio*), then only the federal government could punish transgressions against that power. This seemed an elementary if arguable proposition, and generally in support of *Prigg*. McLean reaffirmed his commitment to the majority opinion in *Prigg v. Pennsylvania* on circuit in *Miller v. McQuerry* (1853), noting there that "a few individuals in Massachusetts may have maintained, at one time, that the power [to pass fugitive slave laws] was with the states." But such views were "long since abandoned" and were being reasserted in the face of the Fugitive Slave Act of 1850 "more as a matter of expediency than principle." To put it bluntly, the abolitionists had lost the argument, and *Prigg v. Pennsylvania* was triumphant in the courts of the United States.

Not that abolitionists gave up. In 1854, just as the Kansas-Nebraska bill reopened the dreaded issue of slavery in the territories, a fugitive slave named Joshua Glover was captured and incarcerated in Milwaukee. Glover was rescued by a crowd that had first laid down the gauntlet before the federal marshal: respect a writ of habeas corpus issued by the county judge for the fugitive or face the consequences. When federal officers refused to comply, the crowd broke the fugitive free and spirited him to freedom. The outraged U.S. commissioner convened an investigation that led to his holding on bond Milwaukee's most vocal abolitionist, Sherman M. Booth. Booth refused the bond and was incarcerated, upon which his attorneys sought a writ of habeas corpus from the Wisconsin Supreme Court. It was a strategic move. Wisconsin law provided that individual justices could hear and determine petitions for habeas corpus when the full bench was not in session. The nearest available justice happened to be Abram D. Smith, an able, pugnacious, and somewhat eccentric man with strong antislavery principles. He heard arguments and then ordered Booth's release on the grounds that the Fugitive Slave Act of 1850 was unconstitutional. His written opinion covered the whole ground, from the violations of trial by jury and habeas corpus occasioned by the Act to its infringements on the reserved sovereignty of the states. Smith also confronted *Prigg v. Pennsylvania*. Before that case was decided, he noted, both slave states and free states had passed laws touching on fugitive slaves. Story's opinion had disrupted this situation by claiming for Congress an absolute power, and this Smith found unpalatable. Smith rejected *Prigg* because he felt that it did not offer legal cover for the substance of the Fugitive Slave Act of 1850 and because he refused to accept the holding of congressional exclusivity and its consequences.

This was the victory for which abolitionists had long hoped. They at least had one appellate judge's opinion questioning the Fugitive Slave Act's constitutionality, which they could put to good use. Most newspapers assumed that the full bench would overturn the decision when it met in July. By then, the federal district attorney had already convened a grand jury that indicted Sherman Booth and two other men for rescue. Then, to everyone's surprise, the Wisconsin court upheld Smith's ruling on a 2–1 vote. It nonetheless declined to interfere with the federal prosecution, which resulted in Booth's conviction in January 1855. Booth then petitioned for another writ of habeas corpus, which the Wisconsin Supreme Court granted yet again, although this time on the narrower grounds of a defective indictment. The U.S. Supreme Court then issued a writ of error that the Wisconsin court refused to enter on its record, thus fulfilling John McLean's prophesy in *Prigg v. Pennsylvania*.

There was no question that this was open revolt, but it was not just a rogue court that repudiated *Prigg v. Pennsylvania*. The November 1854 elections in Wisconsin returned an antislavery majority to Congress. Moreover, a judicial election followed shortly after the Wisconsin court's granting of its second writ of habeas corpus to Sherman Booth in 1855. The seat up for consideration was occupied by the one judge who had held that the Fugitive Slave Act was perfectly constitutional. The election quickly became a referendum on his decision, and he lost the election handily. Through a variety of electoral and political processes, the people of Wisconsin had rejected *Prigg v. Pennsylvania*. More remarkably, they did so repeatedly. While never officially repudiating the fugitive slave clause, Wisconsin insisted that no Supreme Court decision and no act of Congress could ever arbitrarily take away a person's right to habeas corpus and trial by jury. It was a triumph of moderate antislavery constitutionalism.

Although Wisconsin was the first state to take official action against the Fugitive Slave Act in 1855, it anticipated a revived antislavery commitment in the North. Massachusetts passed a personal liberty law in 1855 guaranteeing an alleged fugitive a hearing in a Massachusetts court. Wisconsin would itself pass a law in 1857 that extended state assistance to alleged fugitives. Pennsylvania and New York already had laws on the books that guaranteed these hearings, and abolitionists proved ready and willing to defy *Prigg v. Pennsylvania* as well as Congress's Fugitive Slave Act of 1850. The famous rescue of John Price in Oberlin, Ohio, in 1858 produced a situation similar to that in Milwaukee, with a slightly different outcome. There, as in Milwaukee, the federal government prosecuted the case vigorously and won convictions. The abolitionists sued out writs of habeas corpus, and the case was removed to the Ohio Supreme Court as *Ex Parte Bushnell* (1859). But the Ohio court, unlike Wisconsin's, denied the petition by a vote of 3–2. Once again a judicial election followed the court's decision, this time for the seat occupied by Joseph Swan. An antislavery man himself, Swan had nonetheless felt constrained by the Constitution and by *Prigg v. Pennsylvania*, and he had voted to deny the petition for habeas corpus. His written opinion stressed judicial duty. The established authorities, including the Supreme Court, had declared the

Fugitive Slave Act a constitutional exercise of federal power. Swan considered himself duty bound to accept this reading. In fact, he disdained the notion that a state supreme court might defy the judicial hierarchy, as it could lead only to collision and, potentially, violence. For Swan, the ultimate judicial duty was in putting aside his antislavery sentiments to arrive at the correct, if heartbreaking, legal conclusion — that the Fugitive Slave Act was constitutional. As a reward for his dutiful deference to judicial authority, the voters turned him out on his ear.

Swan's opinion was intellectually honest, but it was not the only credible reading of the constitutional jurisprudence on fugitive slaves. Judges in Wisconsin and Ohio interpreted the fugitive slave clause in concert with the Tenth Amendment and the states' reserved power to protect the liberty of their people. They denied the authority of *Prigg v. Pennsylvania* on the grounds that the decision had not explicitly addressed the fundamental questions of what rights were owed to free blacks claimed as fugitives. This was a demand for equal protection under the law. This idea had deep roots in the antislavery movement, roots that stretched through the abolitionist societies and back to men like James Forten of Philadelphia and Granville Sharp of London. The judges in Wisconsin and Ohio who defied the Fugitive Slave Act grounded their resistance not just in abstract notions of natural law, but in the power of the state to defend real liberty against public or private encroachment. Their claim boiled down to this: alleged fugitives deserved the same protections of their liberty as any other resident of the state. If this was a radical claim, it was so only because alleged fugitives were people of color. Many in the North were reluctant to stand on this color-blind principle and risk driving slaveholders to disunion. But some were now showing the gumption to do so.

Justice Joseph Story's opinion in *Prigg v. Pennsylvania* had no answer for this argument. Its logic worked only if one ignored free blacks' claim to equal protection under the law. Story had not explicitly denied that claim in Prigg, but the Fugitive Slave Act of 1850 institutionalized the unequal application of laws based on skin color. It followed that the only way in which equal protection might be denied to a free person was if his skin color necessarily precluded it, a point Chief Justice Roger B. Taney obliquely addressed in his opinion of the Court in *Dred Scott v. Sandford* (1857). *Dred Scott* was an extremely complicated case that involved issues of diversity jurisdiction, common law pleading, the territories clause, and interstate comity. More than anything else, Taney's opinion promised to solve another contentious constitutional issue — whether Congress could ban slavery in the territories. Taney's answer was no. But part of his decision dealt with whether the descendants of slaves could bring suits in federal court. Taney said they could not because they could never be citizens of the United States. As part of a degraded class of people, blacks had "no rights which the white man was bound to respect." Here was the answer to the claim of equal protection for alleged fugitives which the Wisconsin bench had cited when it declared the Fugitive Slave Act unconstitutional. By the logic of *Dred Scott*, rights could be divided along a color line. Thus was found the answer to a nettlesome question: what separated a kidnapping from a legitimate rendition? For Taney, it did not really matter.

It remained only for the U.S. Supreme Court to make its final ruling on the Fugitive Slave Act. The Court had never given up demanding that Wisconsin submit to its jurisdiction in the Booth cases. Wisconsin continued to refuse. And so, four years after the first writ of error ran, the Supreme Court heard the cases anyway. The Court had to use a copy of the record, as the Wisconsin Supreme Court still refused to send up the official one. And the state declined to participate in oral arguments. In *Ableman v. Booth* (1859), Chief Justice Taney spoke for a unanimous court in upholding the Fugitive Slave Act of 1850 as constitutional. He did not cite *Prigg v. Pennsylvania* in support. He cited no cases, in fact. But the principles of *Prigg* had triumphed, if only to be made a nullity two years later by the fact of civil war.

If one looks only at the appellate record, *Prigg v. Pennsylvania* enjoyed an unvarnished supremacy. It was upheld on three occasions by the U.S. Supreme Court (albeit once tacitly). It also commanded respect in the federal courts, where it was consistently deployed against abolitionist arguments against the constitutionality of the Fugitive Slave Act. Given the turmoil that accompanied slavery in national politics in the 1840s and 1850s, the solidity of this appellate record is admirable. Even the antislavery judge John McLean repeatedly affirmed *Prigg v. Pennsylvania* in jury charges as well as appellate opinions. Moreover, congressional interpretation of the fugitive slave clause in 1850 clearly bowed to the majority opinion in *Prigg v. Pennsylvania*. The new law made rendition entirely a federal affair, refused to allow any "molestation" of the process by state judicial hearings, provided the federal law enforcement apparatus to carry out rendition, and reaffirmed congressional exclusivity in enforcing the fugitive slave clause. The presidents of the 1850s in turn each committed substantial federal resources to the enforcement of the new Fugitive Slave Act. *Prigg v. Pennsylvania*, it would appear, reigned supreme.

But this view can mislead. State judges in the 1840s often neglected to enforce *Prigg* or expressed doubts about whether it had authority when state law was at issue. Some states dutifully repealed their personal liberty laws in its wake, but others did not. Southerners did not care for the opinion much. Its exaltation of national exclusivity had consequences, including (at least potentially) federal protection of free black sailors ensnared by the Negro seamen acts of the southern states. *Prigg*'s subtle conflation of Congress's lack of ability to compel state officers and a duty to enforce the fugitive slave clause suggested that the Constitution was more about power than about mutual duties, a position that threatened southern constitutionalism. Southern ambivalence toward *Prigg* manifested itself in the congressional debate of 1850, where many southern senators denied that the states were bound by the decision. Their states, after all, did not bother to repeal any laws they had on the books that dealt with aiding fugitive slave reclamation.

The revolt against the Fugitive Slave Act of 1850 in the North ran deeper than pushback against *Prigg v. Pennsylvania*. Forcible rescues and violent resistance accompanied rendition attempts. Abolitionists pledged to disobey the law openly, and even moderates found its provisions coercive and repressive. But not all resistance was violent. Many considered the Fugitive Slave Act's constitutional underpinning unsound and fought the law in petitions to legislatures and arguments before courts. Moderate abolitionists articulated theories of reserved states' rights and the police power and demanded equal protection for free blacks. They denied the authority of *Prigg v. Pennsylvania* in part because the decision had failed to solve a critical problem: what separated a kidnapping from a fugitive slave rendition? Abolitionists contended that the right of the free black to liberty was paramount and that alleged fugitives ought to be extended every legal protection the states could offer. Their opponents (not all of them slaveholders) rested on the authority of *Prigg v. Pennsylvania* and its holding of national exclusivity over fugitive slave rendition. Which side one chose in 1859 depended upon one's own political and constitutional commitments. But neither side could claim a definitive interpretation of the fugitive slave clause's true meaning. Nor could either side really claim to have the upper hand in enforcing their interpretation. True, slaveholders had the support of Congress, the President, and the Supreme Court. But slaves kept running, and by the eve of the Civil War southerners would claim that they were losing upwards of one million dollars in property annually. Although more than a thousand fugitives were returned via the Fugitive Slave Act during the 1850s, and even though rescues occurred in only a small fraction of the renditions, slaveholders clearly believed that the fugitive slave clause was being openly flouted. The Fugitive Slave Act could not staunch the flow of refugees northward, slaveholders argued, and no Supreme Court opinion would change that. The slaveholders were right.

1618	In England, Owen Evans confesses to attempting to kidnap young women to press into service in Virginia and Barbados.
1643	New England Confederation articles are adopted, including a provision requiring that fugitive servants be returned across colonial boundaries.
1687	Eleven slaves from South Carolina flee to St. Augustine in Spanish Florida.
1739	Stono Rebellion occurs in South Carolina.
1772	Lord Chief Justice Mansfield reads his opinion in *Somerset v. Stewart*.
1775	Society for the Relief of Free Negroes Unlawfully Held in Bondage founded in Philadelphia.
1780	Pennsylvania passes its Act for the Gradual Abolition of Slavery.
1783	In *Commonwealth v. Jennison* (Quok Walker's Case), Massachusetts Chief Justice William Cushing declares that the Massachusetts Constitution does not permit slaves to be held in Massachusetts. And in *Exeter v. Hanchett* and *Affa Hall*, Chief Justice Cushing declares that out-of-state residents can claim their fugitive slaves in Massachusetts.
1784	Pennsylvania Society for Promoting the Abolition of Slavery and for the Relief of Free Negroes Unlawfully Held in Bondage [Pennsylvania Abolition Society] founded.
August 28, 1787	Charles Pinckney and Pierce Butler propose the fugitive slave clause at the Constitutional Convention. With some modifications, it will be placed in Article IV, Section 2.
1788	Pennsylvania revises its Act for the Gradual Abolition of Slavery and adds an antikidnapping section. John Davis, a free black living in Pennsylvania, is kidnapped by three men at the behest of Davis's former owner.
1790	The Quakers present their petition to Congress for ending the slave trade.

1791	Virginia refuses to surrender three men for the kidnapping of free black John Davis of Pennsylvania. The matter is submitted to Congress for resolution.
1793	Congress passes "an Act respecting fugitives from justice, and persons escaping from the service of their masters," known as the Fugitive Slave Act.
1808	Congress bans participation in the Atlantic slave trade.
1813	James Forten publishes *A Series of Letters by a Man of Color*.
1816	In *Commonwealth v. Holloway* the Pennsylvania Supreme Court rules that the children of fugitive slaves born in Pennsylvania are not fugitive slaves.
1818	In *In re Susan*, the federal circuit court in Indiana rules that the Fugitive Slave Act supersedes Indiana's 1816 law governing the rendition of fugitive slaves.
1819	In *Wright v. Deacon* the Pennsylvania Supreme Court rules that the writ *de homine replegiando* (promising a jury trial to alleged fugitives) cannot interrupt rendition under a certificate of removal.
July 2, 1822	Denmark Vesey hung in Charleston, South Carolina, as the supposed leader of a failed conspiracy to lead free blacks and slaves to Haiti.
December 21, 1822	South Carolina passes its Negro Seamen Act as part of "An Act for the better regulation and government of free negroes and persons of colour, and for other purposes."
1823	In *Commonwealth v. Griffith* the Massachusetts Supreme Court rules that arrest warrants are not necessary to detain fugitive slaves in Massachusetts.
1823	In *Elkison v. Deliesseline*, Justice William Johnson of the U.S. Supreme Court writes (in dicta) that South Carolina's Negro Seamen Act is unconstitutional but disclaims the power to grant relief to black sailors held under its provisions.
1824	John Ashmore of Maryland (the owner of Margaret Morgan's parents) dies. He does not claim Margaret Morgan or her parents in his will.
1826	Pennsylvania passes "an act to give effect to the provisions of the constitution of the United States, relative to fugitives from labor, for the protection of free

	people of color, and to prevent kidnapping," also known as the Pennsylvania Personal Liberty Law of 1826.
1828	New York passes its revised statutes, which include a personal liberty law making a jury trial available to fugitive slaves.
1832	Margaret Morgan moves from Maryland to Pennsylvania following the death of her parents.
December, 1833	William Lloyd Garrison publishes "The Declaration of the National Anti-Slavery Convention" in his newspaper *The Liberator*, announcing the founding of the American Anti-Slavery Society.
1834	In *Jack v. Martin*, Samuel Nelson, chief justice of the New York Supreme Court, rules that the New York personal liberty law is unconstitutional because it conflicts with a power reserved by the Constitution to Congress.
1835	*Jack v. Martin* is affirmed by the Court for the Correction for Errors, although the opinions conflict as to the reason why.
1835	The American Anti-Slavery Society inaugurates its mail campaign, flooding the southern states with antislavery pamphlets.
February, 1836	In *New Jersey v. Sheriff of Burlington*, Joseph C. Hornblower, chief justice of the New Jersey Supreme Court, opines that the Fugitive Slave Act cannot override the state's personal liberty law.
February, 1836	Five southern legislatures pass resolutions demanding that northern states pass penal laws restricting abolitionist speech.
March, 1836	Congress debates, but does not pass, a bill prohibiting the transmission of incendiary publications through the mail.
May, 1836	The U.S. House of Representatives imposes the Gag Rule, immediately tabling all petitions touching on the subject of slavery without officially receiving them.
February, 1837	Edward Prigg and his party cross from Maryland into Pennsylvania to retrieve Margaret Morgan as the fugitive slave of Margaret Ashmore (John Ashmore's widow).

March, 1837	Warrants are served in Maryland for the arrest and rendition of Edward Prigg et al. for kidnapping Margaret Morgan in violation of Pennsylvania's Personal Liberty Law of 1826.
August 30, 1837	A Maryland jury decides, after hearing a freedom petition, that Margaret Morgan is in fact the slave of Margaret Ashmore.
March, 1838	The Maryland Assembly authorizes the governor to appoint commissioners to travel to Pennsylvania and seek dismissal of the kidnapping charges against Edward Prigg et al. or to create a pro forma case that will go before the U.S. Supreme Court.
May, 1839	The Pennsylvania Assembly agrees to the creation of a pro forma case that will go to the U.S. Supreme Court.
May, 1840	Without hearing full arguments, the Pennsylvania Supreme Court issues its pro forma ruling in *Prigg v. Pennsylvania* upholding the conviction of Edward Prigg.
January, 1842	John Quincy Adams presents to Congress the "Haverhill Petition," in which abolitionists seek a peaceable disunion over sectional differences.
February 8-10, 1842	Oral arguments are heard before the U.S. Supreme Court in *Prigg v. Pennsylvania.*
March 1, 1842	*Prigg v. Pennsylvania* decided.
1843	Massachusetts passes its noncooperation law forbidding state officers to help render fugitives, also known as the Latimer Law.
1847	In *Jones v. Van Zandt*, the Supreme Court upholds *Prigg v. Pennsylvania* unanimously.
1850	Congress passes a new Fugitive Slave Act.
1851	In *Sims' Case*, the Massachusetts Supreme Judicial Court refuses to issue a writ of habeas corpus for Thomas Sims, being held under the provisions of the Fugitive Slave Act.
1852	In *Moore v. Illinois* the U.S. Supreme Court upholds *Prigg v. Pennsylvania* and rules that states may punish those who harbor fugitive slaves.
1854	In *In re Booth*, the Wisconsin Supreme Court rules that the Fugitive Slave Act is unconstitutional.
January 1855	The Wisconsin Supreme Court releases from federal

178   { *Chronology* }

	custody Sherman Booth, who was charged with violating the Fugitive Slave Act.
May 1855	Massachusetts passes a personal liberty law guaranteeing alleged fugitives a hearing in a Massachusetts court.
June 1855	The Wisconsin Supreme Court refuses to enter a writ of error from the U.S. Supreme Court on its record.
1857	Wisconsin passes a personal liberty law guaranteeing alleged fugitives a hearing in a Wisconsin court.
1859	In *Ex Parte Bushnell*, the Ohio Supreme Court refuses to interpose itself in the federal prosecution of abolitionists charged with violating the Fugitive Slave Act.
1859	In *Ableman v. Booth*, the U.S. Supreme Court, reviewing the Booth cases from 1854–1855 on a copy of the record, upholds the Fugitive Slave Act of 1850 but does not cite *Prigg v. Pennsylvania*.
December 20, 1860	South Carolina secedes from the Union, citing in its declaration of causes (released December 24) the failure of northern states to give effect to the fugitive slave clause.
June 28, 1864	Congress repeals the Fugitive Slave Act.

BIBLIOGRAPHICAL ESSAY

Note from the Series Editors: The following bibliographic essay contains the major primary and secondary sources the author consulted for this volume. We have asked all authors in the series to omit formal citations in order to make our volumes more readable, inexpensive, and appealing for students and general readers. In adopting this format, Landmark Law Cases and American Society follows the precedent of a number of highly regarded and widely consulted series.

This is the first book-length treatment of *Prigg v. Pennsylvania*. However, numerous articles have been devoted to it, and it plays a prominent part in many books about the antebellum era. There is still some controversy over precisely what *Prigg* decided. The first real revisionist essay was Joseph C. Burke, "What Did the Prigg Decision Really Decide?" *The Pennsylvania Magazine of History and Biography* 93, no. 1 (January 1969): 73–85. Contrary to the standard interpretation, Burke claimed that Justice Story did not have a solid majority on every point. His interpretation was disputed by Paul Finkelman, "Sorting out *Prigg v. Pennsylvania*," *Rutgers Law Journal* 24 (1992–1993): 605–666, who claimed that Story did in fact have a solid majority. The difference in interpretation largely hinged on how to count the two silent justices and what precisely counted for holdings versus dicta.

The primary scholarly question asked of *Prigg v. Pennsylvania* is whether Justice Joseph Story's opinion was proslavery or "a triumph for freedom" (as Story himself claimed). Scholars have generally been kind to Story, placing the opinion within the larger context of his jurisprudential achievement. See Christopher L. M. Eisgruber, "Justice Story, Slavery, and the Natural Law Foundations of American Constitutionalism," *The University of Chicago Law Review* 55, no. 1 (January 1988): 273–327; James McClellan, *Joseph Story and the American Constitution; A Study in Political and Legal Thought with Selected Writings*, reprint ed. (Norman: University of Oklahoma Press, 1990); and R. Kent Newmyer, *Supreme Court Justice Joseph Story: Statesman of the Old Republic* (Chapel Hill: University of North Carolina Press, 1985). Newmyer in particular takes a balanced look at Story's opinion, refusing to call it a "triumph for freedom" but not condemning it either. Others have suggested that Story's opinion was deliberately proslavery. See Paul Finkelman, "*Prigg v. Pennsylvania* and Northern State Courts: Anti-Slavery Use of a Pro-Slavery Decision," *Civil War History* 25 (1979): 5–35; Barbara Holden-Smith, "Lords of Lash, Loom, and Law: Justice Story, Slavery, and *Prigg v. Pennsylvania*," *Cornell Law Review* 78, no. 6 (September 1993): 1086–1151; and Paul Finkelman, "Story Telling on the Supreme Court: *Prigg v. Pennsylvania* and Justice Joseph Story's Judicial Nationalism," *Supreme Court Historical Review* (1994): 247–294. These essays have argued comprehensively that *Prigg v. Pennsylvania* was unnecessarily proslavery. This interpretation has had a big impact on the field. See Joe Lockard, "Justice Story's 'Prigg' Decision and the Defeat of Freedom," *Amerikastudien/American Studies* 52, no. 4 (2007): 467–480.

Recently, several scholars have reconsidered *Prigg v. Pennsylvania* in light of other aspects of antebellum constitutionalism. For an argument that the case was in keeping with antebellum constitutional jurisprudence, see Mark A. Graber, *Dred Scott and the Problem of Constitutional Evil* (New York: Cambridge University Press, 2006) and Austin Allen, *Origins of the Dred Scott Case: Jacksonian Jurisprudence and the Supreme Court, 1837–1857* (Athens: University of Georgia Press, 2006). Earl Maltz makes a similar case, arguing that *Prigg v. Pennsylvania* sought to accommodate both proslavery and antislavery visions of the Constitution. See Earl M. Maltz, *Slavery and the Supreme Court, 1825–1861* (Lawrence: University Press of Kansas, 2009). These three works differ in subtle but fundamental ways in the case each makes, but they all offer a significant challenge to the thesis that *Prigg v. Pennsylvania* was deliberately and unashamedly proslavery. For an argument that Story may have anticipated that his jurisprudence would have positive repercussions for free black sailors and Native Americans, see Leslie Friedman Goldstein, "A 'Triumph of Freedom' After All? *Prigg v. Pennsylvania* Re-examined," *Law and History Review* 29, no. 3 (August 2011): 763–796.

Story's opinion should be put in the larger context of the Supreme Court and slavery under Roger B. Taney. Taney himself is sorely in need of a good biography. An excellent article on him is Timothy S. Huebner, "Roger B. Taney and the Slavery Issue: Looking beyond — and before — Dred Scott," *Journal of American History* 97, no. 1 (June 2010): 17–38. For a more general history of the Taney Court, a good starting point is Peter Charles Hoffer, *The Supreme Court: An Essential History* (Lawrence: University Press of Kansas, 2007). The traditional account of the Taney Court is Carl Brent Swisher, *The Taney Period, 1836–64,* vol. 5 of *The Oliver Wendell Holmes Devise History of the Supreme Court of the United States* (New York: Macmillan, 1974), but Swisher's account is far out of date. Specifically on slavery and the Taney Court, see Austin Allen, *Origins of the Dred Scott Case: Jacksonian Jurisprudence and the Supreme Court, 1837–1857* (Athens: University of Georgia Press, 2006); Don E. Fehrenbacher, *The Dred Scott Case: Its Significance in American Law and Politics* (New York: Oxford University Press, 1978); David Thomas Konig, et al., eds., *The Dred Scott Case: Historical and Contemporary Perspectives on Race and Law* (Athens: Ohio University Press, 2010); Earl M. Maltz, *Dred Scott and the Politics of Slavery* (Lawrence: University Press of Kansas, 2007); and William M. Wiecek, "Slavery and Abolition Before the United States Supreme Court, 1820–1860," *Journal of American History* 65, no. 1 (June 1978): 34–59. The slave cases considered in Chapter 8 are *Brig Caroline v. United States,* 11 U.S. 496

(1813); *Elkison v. Deliesseline*, 8 F. Cas. 493 (C.C. South Carolina 1823); *The Emily and the Caroline*, 22 U.S. 381 (1824); *United States v. La Jeune Eugenie*, 26 F. Cas. 832 (C.C. 1822); *LaGrange v. Chouteau*, 29 U.S. 287 (1830); *United States v. Amistad* 40 U.S. 518 (1841); *Groves v. Slaughter*, 40 U.S. 449 (1841).

Fugitive slaves must be understood within the larger context of labor in North America. The indispensible work is Christopher L. Tomlins, *Freedom Bound: Law, Labor, and Civic Identity in Colonizing English America, 1580–1865* (New York: Cambridge University Press, 2010). I have also drawn here from Douglas Hay and Paul Craven, eds., *Masters, Servants, and Magistrates in Britain and the Empire, 1562–1955* (Chapel Hill: University of North Carolina Press, 2004); John J. McCusker and Russell R. Menard, *The Economy of British America, 1607–1789* (Chapel Hill: University of North Carolina Press, 1985); and John J. McCusker and Kenneth Morgan, eds., *The Early Modern Atlantic Economy* (Cambridge: Cambridge University Press, 2000). On bound labor in Pennsylvania, see Sharon V. Salinger, *"To Serve Well and Faithfully": Labor and Indentured Servants in Pennsylvania, 1682–1800* (Cambridge: Cambridge University Press, 1987), 18–24. Alfred L. Brophy, "Law and Indentured Servitude in Mid-Eighteenth Century Pennsylvania," *Willamette Law Review* 28 (1991–1992): 69–126. On indentured servants' petitions, see Christine Daniels, " 'Liberty to Complaine': Servant Petitions in Maryland, 1652–1797," in *The Many Legalities of Early America*, ed. Christopher L. Tomlins and Bruce H. Mann (Chapel Hill: University of North Carolina Press, 2001), 219–249. The assignment of indentures in colonial Virginia (essentially turning white servants into moveable property) is made quite vivid in John Ruston Pagan, *Anne Orthwood's Bastard: Sex and Law in Early Virginia* (Oxford: Oxford University Press, 2003).

The transition from white indentured servitude to black slavery is still a tendentious issue, largely because of the debate over whether racism preceded or followed slavery. The classic formulation is Edmund S. Morgan, *American Slavery, American Freedom: The Ordeal of Colonial Virginia* (New York: Norton, 1975). However, for an argument that slavery was fully contemplated by the founders of Virginia, see Anthony S. Parent, *Foul Means: The Formation of a Slave Society in Virginia, 1660–1740* (Chapel Hill: University of North Carolina Press, 2003). A review of the so called origins debate can be found in Alden T. Vaughan, "The Origins Debate: Slavery and Racism in Seventeenth-Century Virginia," *The Virginia Magazine of History and Biography* 97, no. 3 (July 1989): 311–354. The indispensable study of slavery in colonial America is Philip D. Morgan, *Slave Counterpoint: Black Culture in the Eighteenth-Century Chesapeake and Lowcountry* (Chapel Hill: University of North Carolina Press, 1998). Also valuable is the forum on "Slaveries in the Atlantic World" in *The William and Mary Quarterly* 59, no. 3 (July 2002), especially Peter Kolchin's "Introduction: Variations of Slavery in the Atlantic World," pp. 551–554. For a survey of slavery across colonial America, see Betty Wood, *Slavery in Colonial America, 1619–1776* (Lanham, Md.: Rowman & Littlefield Publishers, 2005).

The subject of kidnapping in the Atlantic world is brilliantly explored in John Donoghue, " 'Out of the Land of Bondage': The English Revolution and the Atlantic Origins of Abolition," *American Historical Review* 115, no. 4 (October 2010): 943–974. For a reprint of the documents concerning Owen Evans and the kidnapping of Somerset maidens for impressment into slavery, see "Kidnapping Maidens, to Be Sold in Virginia, 1618," *The Virginia Magazine of History and Biography* 6, no. 3 (January 1899): 228–230; and Abbot Emerson Smith, *Colonists in Bondage: White Servitude and Convict Labor in America, 1607–1776* (Chapel Hill: University of North Carolina Press for the Institute of Early American History and Culture, 1947), 67–72. See also John Wareing, "Preventive and Punitive Regulation in Seventeenth-Century Social Policy: Conflicts of Interest and the Failure to Make 'Stealing and Transporting Children, and other Persons' a Felony, 1645–73," *Social History* 27, no. 3 (2002): 288–308.

The "right of recaption" was well grounded in common law and statute law. In the chapter on colonial labor and runaways, I have relied upon Christopher L. Tomlins, *Freedom Bound* (New York: Cambridge University Press, 2010) and Richard B. Morris, *Government and Labor in Early America* (New York: Columbia University Press, 1946). For the Massachusetts law of 1695, see "An Act for Preventing of Men's Sons or Servants Absenting Themselves from their Parent's or Master's Service without Leave" in Chapter 23 of *The acts and resolves, public and private, of the province of the Massachusetts bay: to which are prefixed the charters of the province. With historical and explanatory notes, and an appendix. Published under chapter 87 of the Resolves of the General court of the commonwealth for the year 1867 . . .*, vol. 1, 1692–1714 (Boston: Wright & Potter, Printers to the State, 1896). One can find the New England Confederation and Intercolonial Agreement to return fugitive servants in Ebenezer Hazard, ed., *Historical Collections Consisting of State Papers, and Other Authentic Documents; Intended as Materials for an History of the United States of America* (Philadelphia: T. Dobson, 1792), 2:5, 172. Berkeley's letter requesting rendition can also be found in Hazard, ed., *Historical Collections*, ibid., 1:536.

On the fugitive flight to Spanish Florida, see Jane G. Landers, "Gracia Real de Santa Teresa de Mose: A Free Black Town in Spanish Colonial Florida," *American Historical Review* 95, no. 1 (February 1990): 9–30. See also Sally E. Hadden, *Slave Patrols: Law and Violence in Virginia and the Carolinas* (Cambridge, Mass.: Harvard University Press, 2001); Peter Charles Hoffer, *Cry Liberty: The Great Stono River Slave Rebellion of 1739* (New York: Oxford University Press, 2010); Peter H. Wood, *Black Majority: Negroes in Colonial South Carolina from 1670 through the Stono Rebellion* (New York: Norton, 1975).

On slave law in colonial America, I have generally relied on Peter Charles Hoffer, *Law and People in Colonial America*, Rev. ed. (Baltimore: Johns Hopkins University Press, 1998) and Alan Watson, *Slave Law in the Americas* (Athens: University of Georgia Press, 1989). For an excellent overview and authoritative bibliographic essay, see Sally E. Hadden, "The Fragmented Laws of Slavery in the Colonial and Revolutionary Eras," in *The Cambridge History of Law in America*, vol. 1 of *Early America (1580–1815)*, ed. Michael Grossberg and Christopher L. Tomlins (Cambridge: Cambridge University Press, 2008): 253–287.

Counting fugitive slaves is a precarious endeavor, but some quantitative studies have indicated a rise in numbers over time. For instance, the number of fugitives reported in the *Pennsylvania Gazette* quadrupled in the third quarter of the eighteenth century; see Billy G. Smith and Richard Wojtowicz, *Blacks Who Stole Themselves: Advertisements for Runaways in the Pennsylvania Gazette, 1728–1790* (Philadelphia: University of Pennsylvania Press, 1989), 12–13. Of course, runaway advertisements may have increased with the availability of the print medium; see Graham Russell Hodges and Alan Edward Brown, eds., *"Pretends to Be Free": Runaway Slave Advertisements from Colonial and Revolutionary New York and New Jersey* (New York: Garland Pub, 1994), xvi.

Somerset v. Stewart has a rich historiography. For my general account of the case and its legal antecedents, I have drawn from John H. Baker, *An Introduction to English Legal History*, 3rd ed. (London: Butterworths, 1990); David Brion Davis, *The Problem of Slavery in the Age of Revolution, 1770–1823* (Ithaca, N.Y: Cornell University Press, 1975); James Oldham, *English Common Law in the Age of Mansfield* (Chapel Hill: University of North Carolina Press, 2004); and William M. Wiecek, "Somerset: Lord Mansfield and the Legitimacy of Slavery in the Anglo-American World," *The University of Chicago Law Review* 42, no. 1 (October 1974): 86–146. Somerset's trial is brought vividly to life in Mark Stuart Weiner's excellent chapter on James Somerset in *Black Trials: Citizenship from the Beginnings of Slavery to the End of Caste* (New York: Vintage Books, 2006). Weiner's account, more than any other, has brought me to a deeper appreciation for the multiple meanings of James Somerset's trial. An excellent forum on Somerset's case was published in the *Law and History Review* 24 (March 2006), 601–671, and I must admit to relying especially upon Daniel Hulsebosch's "Nothing but Liberty: 'Somerset's Case' and the British Empire," and Ruth Paley's "Imperial Politics and English Law: The Many Contexts of 'Somerset' " within that forum.

For the influence of Mansfield's opinion on the colonies and on Anthony Benezet, I consulted many of the works cited above. In addition, see Seymour Drescher, *Abolition: A History of Slavery and Antislavery* (Cambridge: Cambridge University Press, 2009); Sally Hadden and Patricia Hagler Minter, "A Legal Tourist Visits Eighteenth-Century Britain: Henry Marchant's Observations on British Courts, 1771–1772," *Law and History Review* 29 (February 2011): 133–179; Maurice Jackson, *Let This Voice Be Heard: Anthony Benezet, Father of Atlantic Abolitionism* (Philadelphia: University of Pennsylvania Press, 2009); and Steven M. Wise, *Though the Heavens May Fall: The Landmark Trial That Led to the End of Human Slavery* (Cambridge, Mass.: Da Capo Press, 2005). On the question of whether the American Revolution was vital to the antislavery movement conceptually, see Christopher Leslie Brown, *Moral Capital: Foundations of British Abolitionism* (Chapel Hill: University of North Carolina Press, 2006).

On black resistance during the Revolutionary era, see Sylvia R. Frey, *Water from the Rock: Black Resistance in a Revolutionary Age* (Princeton, N.J.: Princeton University Press, 1991). On the subject of blacks' revolutionary commitment, abolitionist energy, and the missed opportunity to abolish slavery in the Founding era, see Gary B. Nash, *The Forgotten Fifth: African Americans in the Age of Revolution* (Cambridge, Mass.: Harvard University Press, 2006) and Alfred F. Young, Gary B. Nash, and Ray Raphael, eds., *Revolutionary Founders: Rebels, Radicals, and Reformers in the Making of the Nation* (New York: Knopf, 2011). On the Massachusetts freedom suits, see Emily Blanck, "Seventeen Eighty-Three: The Turning Point in the Law of Slavery and Freedom in Massachusetts," *The New England Quarterly* 75, no. 1 (March 2002): 24–51. Emily Blanck's essay also provides an interpretation of Quok Walker's case, *Exeter v. Hanchett*, and *Affa Hall*, Cushing's two other cases concerning freedom. Douglas R. Egerton, *Death or Liberty: African Americans and Revolutionary America* (Oxford: Oxford University Press, 2009) provides a useful chapter on these cases. Other scholarship on the Massachusetts freedom suits includes John D. Cushing, "The Cushing Court and the Abolition of Slavery in Massachusetts: More Notes on the 'Quock Walker Case,'" *The American Journal of Legal History* 5, no. 2 (April 1961): 118–144; Elaine MacEacheren, "Emancipation of Slavery in Massachusetts: A Reexamination 1770–1790," *The Journal of Negro History* 55, no. 4 (October, 1970): 289–306; Robert M. Spector, "The Quock Walker Cases (1781–83) – Slavery, its Abolition, and Negro Citizenship in Early Massachusetts," *The Journal of Negro History* 53, no. 1 (January 1968): 12–32. For the transcript of the Quok Walker materials, see Roger Bruns, ed., *Am I Not a Man and a Brother: The Antislavery Crusade of Revolutionary America, 1688–1788* (New York: Chelsea House, 1977), 474–475.

The writing on the Constitutional Convention is voluminous, and in no way do I intend to reproduce every relevant work here. For the narrative history, I relied primarily on Richard R. Beeman, *Plain, Honest Men: The Making of the American Constitution* (New York: Random House, 2009); Jack N. Rakove, *Original Meanings: Politics and Ideas in the Making of the Constitution* (New York: Alfred A. Knopf, 1996); and David O. Stewart, *The Summer of 1787: The Men Who Invented the Constitution* (New York: Simon & Schuster,

2007). For primary sources, I relied upon the extensive documentary histories available, including the Library of Congress's *A Century of Lawmaking For a New Nation*, part of its American Memory digitization project (http://memory.loc.gov/ammem/amlaw/lawhome.html); the Avalon Project at Yale Law School (http://avalon.law.yale.edu/default.asp); and print collections such as Donald Lutz, *Colonial Origins of the American Constitution: A Documentary History* (Indianapolis, Ind.: Liberty Fund, 1998).

On the members of the South Carolina delegation, see Marty D. Matthews, *Forgotten Founder: The Life and Times of Charles Pinckney* (Columbia: University of South Carolina Press, 2004); Robert M. Weir, "South Carolinians and the Adoption of the United States Constitution," *The South Carolina Historical Magazine* 89, no. 2 (April 1988): 73–89; Richard Barry, *Mr. Rutledge of South Carolina* (New York: Duell, Sloan and Pearce, 1942); Marvin R. Zahniser, *Charles Cotesworth Pinckney, Founding Father* (Chapel Hill: University of North Carolina Press for the Institute of Early American History and Culture, 1967); C. Gregg Singer, *South Carolina in the Confederation* (Philadelphia: Porcupine Press, 1976); Lewright B. Sikes, *The Public Life of Pierce Butler, South Carolina Statesman* (Washington, D.C.: University Press of America, 1979); S. Sidney Ulmer, "The Role of Pierce Butler in the Constitutional Convention," *The Review of Politics* 22, no. 3 (July 1960): 361–374. In understanding the relationship of South Carolinian planters with their slaves, I have relied primarily upon two works: Ira Berlin, *Generations of Captivity: A History of African-American Slaves* (Cambridge, Mass: Belknap Press of Harvard University Press, 2003), and Jeffrey Robert Young, *Domesticating Slavery: The Master Class in Georgia and South Carolina, 1670–1837* (Chapel Hill: University of North Carolina Press, 1999).

The speculation about whether Pinckney was privy to the discussions about the Virginia Plan prior to the Convention's opening are covered in Beeman, *Plain, Honest Men* (New York: Random House, 2009) and Matthews, *Forgotten Founder* (Columbia: University of South Carolina Press, 2004). The controversy over the Pinckney draft has raged since Pinckney first submitted what he believed to be the draft to John Quincy Adams in 1818 for publication. When Jared Sparks began compiling materials for his history of the Convention in the 1830s, Madison did his best to convince him that Pinckney lied about his contributions. Madison's admirers have never forgiven Pinckney for his arrogance. Marty D. Matthews provides a reasonable discussion of Pinckney's draft in *Forgotten Founder*.

On the imperial model as a foundational example for federalism, see Mary Sarah Bilder, *The Transatlantic Constitution: Colonial Legal Culture and the Empire* (Cambridge, Mass: Harvard University Press, 2004) and Daniel J. Hulsebosch, *Constituting Empire: New York and the Transformation of Constitutionalism in the Atlantic World, 1664–1830* (Chapel Hill: University of North

Carolina Press, 2005). For a rival view, see Alison L. LaCroix, *The Ideological Origins of American Federalism* (Cambridge, Mass.: Harvard University Press, 2010). On the creativity of the Founders in rejecting classical political theory thanks to their provincial mindset, see Bernard Bailyn, *To Begin the World Anew: The Genius and Ambiguities of the American Founders* (New York: Knopf, 2003). On the Constitution's aesthetics, see Eric Thomas Slauter, *The State as a Work of Art: The Cultural Origins of the Constitution* (Chicago: University of Chicago Press, 2009); Robert A. Ferguson, "Ideology and the Framing of the Constitution," *Early American Literature* 22, no. 2 (Fall 1987): 157–165; and Robert A. Ferguson, "The Forgotten Publius: John Jay and the Aesthetics of Ratification," *Early American Literature* 34, no. 3 (1999): 223–240.

The literature on slavery and the Constitutional Convention is also voluminous. Most scholars today have accepted the notion that the Constitution was proslavery insofar as its compromises protected slavery in both intended and unintended ways. Others argue more strongly that the Framers intentionally created a proslavery Constitution. See Robin L. Einhorn, *American Taxation, American Slavery* (Chicago: University of Chicago Press, 2006); Paul Finkelman, "Garrison's Constitution: The Covenant with Death and How It Was Made," *Prologue* 32, no. 4 (2000): 230–245; Paul Finkelman, *Slavery and the Founders: Race and Liberty in the Age of Jefferson*, 2nd ed. (Armonk, N.Y.: M.E. Sharpe, 2001); Gary B. Nash, *Race and Revolution* (Madison, Wisc.: Madison House, 1990); James Oakes, " 'The Compromising Expedient': Justifying a Proslavery Constitution," *Cardoza Law Review* 17 (1996): 2023–2056; and William M. Wiecek, " 'The Blessings of Liberty': Slavery in the American Constitutional Order," in *Slavery and Its Consequences: The Constitution, Equality, and Race*, eds. Robert A. Goldwin and Art Kaufman (Washington, D.C.: American Enterprise Institute for Public Policy Research, 1988), 23–44. The most recent formulations of this thesis are Lawrence Goldstone, *Dark Bargain: Slavery, Profits, and the Struggle for the Constitution* (New York: Distributed by Holtzbrinck, 2005); George Van Cleve, *A Slaveholders' Union: Slavery, Politics, and the Constitution in the Early American Republic* (Chicago: University of Chicago Press, 2010); and David Waldstreicher, *Slavery's Constitution: From Revolution to Ratification* (New York: Hill and Wang, 2009).

On ratification, the definitive text is Pauline Maier, *Ratification: The People Debate the Constitution, 1787–1788* (New York: Simon & Schuster, 2010). I have relied extensively on John P. Kaminski, Gaspare J. Saladino, Richard Leffler, Charles H. Schoenleber, and Margaret A. Hogan, eds., *The Documentary History of the Ratification of the Constitution* (Madison: State Historical Society of Wisconsin, 1976–2012), twenty-four volumes to date, with more to come. All of the citations from the debate over ratification come from the *Documentary History*. My interpretation of slavery's role in the ratification debates departs significantly from that of Kenneth Morgan, "Slavery and the Debate over the Ratification of the United States Constitution," *Slavery & Abolition* 22, no. 3 (2001): 40–65, and David Waldstreicher in *Slavery's Constitution* (New York: Hill and Wang, 2009).

The question of rights, privileges, and the duties of citizenship are the subject of several groundbreaking works, including Linda K. Kerber, *No Constitutional Right to Be Ladies: Women and the Obligations of Citizenship*, 1st ed. (New York: Hill and Wang, 1998) and Rogers M. Smith, *Civic Ideals: Conflicting Visions of Citizenship in U.S. History* (New Haven, Conn.: Yale University Press, 1997). The problem of "citizenship" as an analytical category is discussed by William J. Novak, "The Legal Transformation of Citizenship in Nineteenth-Century America," in *The Democratic Experiment: New Directions in American Political History*, ed. Meg Jacobs, William J. Novak, and Julian E. Zeilizer (Princeton, N.J: Princeton University Press, 2003), 85–119.

On the police power of sovereign entities to regulate broadly the health, welfare, and morals of a society, see William J. Novak, *The People's Welfare: Law and Regulation in Nineteenth-Century America* (Chapel Hill: University of North Carolina Press, 1996); Christopher L. Tomlins, *Law, Labor, and Ideology in the Early American Republic* (Cambridge: Cambridge University Press, 1993); Christopher L. Tomlins, "Necessities of State: Police, Sovereignty, and the Constitution," *Journal of Policy History* 20, no. 1 (January 2008): 47–63. For an extended argument about how the police power informed antislavery jurisprudence, see H. Robert Baker, *The Rescue of Joshua Glover: A Fugitive Slave, the Constitution, and the Coming of the Civil War* (Athens: Ohio University Press, 2006). My thinking about how rights are claimed, negotiated, and won or lost has also been greatly influenced by Hendrik Hartog, "The Constitution of Aspiration and 'The Rights That Belong to Us All,'" *Journal of American History* 74, no. 3 (December 1987): 1013–1034. A sampling of the literature on legal restrictions placed on free blacks in both northern and southern states includes Ira Berlin, *Slaves Without Masters: The Free Negro in the Antebellum South* (New York: Vintage Books, 1976); Stephen Middleton, *The Black Laws in the Old Northwest: A Documentary History* (Westport, Conn.: Greenwood Press, 1993); Stephen Middleton, *The Black Laws: Race and the Legal Process in Early Ohio* (Athens: Ohio University Press, 2005). For a comment on the longitudinal fluctuations in northern commitments to blacks' rights, see Paul Finkelman, "Prelude to the Fourteenth Amendment: Black Legal Rights in the Antebellum North," *Rutgers Law Journal* 17 (Spring and Summer 1986): 415–482.

Any student of the federal government's intimate relationship with slavery must begin with Don E. Fehrenbacher, *The Slaveholding Republic: An Account of the United States Government's Relations to Slavery* (New York: Oxford University Press, 2001). On the congressional debates regarding adoption of an antikidnapping law, see H. Robert Baker, "The Fugitive Slave Clause and the Antebellum Constitution," *Law and History Review*, November 2012. The literature on kidnapping is not extensive. See Carol Wilson, *Freedom at Risk: The Kidnapping of Free Blacks in America, 1780–1865* (Lexington: University Press of Kentucky, 1994) and Daniel Meaders, "Kidnapping Blacks in Philadelphia: Isaac Hopper's Tales of Oppression," *The Journal of Negro History* 80, no. 2 (1995): 47–65. On the adoption of the Fugitive Slave Act of 1793, see Paul Finkelman, "The Kidnapping of John Davis and the Adoption of the Fugitive Slave Law of 1793," *The Journal of Southern History* 56, no. 3 (August 1990): 397–422. On the scope and effect of the internal slave trade, see Ira Berlin, *Generations of Captivity* (Cambridge, Mass: Belknap Press of Harvard University Press, 2003), 161–168 and Steven Deyle, *Carry Me Back: The Domestic Slave Trade in American Life* (New York: Oxford University Press, 2005). Abolitionists documented kidnapping in their petitions and in their reports. See the *American Convention of Abolition Societies 1794–1829: Minutes, Constitution, Addresses, Memorials, Resolutions, Reports, Committees, and Anti-Slavery Tracts* (New York: Bergman Publishers, 1969), passim.

For the 1790 debates on the slave trade in Congress, see David P. Currie, *The Constitution in Congress: The Federalist Period 1789–1801* (Chicago: University of Chicago Press, 1997), 66–67. For the petitioning activities of the Pennsylvania Abolition Society, I have relied on Seymour Drescher, *Abolition* (Cambridge: Cambridge University Press, 2009), 131–133. On James Forten, see Julie Winch, *A Gentleman of Color: The Life of James Forten* (New York: Oxford University Press, 2002). The primary sources covering abolitionist activity are numerous. I have relied extensively on the microfilm of the Papers of the Pennsylvania Abolition Society, 1748–1979, Pennsylvania Historical Society, especially Series IV, which covers much of the society's legal activities. James Forten's letter can be found in James G. Basker, ed., *Early American Abolitionists: A Collection of Anti-Slavery Writings, 1760–1820* (New York: Gilder Lehrman Institute of American History, 2005). For a nuanced analysis of the ways in which abolition worked in Pennsylvania, see Gary B. Nash and Jean R. Soderlund, *Freedom by Degrees: Emancipation in Pennsylvania and Its Aftermath* (New York: Oxford University Press, 1991). For New York, see Graham Russell Hodges, *Root & Branch: African Americans in New York & East Jersey, 1613–1863* (Chapel Hill: University of North Carolina Press, 1999). See generally Richard S. Newman, *The Transformation of American Abolitionism: Fighting Slavery in the Early Republic* (Chapel Hill: University of North Carolina Press, 2002).

The jurisprudence of Chief Justice William Tilghman of Pennsylvania was key to the development of fugitive slave jurisprudence. The classic work on judges and slavery is Robert M. Cover, *Justice Accused: Antislavery and the Judicial Process* (New Haven, Conn.: Yale University Press, 1975). Cover's analysis suggests that judges retreated into formalism to justify sending fugitives back into slavery. A more critical look at Tilghman is Eric W. Plaag, " 'Let the Constitution Perish': *Prigg v. Pennsylvania*, Joseph Story, and the Flawed Doctrine of Historical Necessity," *Slavery & Abolition* 25, no. 3 (2004): 76–101. On the Pennsylvania Abolition Society's actions toward creating a free space within Pennsylvania, see Richard S. Newman, " 'Lucky to be born in Pennsylvania': Free Soil, Fugitive Slaves and the Making of Pennsylvania's Anti-Slavery Borderland," *Slavery & Abolition* 32, no. 3 (2011): 413–430. Contrast this with Gautham Rao, "The State the Slaveholders Made: Regulating Fugitive Slaves in the Early Republic," in *Freedom's Conditions in the U.S.-Canadian Borderlands in the Age of Emancipation*, eds. Tony Freyer and Lyndsey Campbell (Durham N.C.: Carolina Academic Press, 2011), 77–100. Any look at judges and slavery must also consider the changing nature of the judicial power and judicial function in antebellum America. See Mary Sarah Bilder, "Idea or Practice: A Brief Historiography of Judicial Review," *Journal of Policy History* 20 (January 2008): 6–25; Barry Friedman, "The History of the Countermajoritarian Difficulty, Part One: The Road to Judicial Supremacy," *New York University Law Review* 73 (1998): 333–433; Mark A. Graber, "Desperately Ducking Slavery: Dred Scott and Contemporary Constitutional Theory," *Constitutional Commentary* 14 (1997): 271–318; Mark A. Graber, "Resolving Political Questions into Judicial Questions: Tocqueville's Thesis Revisited," *Constitutional Commentary* 21 (2004): 485–546; Larry D. Kramer, *The People Themselves: Popular Constitutionalism and Judicial Review* (Oxford: Oxford University Press, 2004); Keith E. Whittington, "An 'Indispensable Feature'? Constitutionalism and Judicial Review," *New York University Journal of Legislation & Public Policy* 6 (2002/2003): 21–33; Gordon S. Wood, "The Origins of Judicial Review Revisited, or How the Marshall Court Made More out of Less," *Washington & Lee Law Review* 56 (Summer 1999): 787–808.

The early court cases concerning fugitive slaves (through 1824) are *Commonwealth v. Holloway*, 2 Serg. & Rawl 305 (Pennsylvania, 1816); *Kitty's Case* (1815) went unreported—for a report on *Kitty's Case*, see Richard S. Newman, *The Transformation of American Abolitionism* (Chapel Hill: University of North Carolina Press, 2002), 78–79; *Wright v. Deacon*, 5 Serg. & Rawl 62 (Pennsylvania 1819); *Worthington v. Preston*, 30 F. Cas. 645 (C.C.E.D. Pennsylvania 1824); *In re Susan*, 23 F. Cas. 444, Case No. 16,632 (C.C.D. Indiana, 1818); *Commonwealth v. Griffith*, 19 Mass. 11 (Massachusetts, 1823).

The sectional conflict that accompanied the Missouri crisis had deep roots, both constitutionally and culturally. See Matthew Mason, *Slavery and Politics in the Early American Republic* (Chapel Hill: University of North Carolina Press, 2006) and Peter S. Onuf, *Jefferson's Empire: The Language of American Nationhood* (Charlottesville: University Press of Virginia, 2000). Specifically on the Missouri Compromise, see Robert Pierce Forbes, *The Missouri Compromise and Its Aftermath: Slavery and the Meaning of America* (Chapel Hill:

University of North Carolina Press, 2007); Peter B. Knupfer, *The Union as It Is: Constitutional Unionism and Sectional Compromise, 1787–1861* (Chapel Hill: University of North Carolina Press, 1991); William M. Wiecek, *The Guarantee Clause of the U.S. Constitution* (Ithaca, N.Y.: Cornell University Press, 1972); Joshua Michael Zeitz, "The Missouri Compromise Reconsidered: Antislavery Rhetoric and the Emergence of the Free Labor Synthesis," *Journal of the Early Republic* 20, no. 3 (October 2000): 447–485.

On the passage of the Pennsylvania Personal Liberty Law of 1826 (and for that matter all the personal liberty laws), the indispensible work is Thomas D. Morris, *Free Men All: The Personal Liberty Laws of the North, 1780–1861* (Baltimore, Md.: Johns Hopkins University Press, 1974). The primary sources drawn upon for the legislative debates were from the Pennsylvania session laws and the *Aurora and Franklin Gazette* (Philadelphia, Pa.), accessed through 19th Century Newspapers Database http://infotrac.galegroup.com. The subject of legal conflict between free and slave jurisdictions is given ample treatment in Paul Finkelman, *An Imperfect Union: Slavery, Federalism, and Comity* (Chapel Hill: University of North Carolina Press, 1981). On southern jurisprudence, see all the essays in Kermit Hall and James W. Ely, eds., *An Uncertain Tradition: Constitutionalism and the History of the South* (Athens: University of Georgia Press, 1989). On South Carolina's Negro Seaman Act—and *Elkison v. Deliesseline*, 8 F. Cas. 493 (C.C. South Carolina, 1823) in particular—see David M. Golove, "Treaty-Making and the Nation: The Historical Foundations of the Nationalist Conception of the Treaty Power," *Michigan Law Review* 98, no. 5 (March 2000): 1075–1319; Philip M. Hamer, "Great Britain, the United States, and the Negro Seamen Acts, 1822–1848," *The Journal of Southern History* 1, no. 1 (February 1935): 3–28; Herbert A. Johnson, "The Constitutional Thought of William Johnson," *The South Carolina Historical Magazine* 89, no. 3 (July, 1988): 132–145; Earl M. Maltz, "Slavery, Federalism, and the Structure of the Constitution," *The American Journal of Legal History* 36, no. 4 (October 1992): 466–498; Edward T. Swaine, "Negotiating Federalism: State Bargaining and the Dormant Treaty Power," *Duke Law Journal* 49, no. 5 (March 2000): 1127–1278.

Regarding abolitionist constitutional thought, I have been guided by William M. Wiecek, *The Sources of Antislavery Constitutionalism in America, 1760–1848* (Ithaca, N.Y.: Cornell University Press, 1977). On the trial trope in abolitionist rhetoric, see Jeannine Marie DeLombard, *Slavery on Trial: Law, Abolitionism, and Print Culture* (Chapel Hill: University of North Carolina Press, 2007); Elizabeth B. Clark, "'The Sacred Rights of the Weak': Pain, Sympathy, and the Culture of Individual Rights in Antebellum America," *Journal of American History* 82 (1995): 463–493; Helen J. Knowles, "The Constitution and Slavery: A Special Relationship," *Slavery & Abolition* 28, no. 3 (2007): 309–328; and Andrea McArdle, "The Confluence of Law and Antebellum Black Literature: Lawyerly Discourse as a Rhetoric of Empowerment," *Law and Literature* 17, no. 2 (Spring 2005): 183–223. On the Underground Railroad, see David W. Blight, ed., *Passages to Freedom: The Underground Railroad in History and Memory* (Washington, D.C.: Smithsonian Books in association with the National Underground Railroad Freedom Center, 2006) and Fergus M. Bordewich, *Bound for Canaan: The Underground Railroad and the War for the Soul of America* (New York: Amistad, 2005).

On the abolition movement in world history, see David Brion Davis, *Inhuman Bondage: The Rise and Fall of Slavery in the New World* (New York: Oxford University Press, 2006); David Brion Davis, *The Problem of Slavery in the Age of Revolution, 1770–1823* (Ithaca, N.Y.: Cornell University Press, 1975); Seymour Drescher, *Capitalism and Antislavery: British Mobilization in Comparative Perspective* (New York: Oxford University Press, 1987); Rebecca J. Scott, *Degrees of Freedom: Louisiana and Cuba after Slavery* (Cambridge, Mass.: Belknap Press of Harvard University Press, 2005). See especially "Law, Slavery, and Justice: A Special Issue," in *Law and History Review* 29, no. 4 (November 2011) with essays by Rebecca J. Scott, Natalie Zemon Davis, Malick W. Ghachem, and Martha S. Jones. On the abolition of slavery in the British Caribbean and U.S. slaveholders' reactions, see Robin Blackburn, *The Overthrow of Colonial Slavery 1776–1848* (London: Verso, 1988); Michael Craton, *Testing the Chains: Resistance to Slavery in the British West Indies* (Ithaca, N.Y.: Cornell University Press, 1982); and Edward Bartlett Rugemer, *The Problem of Emancipation: The Caribbean Roots of the American Civil War* (Baton Rouge: Louisiana State University Press, 2008).

For the court cases concerning fugitives in the 1830s, 1840s, and 1850s, an indispensable resource is Paul Finkelman, ed., *Fugitive Slaves and American Courts: The Pamphlet Literature*, 4 vols. (Clark, N.J.: Lawbook Exchange, 2007), which contains both the report of the case of Charles Brown and the opinion of Chief Justice Hornblower in *New Jersey v. Sheriff of Burlington*. On the latter case, see also Paul Finkelman, "Chief Justice Hornblower of New Jersey and the Fugitive Slave Law of 1793," in *Slavery & the Law*, ed. Paul Finkelman, 1st ed. (Madison, Wisc.: Madison House, 1997), 113–141. Justice Henry Baldwin's charge to the jury can be found in *Johnson v. Tompkins*, 13 F. Cas. 840 (Circuit Court, E.D. Pennsylvania 1833). On *Jack v. Martin*, find Chief Justice Samuel Nelson's opinion at 12 Wend. 311 (Supreme Court of New York, 1834) and the opinions on appeal at 14 Wend. 506 (New York Court for the Correction of Errors, 1835). See also *In re Martin*, 16 F. Cas. 881 (undated) (No. 9, 154).

A helpful article that sorts out the facts and fictions of the arrest of Margaret Morgan is Paul Finkelman, "Story Telling on the Supreme Court: *Prigg v. Pennsylvania* and Justice Joseph Story's Judicial Nationalism," *Supreme Court Historical Review* (1994): 247–294. A dearth of archival evidence regarding the arrest has led scholars to rely on reports of it in the abolitionist press, some of which ended up in the official record of *Prigg v. Pennsylvania*. For information on John Ashmore, Margaret Ashmore, Edward Prigg, and the other actors involved in the arrest of Margaret Morgan, I consulted the vertical files at the Historical Society of Harford County in Bel Air, Maryland. Amongst the published sources I consulted were the U.S. Census and Carolyn Greenfield Adams, ed., *Hunter Sutherland's Slave Manumissions and Sales in Harford County, Maryland, 1775–1865* (Bowie, Md.: Heritage Books, 1999). The Maryland freedom petitions cited in this chapter are: *Burke v. Negro Joe*, 6 G. & J. 136 (Court of Appeals of Maryland, 1834); *Wilson v. Ann Barnet*, 8 G. & J. 159 (Court of Appeals of Maryland, 1836); and *Bland v. Beverly*, 9 G. & J. 19 (Court of Appeals of Maryland, 1837). The primary sources for Maryland's correspondence with Pennsylvania can be found in "Communication from the Executive, Enclosing a Correspondence, etc. Relative to Bemis, and others," Reports to the Maryland General Assembly, Public documents 1838–1840, pp. 519–538; MSA SC M3171; the Maryland State Archives, Early State Records Online; http://www.msa.md.gov/megafile/msa/speccol/sc4800/sc4872/003171/html/m3171-0519.html.

For scholarship on the political and constitutional crises of the 1830s pertaining to slavery, see Michael Kent Curtis, *Free Speech, "The People's Darling Privilege": Struggles for Freedom of Expression in American History* (Durham, N.C.: Duke University Press, 2000); Richard E. Ellis, *The Union at Risk: Jacksonian Democracy, States' Rights, and the Nullification Crisis* (New York: Oxford University Press, 1987); David C. Frederick, "John Quincy Adams, Slavery, and the Disappearance of the Right of Petition," *Law and History Review* 9, no. 1 (Spring 1991): 113–155; William W. Freehling, *The Road to Disunion* (New York: Oxford University Press, 1990); Harold Melvin Hyman and William M. Wiecek, *Equal Justice Under Law: Constitutional Development, 1835–1875* (New York: Harper & Row, 1982); David L. Lightner, *Slavery and the Commerce Power: How the Struggle Against the Interstate Slave Trade Led to the Civil War* (New Haven, Conn.: Yale University Press, 2006); James M. McPherson, "The Fight Against the Gag Rule: Joshua Leavitt and Antislavery Insurgency in the Whig Party, 1839–1842," *The Journal of Negro History* 48, no. 3 (July 1963): 177–195; Phillip S. Paludan, *A Covenant with Death: the Constitution, Law, and Equality in the Civil War Era* (Urbana, Ill.: University of Illinois Press, 1975); Bertram Wyatt-Brown, "The Abolitionists' Postal Campaign of 1835," *The Journal of Negro History* 50, no. 4 (October 1965): 227–238. The southern resolves and Massachusetts's response are found in *Report and resolves on the subject of slavery* (Massachusetts General Court, 1836), Samuel J. May Collection, Cornell University Library. For an overview of the political history of the period, compare Daniel Walker Howe, *What Hath God Wrought: The Transformation of America, 1815–1848* (Oxford: Oxford University Press, 2007) with Sean Wilentz, *The Rise of American Democracy: Jefferson to Lincoln* (New York: Norton, 2005). On Maryland's politics during the *Prigg* affair, see Robert E. Shalhope, *The Baltimore Bank Riot: Political Upheaval in Antebellum Maryland* (Urbana: University of Illinois Press, 2009) and A. Clarke Hagensick, "Revolution or Reform in 1836: Maryland's Preface to the Dorr Rebellion," *Maryland Historical Magazine* 57, no. 4 (1962): 346–366.

On the transformation of the abolitionist movement in the 1840s and 1850s, I have found it useful to compare the work of James Brewer Stewart, *Abolitionist Politics and the Coming of the Civil War* (Amherst: University of Massachusetts Press, 2008) with Bruce Laurie, *Beyond Garrison: Antislavery and Social Reform* (Cambridge: Cambridge University Press, 2005). On Salmon P. Chase in particular and abolitionism more generally, I have also consulted the work of Frederick J. Blue, *Salmon P. Chase: A Life in Politics* (Kent, Ohio: Kent State University Press, 1987) and Frederick J. Blue, *No Taint of Compromise: Crusaders in Antislavery Politics (Antislavery, Abolition, and the Atlantic World)* (Baton Rouge: Louisiana State University Press, 2005). On Wendell Phillips, the classic work is James Brewer Stewart, *Wendell Phillips, Liberty's Hero* (Baton Rouge: Louisiana State University Press, 1986).

The Fugitive Slave Act of 1850 and its aftermath are nicely summed up in Don E. Fehrenbacher, *The Slaveholding Republic* (New York: Oxford University Press, 2001). See also H. Robert Baker, *The Rescue of Joshua Glover* (Athens: Ohio University Press, 2006); Stanley W. Campbell, *The Slave Catchers: Enforcement of the Fugitive Slave Law, 1850–1860* (Chapel Hill: University of North Carolina Press, 1970); Gerald G. Eggert, "The Impact of the Fugitive Slave Law on Harrisburg: A Case Study," *The Pennsylvania Magazine of History and Biography* 109, no. 4 (October 1985): 537–569; Leonard W. Levy, "Sims' Case: The Fugitive Slave Law in Boston in 1851," *The Journal of Negro History* 35, no. 1 (January 1950): 39–74; Steven Lubet, *Fugitive Justice: Runaways, Rescuers, and Slavery on Trial* (Cambridge, Mass.: Belknap Press of Harvard University Press, 2010); Earl M. Maltz, *Fugitive Slave on Trial: The Anthony Burns Case and Abolitionist Outrage* (Lawrence: University Press of Kansas, 2010); Gautham Rao, "The Federal Posse Comitatus Doctrine: Slavery, Compulsion, and Statecraft in Mid-Nineteenth-Century America," *Law and History Review* 26, no. 1 (Spring 2008): 1–56; Jeffrey M. Schmitt, "The Antislavery Judge Reconsidered," *Law and History Review* 29, no. 3 (August 2011): 797–834; Thomas P. Slaughter, *Bloody Dawn: The Christiana Riot and Racial Violence in the Antebellum North* (New York: Oxford University Press, 1991); Albert J. Von Frank, *The Trials of Anthony Burns: Freedom and Slavery in Emerson's Boston* (Cambridge, Mass.: Harvard University Press, 1998).

The newspapers and periodicals I cite frequently throughout this study come largely from two databases: 19th Century U.S. Newspapers, Galegroup, http://infotrac.galegroup.com and American Periodicals, Proquest, http://

search.proquest.com/americanperiodicals. I have also availed myself of the Samuel J. May Anti-Slavery Collection, Cornell University Library http://ebooks.library.cornell.edu/m/mayantislavery/. For this project I also consulted archival materials in the National Archives, Great Lakes Regional Branch, Chicago, Illinois, and books held by the Newberry Library, Chicago, Illinois. The other primary source collections I used (archival, printed, and digital) I have dispersed throughout this bibliographical essay by topic.